307.

PUBLIC POLICY ISSUES
IN RESOURCE MANAGEMENT

WATER RESOURCES
MANAGEMENT
AND PUBLIC POLICY

Edited by Thomas H. Campbell
and Robert O. Sylvester

UNIVERSITY OF WASHINGTON PRESS

SEATTLE AND LONDON

PREFACE

ONLY a decade ago water was mainly taken for granted by the population at large, both in and out of the academic community, except for those engineers, physical scientists, and agriculturists who had reason to combat pollution or to seek knowledge regarding the supply, quality, or behavior of water, and for a handful of social scientists exploring its economic and social implications. Since that time the needs of a rapidly growing population for water supplies, waste disposal, and clean waters have focused sharp attention on water as a natural resource. Agronomists, biologists, chemists, economists, engineers, fisheries researchers, foresters, geographers, lawyers, mathematicians, and representatives of many other branches of learning are now actively engaged in their own studies regarding water. Current periodical literature, both scientific and popular, reflects this activity.

Among those interested in water supplies and their uses are political scientists and others interested in public policy. At the University of Washington, the Graduate School of Public Affairs for several years has sponsored a series of seminars on natural resources. These meetings have been open to both faculty and students, and off-campus participants have been welcome. The emphasis has been largely upon regional problems relating to the Pacific Northwest, but the scope of the seminars has been general enough to encompass issues of national importance. In 1963 the seminars were concerned with many aspects of fisheries, and a publication resulted based on papers presented for these discussions.* Since that time two seminars have

* *The Fisheries: Problems in Resource Management,* ed. James A. Crutchfield (Seattle: University of Washington Press, 1965).

been concerned with water as a resource and as a commodity, among other topics. For the academic year of 1964–65 water quality received attention, and during the following year the discussions centered on water supply.

Since this collection is based largely on papers prepared primarily for presentation at seminars where each speaker was concerned with acquainting laymen and academicians of various disciplines with approaches to policy issues of his own discipline, it makes no pretense of being definitive in scope, nor does it contain many new revelations from original research. Much of the merit of these papers consists of looking at existing problems and knowledge in a manner sufficiently challenging to warrant discussion. This book, therefore, represents an attempt to outline, for laymen, academicians, legislators, and the public, many of the relevant technical, scientific, and policy issues that should be considered in the management of water resources.

In the West, the desire for more water comes largely from pressures of government agencies and agricultural interests concerned with initiating or increasing agricultural production on arid or water-short land. In the first paper in this volume, Dr. E. Roy Tinney discusses project analysis and agricultural demand for water in the West in relation to land development, water transfers, and other socioeconomic goals. One result of the present increasing desire for more water is the appearance of large-scale water transfers from one region to another, as typified by the California Water Project. This project is initially to transfer 4.23 million acre-feet of water yearly from the northern part of the state to the southern, a distance of over 440 miles. The development of the surface waters of California's Central Valley is examined by Dr. Joe S. Bain in the second paper. In this study Dr. Bain uses benefit-cost comparisons and other criteria to evaluate the relative efficiencies of performance of private and governmental agencies which have been active in the development of the water resources of this valley, and postulates reasons for differences in performance and efficiency between the types of agencies. Benefits and economic efficiency also become the yardstick in Dr. Gardner Brown's paper on the economics of agricultural water use. He proposes a project reimbursability ratio and a contractor reimbursability ratio as measures of relative economic feasibility of irrigation projects. The first three papers make such heavy use of the benefit-cost comparison that it seems appropriate to study this concept in detail. Dr. Robert C. Lind, in the fourth paper, analyzes the benefit-cost technique, states its limitations, and discusses its range of applicability.

Research is emphasized in the next seven contributions. Professor Thomas

H. Campbell calls attention to the fact that while analytical technology and scientific knowledge with respect to water are growing rapidly, the fund of quantitative information in some regions is sadly inadequate, and that research is needed in order to provide these data. The paper of John S. Gladwell, which follows, presents a stochastic model for analyzing the runoff of the Columbia River, as an example of the approach and type of data needed for surface-water hydrology as the basis for project design. Professor James Crosby III states the need for similar information and research in regard to our ground-water resources, and tells of an interesting case study of the Pullman-Moscow aquifer on the eastern boundary of Washington, in which the age of the waters are determined as an aid in determining their movements.

Professors Robert O. Sylvester and Carl A. Rambow discuss concepts of water quality, differing quality objectives, and the difficulties in setting water-quality standards. They then propose a methodology for setting water-quality standards and present suggested standards for the state of Washington which are based on an objective for "clean" water. That the majority of Washington yet enjoys most of the benefits of clean water is pointed out by Professors Dale A. Carlson and Robert O. Sylvester, who then make a plea for research aimed at the development of treatment technology to ensure continuation or achievement of high water quality. In the following paper Professor James Crutchfield calls attention to the fact that it is costly to maintain this high quality, and forcefully points out how economic analysis can aid both policy formation and the effectiveness of research in the field of water quality.

As a result of a comprehensive research project on Lake Washington, now surrounded by metropolitan Seattle, Dr. W. Thomas Edmondson presents a detailed case study on the water-quality problems of this large lake. He also puts this case in perspective with other lakes and associates these findings with water resource management problems. The impending eutrophication of Lake Washington helped prompt the formation of the Municipality of Metropolitan Seattle (or Seattle Metro). It is, then, appropriate to have as the next contribution a description by Mr. Charles Gibbs of the program of water-quality monitoring of receiving waters, a key element in Seattle Metro's pollution-abatement program. It should be noted that the Seattle area has been plagued not only by pollution of its lakes, but also of the salt water of Puget Sound which forms its western boundary. The next paper in this volume, by Mr. Donald Benson, presents a zoning plan to cope with problems of pulp mill waste-water discharges into Puget Sound.

A work which purports to deal with the public policy of water resources management could not be concluded without considering water law, and indeed, the discussion may well have started at that point. Lawyers and the courts, however, usually have the last word in most cases surrounded by controversy, and since water currently qualifies as a controversial topic it is appropriate that the lawyers be given the last word here. Water law is both a tool of and a constraint on the operation of public policy with respect to water resources. In the final two papers, Ralph W. Johnson first discusses water law broadly, especially as it applies to water quality, pointing up the limitations of court-centered common-law actions on water-quality problems in the interest of the general public. For this reason, Johnson points out, the trend in water legislation has been a movement away from the courts and towards establishment of administrative agencies for water resources management. Finally, William Van Ness surveys in some detail the body of water law in the state of Washington as interpreted by the courts. While the water code in Washington differs in some respects from the codes of other states, the similarities are strong enough to permit generalization to other areas in the West. Van Ness discusses the general history of water law, the riparian and appropriation systems of water rights, pollution-control laws on state and federal levels, and concludes by discussing interstate water problems, water law and the federal-state relationship, and the implications for water resources planning.

A collection of papers such as these is only a part of the dialogue. High-quality interdisciplinary discussion of critical public policy issues is difficult, sorely needed, and, when successful, richly rewarding. To be interdisciplinary, the discussion must be more than a potpourri of technical analysis and policy discussion by scientists, engineers, economists, geographers, lawyers, and political scientists on a topic of broad mutual interest and genuine intellectual challenge. The connecting tissue of the personal equation, the sharp exchanges of discussion, and the resulting shifts in position over time are the real substance of the interdisciplinary interaction. These papers cannot show all that, but they have been tempered and shaped by it. The book should be read, then, in the light of this modest claim to an important role in the development of the significant interdisciplinary dialogue, which hopefully can continue more fruitfully by virtue of publication of the papers.

The reader will not fail to note, however, that there are some sharp differences in the viewpoints of the various writers, divided along disciplinary lines. From the standpoint of "the interdisciplinary view," then, if indeed there is such a thing, the value of a book such as this lies in illuminating the differences among the various disciplines so that attention and efforts can be focused on their resolution. The aim of the present book is to help the reader to gain an understanding and appreciation of the viewpoints of the various disciplines on water resources.

THOMAS H. CAMPBELL
ROBERT O. SYLVESTER

ACKNOWLEDGMENTS

THE EDITORS wish to express their thanks to the contributors to this volume and to the Natural Resources Public Policy Seminars. We particularly wish to acknowledge the assistance of Professor James A. Crutchfield, chairman of the Natural Resources Public Policy Seminars, for his leadership throughout. Our largest debt is to Mr. John Grobey, for his editorial assistance, and for keeping a fire built under all participants and contributors. We owe a special debt to the faculty and student audience whose loyalty and stimulating participation were essential to these proceedings. The seminars and papers benefited substantially from opportunities to discuss critical issues in water resources with national and state officials and with the management personnel of major resource industries. The cooperation and participation of Dr. E. Roy Tinney of Washington State University and his and our colleagues in the State of Washington Water Research Center, a joint enterprise of Washington State University and the University of Washington, were invaluable. We also wish to thank the National Science Foundation, the National Institute of Public Affairs, and the Graduate School of Public Affairs of the University of Washington for their financial support of portions of this effort.

CONTENTS

FIGURES

WATER RESOURCES MANAGEMENT AND PUBLIC POLICY

I

WATER FOR WESTERN FEDERAL IRRIGATION PROJECTS

E. Roy Tinney

Agricultural Goals

ALMOST three and a half centuries ago the Pilgrim Fathers signed the Mayflower Compact in which they did "covenant and combine" for the "general good" of the colony. The history of American agriculture since that time has developed in this spirit of mutual aid derived from our Judeo-Christian heritage. We have also had an almost religious conviction that agricultural pursuits are the very foundation of national development and strength. With these two guiding principles we have, as a relatively free society, eliminated the fear of famine that persists throughout so much of the world and attained an affluence unparalleled in history.

After the end of the Indian wars in the West and even before three southwestern states (Arizona, New Mexico, and Oklahoma) had joined the Union, the nation signed the Reclamation Act of 1902, in which the peoples of the United States did again covenant and combine for the common welfare by initiating the development of the virgin lands of the West. Within four decades, during which the nation was involved in two global wars, our agricultural output had surpassed the needs of our people. Now, after two decades of surplus crops and controlled acreage, we see signs of decreasing surpluses, but our remarkably successful agricultural system still retains great opportunities for expansion.

Testimony presented at a hearing of the Commission on Food and Fiber, Tucson, Arizona, December 1, 1966.

E. Roy Tinney is professor of civil engineering at Washington State University, Pullman, and director of the State of Washington Water Research Center.

3

One cannot deny the central role that mutual aid, or, in economic terms, federal subsidy, has played in maintaining a successful agriculture. The motive for mutual aid today is based less on fear and more on a desire for an ever-higher standard of living. We should be grateful for this fortunate change and constantly remind ourselves that the cardinal goal of our agriculture is to provide a fully adequate supply of food and fiber under the most adverse conditions.

The second purpose of agriculture is to develop our land and water resources for the betterment of the general welfare. As our affluence grows, a third objective is emerging, namely, the use of agriculture as a means of channeling aid and economic stimulation to specific depressed areas. It is in the context of these goals that we must approach the subsidization of agriculture by asking in each instance whether more or less subsidy is necessary for and would indeed provide: (1) assurance of a fully adequate food and fiber supply, (2) improvement of the general economy, and (3) aid to specific depressed areas.

The abandonment of these historically based socioeconomic goals would be risky at best unless the change were made sufficiently slowly to observe the consequences at intermediate steps. Professional people accept these goals as valid for agriculture, but they do question whether the individual projects constructed or proposed have been or will be efficient means for improving the general economy or for aiding depressed areas (Ruttan, 1965:85–88).

Western Land and Water Development

Western agricultural development programs in the last sixty years from the Canadian to the Mexican borders have produced a series of projects for bringing large quantities of water to huge tracts of arid lands. The Columbia Basin project in Washington, several projects in southern Idaho, the Colorado–Big Thompson project, the Salt River project in Arizona, Elephant Butte in New Mexico, and the Friant-Kern Canal in California are typical examples of projects that now irrigate 37 million acres in the western United States.

Unfortunately, the enthusiasm for irrigation has led to many excesses. Lands have been brought under irrigation without adequate attention to either drainage or increasing salt concentration and without proper evaluation of the random nature of the supply. One of the most serious mistakes has been the exploitation of ground waters in many arid areas that has resulted in a large irrigated acreage dependent on a nonrenewable, almost exhausted ground-water mine. It is incredible that this last error has been repeated so often. The tragedy is that so many farmers, businessmen, and communities have made long-term commitments and investments apparently assuming that the water supply would last indefinitely. As acreage expands and pumpage increases, the water table drops so low that high pumping costs prohibit further operation.

A similar situation arises with regularity in ore mining as mines are depleted. When an ore deposit is exhausted the mine is abandoned, and production is moved to a new site with more cheaply obtained ore. The mine-based community finds another basis for economic activity or workers and townspeople move on to an area that has such a base.

But with water and agriculture there is a tendency to think along other lines. Farmers, businessmen, and communities in the water mining area assume that someone—presumably the federal government—will replenish their mine. But one might ask whether there is any more basis for replenishment here than in an ore mine. Is the rest of the country really obligated to provide what is needed to protect local commitments and investments based on an erroneous assessment of the period of time that the resource would last? Or is it not more reasonable that areas which have used up their water compete on an equal basis with new areas for remaining unallocated water supplies? Is it really essential to our national food and fiber production capability that these particular areas have the water needed to keep them in production? Or is it not true that there are other areas and other means from which we could obtain our needed supplies—perhaps with much less outlay of federal funds?

Another troublesome feature of water supply is the fact that it has now become the rule rather than the exception to transport water hundreds of miles (and transfers of thousands of miles are eagerly proposed) to supply water for acreage developed earlier by ground-water mining or for additional irrigated acreage. The arguments presented for these superdiversions are the same as those for local developments discussed earlier, but the two situations are vastly different. I submit that subsidizing proposed superdiversions for far distant farms at water costs equal or greater than the value of the additional crop produced is not mutual aid—it is a national folly representing a very major income transfer without specific social objectives.

Consider a parallel case in the metals resource area. The Pacific Northwest has deposits of limestone, hydroelectric power, and coal with an interconnecting inland waterway. A federally subsidized importation of iron ore from the Midwest would permit the development of a substantial steel industry adjacent to the Puget Sound shipyards. Certainly this would improve the local economy, but the real question is whether or not it would be to the general good of the nation. I submit that until the natural opportunities for resource development within a region are exhausted, it is not in the nation's interest to subsidize major resource transfers of either water or ores. Aid to depressed local economies must first take the form of subsidizing the readjustment of local economic patterns for intensive utilization of the productive factors within those localities, patterns that may reduce or even exclude irrigated farming.

Confusion in Project Analysis

The development of irrigated lands in the West is a complex issue, because we have deliberately made it so. The social and economic factors are so intertwined in project analysis that only professional economists can unravel the situation. Much of this confusion could be eliminated if the federal government would adopt a two-phase analysis—an economic efficiency analysis and a social objectives or income distribution analysis. At the present time benefit-cost analyses contain hidden subsidies in the form of arbitrary allocation of costs to power generation, abnormally low discount rates, subsidized crop values, and a stretching of secondary benefits. The full cost of supplying water to the land is difficult for economists to determine and certainly beyond the comprehension of laymen and legislators who must make the final decision.

It does not appear to be difficult, nor does it seem to be an unwarranted simplification, to insist that project analyses indicate full costs and that they state explicitly the true, total amount of federal subsidy required. The argument for subsidy could then be presented in terms of social or nonmeasurable parameters. Indeed the nation is spending 30 per cent more on space exploration than on agricultural development, and the nation accepts the space program, albeit with some debate, without any evidence of a direct consumer product or other measurable returns. The apologists for increased irrigation should have the courage to be forthright in stating the true cost of irrigation and then defending that cost. To do otherwise is to betray the confidence of the taxpayer, to widen an already large credibility gap in subsidized irrigation, and to defeat the legitimate interests of agriculture. Confusion and misrepresentation have seldom succeeded long. The only course is an accurate and understandable presentation of facts.

Large Water Transfers

In much of the Southwest there is no longer an adequate water supply to develop additional acreage. Indeed we are told that Arizona is forced to take land out of production because of the mined ground-water reservoir and the rapidly growing demand for municipal and industrial supply. The Southwest is therefore at a very critical stage in agricultural development, since many local surface waters have long been committed. The Southwest's answer is to propose importation of waters from remote sources. This situation has, surprisingly, clarified the issue, because the discussion of interregional transfer of water has sharpened the debate on water for irrigation.

In addition to the clarification of project analysis methodology to present true costs and total subsidies as mentioned earlier, there are several other criteria applicable to the consideration of large interregional water transfers. First, large transfer schemes are monuments of concrete, steel, and rock with a service life of more than a century (indeed the Roman aqueducts have stood for sixteen centuries). The useful economic life, however, may be very short because of technological obsolescence of the demand in the recipient area. Consider, for example, cotton fiber production, a major water use in several southwestern states. A significant advance in the production of synthetic fibers would drastically reduce irrigation water demands in the Southwest. Our present rate of technological advance holds considerable promise for such a change in the next three or four decades. How would we then amortize the huge federal investment in an inflexible system of dams, canals, and pumps?

Other aspects of interregional transfers are the comparative costs, both in monetary terms and in the water consumed, and the value of irrigation water in areas of water abundance. The state of Washington, for example, now irrigates only 1.3 million acres out of a total of 9.2 million irrigable acres adjacent to the Columbia and Snake rivers. These lands are suitable for a variety of crops, particularly sugar beets, alfalfa, hops, and tree fruits and vegetables. Moreover, the added value of the crop produced by irrigation is quite similar in this region to that of the Southwest, as indicated in Table 1.

A careful examination of water values by Nathaniel Wollman (1962: XIII) indicates a net value of $44 to $51 per acre-foot for agricultural uses in the Rio Grande Valley, which would agree with the higher figures in Table 1 if production costs are added for the Rio Grande Valley.

TABLE 1

TYPICAL VALUES OF IRRIGATION WATER *

Project	Size (acres)	Farm Delivery (ac.-ft./acre)	Water Value † ($/ac.-ft.)
Southwest			
Arizona			
Boulder Canyon	492,502	5.28	$ 67.44
Gila	91,684	7.07	43.38
Yuma	56,939	5.52	113.08
California			
Klamath	197,231	1.93	64.03
Orland	17,200	2.40	45.31
Nevada			
Newlands	61,348	2.53	29.12
Pacific Northwest			
Idaho			
Michaud Flats	9,232	2.11	78.64
Rathdrum	4,036	2.72	40.38
Washington			
Columbia Basin	410,645	4.25	40.72
Chief Joseph	5,428	3.51	174.36

* Source: "1965 Crop Report and Related Data," United States Bureau of Reclamation, July 21, 1966.

† The value of water taken to be equal to the gross value of crop produced per acre-foot of irrigation water delivered.

Another useful comparison is that the 234,000 acres of irrigated lands in the Yakima project in central Washington, with a wide variety of crops, yielded $197 of crop per acre in 1965 while the average for all Bureau of Reclamation projects was $194. The smaller Chief Joseph project (5,428 acres) in eastern Washington yields $612 per acre with a tree fruit crop, which is comparable to $624 for the Yuma project.

The values of irrigation water derived above are for a variety of crops in each project. A more useful index for presenting water efficiency is the amount of a given crop grown per acre-foot of water, as indicated in Table 2.

Still another aspect of irrigation in the areas of water abundance is the relatively inexpensive cost of water delivery. In a recent study at Washington State University (Sutherland, 1967), it has been estimated that the cost of delivering irrigation water by pumping directly from the Columbia and Snake rivers, when all costs are included as in a privately financed development, ranges from about $8.00 to $18.00 per acre-foot depending on plant size and lift as shown in Table 3.

TABLE 2

CROP YIELD PER ACRE-FOOT OF WATER DELIVERED
TO THE FARM IN EASTERN WASHINGTON *

Crop	Unit	Yield/Ac.-Ft. of Water Consumed
Sugar beets	Tons	19.30
Potatoes	Tons	15.80
Alfalfa	Tons	2.54
Corn	Bushels	56.00

* Source: private communication with J. S. Robins, superintendent of the Irrigation Agricultural Center, Prosser, Washington, November 28, 1966.

TABLE 3

COST OF WATER DELIVERY IN EASTERN WASHINGTON

Assuming a 30-year amortization period at 4½ per cent interest, power cost at 5 mils/kwh, and a 3-mile pumping main

Plant Size (cfs)	Pumping Lift-Feet				
	200	300	400	800	1,200
30	$11.80	$12.50	$13.50		
90	7.90	8.50	9.30		
600			9.05	$14.00	$18.25

The proponents of major interregional transfers to supply irrigation water must recognize first that crop production per acre and per unit of water is competitive in the areas of origin, and second that water deliveries can be made in the area of origin at a fraction of the cost of conveyance between regions, which may run as high as $65–$120 per acre-foot depending on the size and location of the transfers.

Admittedly, denying the Southwest imported water will leave many local problems unsolved where the ground water has been mined or where salt concentration is prohibitive. Agricultural policies, however, have long-term consequences and should not be framed to answer a local problem. It may be less costly for the nation to subsidize immediate reallocation of land and water use within specific areas of the Southwest and then to plan the long-range development to utilize the productive factors within the Southwest. To do otherwise would be to wed certain states to heavily subsidized importations for many decades and retain the imbalance of federal support to those states.

In a region of great water shortages and abundant irrigable lands, the national interest would perhaps be best served by adopting a policy that all federal irrigation projects within that region must be optimal in terms of water use. The opportunities for greater economic efficiency are still available in the Southwest. In the first place greater allocations of Colorado River water southeastward with simultaneous development of northern California rivers and desalinization to meet the demand in the South Pacific region would serve both regions less expensively than tapping a new source more than fifteen hundred airline miles from either region. Second, the available waters in the Southwest could be reallocated in part to higher value uses along the lines indicated by Nathaniel Wollman's analyses (1962:XIII). It does not seem that such a reallocation need impinge, in the foreseeable future, on the ability of the Southwest to supply those specialty crops that require or are specially favored by the unique climate.

Summary

1. The chief agricultural problem of the West is the supply of irrigation water.
2. Future federal irrigation development should follow the general policy of
   a. assuring the nation of a fully adequate supply of the varieties of food and fiber
   b. improving the general economy
   c. aiding specific depressed areas.
3. In regions of extreme water shortage, federal projects should consider optimal use of water and reallocation to higher value uses within that region.
4. Governmental control of ground-water mining for irrigation should be developed.
5. Project analysis methodology should be clarified to indicate actual total costs and total federal subsidies required.
6. Future federal projects should be ranked in ascending order of economic efficiency for each crop pattern so that Congress can make a more rational selection, recognizing that social goals weigh significantly in the final decision.
7. Interregional transfers, as a solution to regional water shortages, should be analyzed on the basis of technological obsolescence of demand, crop production factors in the area of water abundance, relative cost of water delivery at each end of the transfer, water losses incurred by the transfer,

and alternative means of increasing the water supplies in the recipient regions.

REFERENCES

Ruttan, Vernon W.
  1965 The economic demand for irrigated acreage. Johns Hopkins Press, Baltimore, Md.
Sutherland, R. A.
  1967 Cost of pumping water for irrigation. Appendix C in Irrigation atlas of the state of Washington (Volume III in An initial study of water resources of the state of Washington). State of Washington Water Research Center, Pullman.
Wollman, Nathaniel
  1962 The value of water in alternative uses. University of New Mexico Press, Albuquerque.

II

WATER RESOURCE DEVELOPMENT IN CALIFORNIA: THE COMPARATIVE EFFICIENCY OF LOCAL, STATE, AND FEDERAL AGENCIES

Joe S. Bain

In bringing their powers of analysis to bear on problems of water resource development, economists have emphasized a number of related things, including:

1. Norms or criteria of efficiency for the design of water projects or for river-basin development.

2. Rectified and refined principles of cost-benefit analysis.

3. Planning of individual projects or basin developments.

4. Evaluation and explanation of the actual performance of water agencies.

Two coauthors (Richard E. Caves and Julius Margolis) and I currently have in press a study of water resource development in Northern California with the last-mentioned emphasis. We have appraised the actual economic performance of water agencies in that region, and tried to explain the quality of that performance in terms of the behavioral tendencies of these agencies and the structural setting in which they operate. Here, I should like to report and comment on three related aspects of our findings concerning the development of surface waters for and from the Central Valley of California. These concern:

1. The quality of the performance of local, state, and federal water agencies with respect to:

This paper is a revised version of "Northern California's Water Industry," by Joe S. Bain, Richard E. Caves, and Julius Margolis, a study that appears in *Water Research* (Baltimore, Md.: Johns Hopkins Press, 1966), published for Resources for the Future.

Joe S. Bain is professor of economics at the University of California at Berkeley.

a. the level of water resource development, and
b. the allocation of water among types, sites, and times of use.
2. The comparative efficiency in these respects of local water agencies as one group and the federal agencies together with the California Department of Water Resources as another.
3. Some apparent historical and structural reasons for differentials in efficiency between the two groups of agencies.

Although our findings relate specifically to one region, with its own hydrologic and other peculiarities, they may suggest hypotheses concerning sources of deficient performance by local and federal water agencies in other regions as well.

Some Basic Concepts

Let us begin with a few remarks on concepts invoked in analyzing Central Valley development, mentioning first two possible related concepts of the level of water resource development: (1) the level of water-usage development, and (2) the level of water-facilities development.

The level of water-usage development refers roughly to the extent to which available water resources have been put to economic uses as a whole. Water from any source may be less than fully used or fully used; it becomes fully used as soon as it is an economically scarce good with a positive shadow price at the source. This would mean in turn that if properly allocated it would have a positive net marginal value at the source in all alternative uses. It is then clear that the level of water-usage development definitionally hits a ceiling as soon as the water becomes economically scarce.

One corollary of this definition is that you cannot overdevelop scarce water by further investment in water facilities, but can only reallocate it among uses. Other corollaries are that we may distinguish among water-development projects according to whether they are drawing on free water or scarce water, and that if they are drawing on the latter we must insist on counting the opportunity cost of the scarce water as a legitimate part of project costs. To avoid ambiguity, we should perhaps underline the fact that in determining the existence or nonexistence of scarcity and of full water usage we include all demands for water, including those for nonreimbursable in-stream use. It is thus quite possible that a full level of water-usage development is entirely consistent with appreciable amounts of water wasting to sea, though this situation may be or may not be consistent with ideal allocation of the scarce resources.

The level of water-facilities development of course refers generally to the quantum of nonwater resources which have been committed to developing water for use. For rough-and-ready purposes we can observe that an increased level of facilities development is generally matched by a corresponding increase in usage development as long as the facilities development can only reallocate scarce water. Thus, once a threshold of scarce water is passed, the appraisal of the level of water-facilities development becomes essentially also an appraisal of the allocation of water among uses.

Before proceeding further with conceptualization, we might note that by 1960 water had evidently become a scarce good in all seasons in practically all of the numerous medium-sized and small rivers which flow into the Central Valley (there are no really big ones), with the possible exception of winter water in a few rivers feeding the Sacramento Valley. And on those, nonscarcity was being rapidly remedied by construction to augment interseasonal transfers. In the only source outside the hydrographic region that was being tapped for water for the Central Valley—the Trinity River of the North Coastal region—we offer the rebuttable presumption that in-stream recreational uses gave the flow an appreciable year-round scarcity value; if not, Trinity water is free water so far. Thus, all or practically all of our appraisal of the level of water-facilities development in or for the Central Valley refers also to water allocation—we are really not concerned with the question of whether or not free water is being used enough.

Returning to conceptualization, the task of analyzing the allocational accomplishments wrought by water-facilities development (and identifying any allocational distortions attributable to insufficient, excessive, or misplaced water facilities) is assisted if we distinguish several allocational frontiers:

1. The frontier of allocation among different types of use—such as irrigation, urban water, power, support of navigation, saline repulsion, in-stream recreational use, and so on.

2. The frontier of allocation among times of use, involving interseasonal or interannual transfers, generally through the use of dams and reservoirs.

3. The frontier of allocation among places of use, involving particularly interbasin and long intrabasin transfers of water, but also more local patterns of water distribution within subregions or individual river subbasins.

4. The frontier of allocation among customer-members of particular local water agencies, and among the lands of these constituents.

The meaning of these frontiers is presumably clear enough to require no definition. It should also be obvious that the first three frontiers mentioned tend to be highly interrelated either of necessity or in practice; for example, interseasonal transfers generally involve shifting emphasis as among types of use, and the major projects of the Bureau of Reclamation and the California Department of Water Resources have clearly conjoined long-distance water transfers with movements on the first two frontiers. For present purposes, we confine our attention to the interuse, intertemporal, and interspatial allocative frontiers, neglecting the fourth one listed.

Two Spheres of Central Valley Water Development

Now let us turn to an appraisal of the level of water-facilities development and the character of water allocation in and from the Central Valley as of approximately April, 1966. To simplify this appraisal, let us initially suggest one conclusion which emerged from our study after analysis of some evidence referred to below. This is that in the Central Valley there are presently two spheres of water development, the performance of which should be distinguished. One is the sphere of local-agency development, undertaken mostly by a variety of types of local public agencies (including irrigation districts and some municipalities) and by two private electric-utility companies—Pacific Gas and Electric and Southern California Edison. The other is the sphere of the large federal and state producer-wholesalers, occupied by the Bureau of Reclamation, the Corps of Engineers, and the California Department of Water Resources.*

These spheres have made contact and developed economic relationships, as yet to a relatively minor degree, but they are still a very long way from integration and coordination into a unified system for water development, whatever there is on the drawing boards, and there are very good explanations of the persistence of this situation. Moreover, the agencies in the federal-state sphere have performed differently than those in the local agency sphere—enough differently that separate appraisals should be made of the two spheres of Central Valley development—for evident reasons: as comparative newcomers to the Central Valley, they have had to superimpose their operations on the local-agency sphere; and though possessing some inherent advantages over their predecessors, they have also encountered very important disabilities because of prior development.

How this came about probably deserves a synoptic explanation. After the Civil War, the Central Valley began a slow shift from cattle range plus a little dry farming to irrigated agriculture. This movement was greatly accelerated after 1887 with the passage of the Wright Act, which permitted the

---

* The two spheres are further distinguished by the fact that they have, in large part, developed different groups of rivers within or for the Central Valley.

establishment of public irrigation districts with taxing and bonding powers and provided vehicles for local development of irrigation which lacked the fatal flaws of private water companies as alternative vehicles. Development of rivers for irrigation thereafter proceeded rapidly and progressively, mostly through local entrepreneurship using public districts as devices—first through the stage of diverting run-of-the-stream flow and then into that of building reservoirs for storage and interseasonal transfer. Concurrently, two large private electric-utility companies or their predecessors picked out the most likely rivers for intensive development for hydropower, constructing among other things a good deal of large-capacity reservoir storage for interseasonal transfers.

If their accomplishment is measured against the present stage of development, local agencies and electric utilities did not proceed too far with reservoir development before the bureau and then other big agencies really entered the area. By 1940 their total water storage capacity in reservoirs with individual capacities of 40,000 acre-feet or more was only about 28 per cent of the large-reservoir capacity of 1962, although they later added another 8 per cent of that total (California Department of Water Resources, 1963). But we should not be misled by these numbers. A process of economic selection was operating as local agencies developed water. It should thus surprise no one that in general local irrigation agencies concentrated their efforts—within a general pattern of development of local sources for local use—on the most attractive riverland combinations (good river flow, good dam sites, and high-grade land adjacent), although they did not necessarily exploit every attractive opportunity. Similarly, the electric-utility companies chose to exploit the most promising rivers for power generation (especially the Feather, the San Joaquin, and the Pit), and the metropolitan agencies of the San Francisco Bay area, when they reached across the Valley to the Sierra Nevada for pure water supplies, for geographical reasons hit on the same set of rivers developed by local irrigation agencies. In effect, the local agencies took advantage of their temporal priority to skim much of the cream of economically attractive water-development opportunities in the Central Valley.

To be sure, these agencies did not and still generally have not developed the "full physical potentials" of their chosen rivers. They frequently built reservoirs which were suboptimal in scale from the standpoint of multipurpose development and for a number of reasons, including budgetary constraints and insularity. But they tied up the water rights and the dam sites (as well as the natural service areas) of a band of significant rivers of prime economic potential, thus placing severe barriers in the way of late-coming federal and state agencies should they seek to stir cream into their project benefits or really to incorporate this significant series of rivers into any comprehensive plan. The strategic band of rivers which local-agency and electric-utility development had pretty well pre-empted before the bureau got into operation included the Kings; the San Joaquin and its three principal tributaries, the Merced, Tuolumne, and Stanislaus; some lesser rivers like the Mokelumne just to the north; and in lesser but significant degree the Feather and the Yuba, which feed the Sacramento River about forty miles north of the Delta (for various reasons more or less skipping the American River in between). In the Central Valley, these are the prime rivers serving prime adjacent land in the center of the Central Valley's eastern slope. As we will see, the level of water development and allocation in this area deserves an appraisal apart from that of the federal-state areas.

Although this choice area had been more or less carved out of the middle by local development and pre-emption, there of course remained many good physical or engineering opportunities for bringing water to valley lands of from moderate to very high grade, especially after ground-water mining began to reach its limit in the Tulare Basin area south of the Kings River. Classified economically, what was left for the federal and state agencies consisted mainly of (1) numerous marginal or submarginal opportunities which could be exploited independently; * (2) a very few better opportunities for augmenting development on rivers already solidly occupied by local agencies, which had not been exploited because of tangled water-rights situations (Pine Flat and Friant on the Kings and the San Joaquin); and (3) a very few better opportunities which had been bypassed by local agencies because of huge financial requirements (Shasta on the Sacramento and possibly Oroville on the Feather). Economically feasible projects of certain scales and designs could probably have exploited the opportunities in the latter two categories, though not evidently in such a fashion as to effect very much more integration in the development of the valley's water resources, given the barriers mentioned. Even then, these possible projects did not offer the superior economic payoffs reaped, for example, by watering the alluvial fans of the Kings, Merced, Tuolumne, and Stanislaus from the river flows that traversed them.

---

* It should be noted that in any array of water resource development opportunities in this region according to "quality" or potential economic payoff, there are distinct discontinuities in quality, so that increasing demand for water over time did not "promote" most neglected opportunities into a supramarginal class.

In this setting, the federal and state agencies encountered severe disabilities in any endeavor to effect comprehensive river-basin development, though there was some good "project material" left. At the same time, these agencies or the legislatures above them were acutely responsive to the pleas and pressures of prospective clients who had been left short of surface water in the course of local-agency development or who were running out of ground water. In consequence, they were led not only to exploit marginal or submarginal opportunities as available, but also to exploit the few better opportunities generally with projects of excessive and uneconomic scale (*cum* design) at the dam-reservoir level and then to connect in other excessively scaled or otherwise uneconomic facilities to deliver the water.* This was done, of course, in the context of a policy of working around the edges of the going concern which the local agencies had established, and which the federal and state agencies did not wish to disrupt, even where the precommitment of fixed facilities by the local agencies might not have made this disruption *ex ante* uneconomic (when the bureau did break the bind to a limited extent with the basic features of the Central Valley Project, it did so at a very high economic cost as well as by transfer payments).

Thus it was that the basic features of the bureau's CVP essentially involved placing a very large dam on the Sacramento River to set in motion a transfer of water to the Tulare Basin five hundred miles away, and that it then proceeded further in parallel and comparable endeavors. It is not plausible that the bureau would have done what it did or in the order that it did it had the bureau been able to develop the Central Valley *de novo*. Thus it was also with the developments of the minor rivers feeding the Tulare Basin—the Daweah, Tule, and Kern—that though none involved a huge investment, each awaited the entrance of the Corps of Engineers to augment the local irrigation water supply while charging most of the cost off to flood control. With respect to the bureau's CVP works, it is true that the investments involved were beyond the resources of local agencies, so that budgetary constraints alone could have deterred earlier development. But this fails to establish a *prima facie* case to the effect that these investments were all along justified on the basis of economic efficiency, if only someone could dig up the money. So much for the sketchy establishment of a "second-sphere" classification of bureau and corps developments in or serving the Central Valley.

The California Department of Water Resources joined this second sphere

---

* A possible exception to this rule is found in the Pine Flat Reservoir on the Kings, built by the Corps of Engineers.

by initiating its Feather River Project, which is principally designed to capture 4 million acre-feet per year of winter water from near the mouth of the Feather River, carry about half of it to the southern end of the Tulare Basin for irrigation, and pump the other half across a range of mountains for urban use in the area of Los Angeles. The department's operation and position as a marginal operator are quite comparable to those of the bureau so far as the transfer of irrigation water is concerned, though its pricing policies differ. In its interbasin export of urban water, the demand-and-benefit situation differs but the marginality of the project is reasonably clear.

Development and Allocation in the Local-Agency Sphere

Hard evidence on the level of water-facilities development and allocation by local agencies is difficult to amass, but we have built up some by supplementing published data with primary research, and have expanded our findings by drawing a few inferences from institutional arrangements. A principal finding, referring to a random sample of eighteen irrigation districts (Table 4), is that on the average from 1952 through 1960 these districts

TABLE 4

DISTRIBUTION OF AVERAGE
ANNUAL RATES OF RETURN
ON INVESTMENT, 1952–60, FOR
EIGHTEEN IRRIGATION
DISTRICTS *

Rate of Return	Number of Districts
−3.1 to −5.0	1
−1.1 to −3.0	2
−1.0 to 1.0	9
1.1 to 3.0	3
3.1 to 5.0	0
5.1 to 10.0	0
over 10.1	

* Source: Bain, Caves, and Margolis (1966).

averaged about a zero per cent return on price-level-adjusted depreciated investment, which is to say that average revenue was appreciably below long-run average cost. (The dispersion in rates of return within the sample appears principally attributable to differences in the age of district and to the fact that district revenues are set to cover bond amortization rather than calculated depreciation.) General evidence concerning the incidence and importance of water rationing other than by price suggests that the marginal value of water to users in these districts does not greatly exceed average revenue. Furthermore, economic costs are systematically understated by a failure to include any charge for the opportunity cost of scarce water, or any payment for the stream-flow regulation service provided to most of these eighteen districts by others on which these districts freeload.

Taking these factors into account, it seems reasonably clear that Central Valley irrigation districts, so far as they are fairly represented by this random sample, have tended to invest excessively in water facilities for the service of their own lands, and correspondingly to overallocate water to irrigating these lands, at the expense of its use elsewhere for irrigation or for other purposes.* On the other hand, surrounding evidence that irrigation districts have secured larger water allocations than neighboring actual or potential irrigators suggests it to be quite possible that the total development of water facilities for local irrigation is not excessive, but simply maldistributed among irrigators.

Another study of twenty-four irrigation districts and water districts served by the Bureau of Reclamation with wholesale water showed that ten of these were predicted to grow crops at an extensive margin, having net values of average product (payment capacities) below the long-run marginal costs of supplying water (even with subsidized bureau water rates being taken at face value). These findings are subject to about the same interpretation as the rate-of-return findings just cited.

Neither of these samples happens to pick up members of that small but important group of irrigation districts which operate joint reservoir facilities with Pacific Gas and Electric Company, under contracts by which the electric utility pays for a dam in return for exploiting it for power yield for a fifty-year period. The character of these contractual arrangements, however, strongly suggests that these districts also probably have excessive water-facilities development imputable to irrigation use and excessive interseasonal transfer for this purpose, relative to their own service areas, though the level of facilities development relative to all irrigable land (including that excluded from district service) may not be excessive. Thus, in the sector examined, a generally excessive level of water-facilities development is not

* This finding is potentially quite consistent with local agencies having realized benefit-cost ratios (but not marginal benefit-cost ratios) generally in excess of unity, if buyers' surpluses are included in benefits.

clearly identified, though its possible existence is not excluded. The major misallocation so far identified is probably more among users than among uses, and no clear indication of excessive over-all interseasonal transfer is found.

Some attention should also be given to water-facilities development in the form of single-purpose (though generally dual-function) large reservoirs which are operated on their own accounts by Pacific Gas and Electric Company and Southern California Edison Company. These include sixteen Central Valley reservoirs with individual capacities above more than 40,000 acre-feet and an aggregate capacity comprising about 15 per cent of all major reservoir capacity in the valley region. All circumstantial evidence suggests that these do not embody overdevelopment or generate excessive interseasonal transfer of water. There is a possibility, but not a clear probability, that their lack of dual- or multi-purpose orientation has led to a deficient level of reservoir development, though the rather abundant development of facilities for irrigation casts some doubt on this hypothesis.

Given the level of water-facilities development in the local-agency sector, and whatever it implies directly for water allocation, we may also consider other allocational impacts of local development. The following stand out: as regards the interseasonal pattern of releases from storage, utility-owned reservoirs evidently deviate significantly from an ideal multipurpose pattern of releases; reservoirs jointly controlled by utilities and irrigation districts probably do not; reservoirs controlled by irrigation districts and not supporting power generation, and the few reservoirs controlled by urban agencies, evidently tend to deviate from an optimal multipurpose operation and in particular to give insufficient weight in allocation to recreational in-stream uses and to fish habitat. Interferences by the state Fish and Game Department or through Federal Power Commission hearings do not seem generally to have been sufficient to secure an adequate attention to in-stream recreational uses in water allocations and in reservoir release patterns, except in those categories in which these uses are pretty well served as a by-product of commercial development. Such commercial development clearly does not include that oriented very heavily to supporting diversions for irrigation. The only significant interbasin or long-distance transfers of water encountered in the local-agency sector involve the transfer of relatively trivial amounts of water (perhaps 2 per cent of Central Valley surface diversions) from the Sierra to the San Francisco Bay region, and no appreciable misallocation is ascertainable here.

Development and Allocation in the Big-Agency Sphere

The most solid evidence that emerged from our study of federal and state development in and for the Central Valley consists of two benefit-cost analyses: one for the basic features of the Central Valley Project of the Bureau of Reclamation, and one for the Feather River Project of the California Department of Water Resources. Since the bureau has by now gone beyond the basic features of CVP and plans to go further, and since the Feather River Project is viewed as only the first unit in a very much larger California Water Plan, some might argue that an evaluation of the accomplishment of these agencies on the basis of these two appraisals is premature. However, a preliminary analysis of available evidence on subsequently constructed plus ongoing added features of the CVP suggest that any amalgamated benefit-cost ratio for a fuller or full CVP is going to get worse rather than better. In particular, a subsequent benefit-cost study of the Trinity River–Sacramento Canals Divisions of the CVP, construction of which is partly completed and partly under way, finds this major addition to CVP's features to be much further below the margin of economic feasibility than the basic features. And any careful reading of the California Water Plan makes it unmistakably clear that the Feather River Project offers by far the least expensive feature of that plan for getting water from Northern California to the southern San Joaquin Valley, the Los Angeles area, and the Mojave and Colorado deserts. Thus, we offer a *prima facie* finding that the basic features of CVP and the FRP respectively show the bureau and the California department at their own best in terms of economic efficiency of accomplishment.

The basic features of the CVP include Shasta Dam on the Sacramento River at the north end of its valley; connected hydro facilities that supply power for pumping water south from the Delta as well as power for sale; a major pumping plant at the Delta; and the Delta-Mendota Canal, which carries water from the Delta to the San Joaquin River below Friant Dam to replace river water cut off by Friant from rights-holders on the lower San Joaquin (and incidentally delivers some water en route). They include also Friant Dam; the Friant-Kern Canal, which carries most of the flow of the San Joaquin southward to the east valley slope of the Tulare Basin area; lesser Madera Canal, which carries water northward from Friant to augment irrigation water supplies in another service area; and a Contra Costa Canal running from the Delta to the northeast corner of the San Francisco Bay area. For this complex of interrelated facilities, we have calculated * in Table 5 two benefit-cost ratios (each for fifty- and one-hundred-year time horizons and each at several discount rates) with painstaking attention to all details, these ratios including: (1) a "standard" ratio of primary benefits to costs, B'/C,† wherein benefits are measured at average values inclusive of buyers' surpluses (payment capacities in the case of irrigation water); (2) the same ratio where agricultural benefits are based on adjusted ‡ world prices for price-supported crops (especially cotton), rather than on support prices, on the theory that support prices clearly overstate any addition to national net income.

TABLE 5

BENEFIT-COST RATIOS (B'/C) FOR BASIC FEATURES OF THE CENTRAL VALLEY PROJECT IN TERMS OF DISCOUNTED PRESENT VALUES AS OF 1950 *

	Time Period	Rate of Discount per Annum			
		3%	4%	5%	6%
B'/C without adjustment for surplus crops	50 years	1.21	1.03	0.89	0.77
	100 years	1.45	1.16	0.96	0.81
B'/C using adjusted world prices for surplus crops	50 years	0.72	0.61	0.53	0.47
	100 years	0.85	0.69	0.57	0.49

* Source: Bain, Caves, Margolis (1966).

The basic features of the CVP appear to be marginally efficient at discount rates of 3 or 4 per cent, and inefficient at higher rates even if surplus crops are valued at support prices in calculating benefits. Except for those who believe that a rate as low as 4 per cent is appropriate in calculating the efficient allocation of investible funds among all uses, public and private, the CVP is a nonfeasible project, embodying overdevelopment of water facilities and misallocations in the form of excessive interseasonal transfer, excessive long-distance transfer, and excessive allocation of water to irrigation as opposed to other commercial and noncommercial uses. If the value of the surplus crops grown with CVP water is measured realistically from a national-welfare standpoint, the project is a loser at any faintly plausible interest rate.

* The benefit-cost analysis of CVP has been made almost entirely by Professor Caves.
† We add the prime sign to the B to designate inclusion in benefits of buyers' surpluses, and to distinguish this B' from a different measure of benefits referred to below.
‡ Adjusted for storage costs and losses.

There are rather clear indications, moreover, that the basic features are of excessive scale, so that $\Delta B'/\Delta C$ for the project falls below unity at any interest rate from 4 per cent up. The ratio of revenues to cost for fifty years at 5 per cent is about 0.3. Reading up from this to the probability that the ratio of benefits prices at marginal values to costs is slightly higher, and making a liberal allowance for increasing returns to scale, we conclude that $\Delta B'/\Delta C$ must be below unity. This suggests the possibility that the basic features of the CVP might have been economically feasible at an appreciably smaller scale, but it does not suggest it very strongly. The only ground for showing that an excessive level of water-facilities development was not embodied in the basic features of CVP would be a demonstration that its irrigation water was irrationally allocated among service areas, and there is little to support this hypothesis.

TABLE 6

BENEFIT-COST RATIOS (B'/C) FOR THE TRINITY RIVER
AND SACRAMENTO CANALS DIVISIONS OF THE CENTRAL
VALLEY PROJECT, CALCULATED FROM 1966 ESTIMATES
OF 1964—PRESENT VALUES OF DIVISION BENEFITS
AND COSTS *

Time Period	Rate of Discount per Annum			
	3%	4%	5%	6%
50 years	.67	.59	.50	.43
100 years	.79	.66	.54	.46

* Source: David L. Shapiro, "Statistical Appraisal of the Economic Efficiency of the Trinity River Diversion of the Central Valley Project" (Doctoral dissertation, University of California, Berkeley, 1966).

The Trinity River–Sacramento Canals Division of CVP includes a large dam-reservoir complex on the upper Trinity River, tunnel and aqueduct facilities to divert about a million acre-feet of water annually from the Trinity into the Sacramento River below Shasta, large connected hydro facilities, and two major and some lesser canals to deliver this water mainly to lands west of the present irrigated belt on the west side of the Sacramento River. Some Trinity water is also scheduled to augment deliveries from the Delta through the Delta-Mendota Canal. The investment outlay for the project is almost as large as that for all basic features of the CVP.

The "standard" ratios of primary benefits to costs for the division (for fifty and one hundred years, at several discount rates and with no adjustment for surplus crops) are shown in Table 6. This addition to the CVP promises to return about fifty cents in benefits for every dollar of costs that include a 5 per cent interest charge, and is distinctly submarginal even when a discount rate of 3 per cent is used. The project would not appear to have a chance of being economically feasible at any scale, nor would any of its separable segments.

The major features of the Feather River Project of the California Department of Water Resources are shown in Tables 7 and 8. Our benefit-cost analysis of this project * has been prospective, since the project is still being built even though practically all of its ultimate deliveries are under contractual commitments. As the tables show, over half of its deliveries will go to Southern California in a very long aqueduct and pumping system, and most of the remainder to the southern San Joaquin Valley. Delivery schedules, costs, and revenues have been taken directly from state estimates. Irrigation-water benefits have been taken, both as marginal (B) and average (B') values, from detailed studies made for the purchasing agencies, with no deductions being made for surplus crops. Urban water benefits have also been calculated both as quantity times marginal value and as quantity times average value inclusive of consumers' surplus $(B$ and $B')$. This calculation follows the principle that marginal value is any year in any service area the lower of marginal value in use (liberally equated to the FRP contract price to purchasers) and cost from the marginal alternative source of water (calculated area by area in some detail). A correlative principle is that average value cannot exceed cost from the marginal alternative source, but where this alternative cost is above marginal value, average value lies between them as calculated on the supposition of a price elasticity of demand for urban water of −0.25. The most important alternative cost is that of demineralized ocean water in Southern California after 1984 (when lower-cost alternatives would be exhausted in meeting scheduled FRP deliveries); we have set this at one hundred dollars per acre-foot, on the basis of best projections of current evidence.

Table 9 shows the variety of ratios we have calculated at various discount rates, all for a fifty-year and an eighty-year period. The latter ends in 2039 and is the payout period of the project and the reference period for most state data. These ratios include revenue cost, benefit cost with benefits priced at marginal values, and conventional benefit cost with benefits including buyers' surpluses, with all values discounted to the beginning of 1960.

This project rates about the same in terms of efficiency as the basic features

---

* The benefit-cost analysis of the FRP has been made primarily by Professor Margolis.

TABLE 7

MAJOR FACILITIES OF THE FEATHER RIVER PROJECT, AS PLANNED IN 1964 *

Facilities	Location	Capacity (Reservoir Storage or Aqueduct Head Flow)	Length in Miles
On-stream storage and regulation facilities			
Oroville Dam and Reservoir †	Lower Feather River	3,484,000 af.	. . . . . .
Five Feather River reservoirs above Oroville	Forks of Feather River	187,900 af.	
Spencer and Dos Rios Reservoirs and conveyance facilities	Middle Fork of Eel River	800,000 af. ‡	
Delta facilities			
Barriers, control works, and canals	Lower Delta	. . . . . .	. . . . . .
Delta pumping plant	Tracy	10,330 cfs.	. . . . . .
Aqueducts			
North Bay Aqueduct	Delta west to Napa Valley	138 cfs.	32
South Bay Aqueduct	Delta § south to Santa Clara Valley	363 cfs.	44
Main Southern California Aqueduct ‖	Delta south to Tehachapi	10,000 cfs. #	322
West branch of Southern California Aqueduct	Division point south to Castaic Reservoir	1,500 cfs.	13
East branch of Southern California Aqueduct	Division point east and south to Perris Reservoir	1,842 cfs.	118
Central Coastal Aqueduct	Main Southern California aqueduct west to Santa Maria River	329 cfs.	110
San Joaquin Drainage Facilities **	South of Bakersfield north to Delta	1,100 cfs. ††	288

* Source: California Department of Water Resources, Bulletin No. 132–64, *The California State Water Project in 1964* (Sacramento, 1964), chap. iii.

† With connected power plant and other facilities.

‡ Estimated annual yield of water; storage capacity n.a.

§ Strictly from elevated reservoir above the Delta pumping plant.

‖ 103 miles of this aqueduct, from San Luis Reservoir south to Kettleman City, is a joint facility of the FRP and the Bureau of Reclamation, having a head capacity of 13,100 cfs. of which the FRP share is 7,100 cfs.

Capacity tapers to 3,800 cfs. at the south end of the San Joaquin Valley.

** Joint facility of FRP and Bureau of Reclamation.

†† Terminal capacity near Delta.

TABLE 8

ESTIMATED ULTIMATE ANNUAL DELIVERIES OF FEATHER RIVER PROJECT WATER
BY SERVICE AREA *

Service Area	Aqueduct Source	Ultimate Annual Deliveries in Thousands of Acre-Feet	Year Deliveries Are Scheduled to Begin
Feather River area	Local canals	38.5	1967
San Francisco Bay area, northeast	North Bay Aqueduct	73.0	1980
San Francisco Bay area, south	South Bay Aqueduct	194.0	1962
San Luis Obispo and Santa Barbara	Central Coastal Aqueduct	75.0	1980
Southern San Joaquin Valley	Main Southern California Aqueduct	1,362.0	1968
South Coastal Basin	West and east branches of Southern California aqueduct	1,925.0	1971
Antelope Valley—Mojave Desert	East branch of Southern California aqueduct †	264.0	1971
Coachella Valley—Palm Springs	Purchasers' spur aqueduct from East branch	68.0	1972
	TOTAL deliveries	4,000.0	

* Source: California Department of Water Resources, Bulletin No. 132–64, Table 7.
† And southern end of main Southern California aqueduct just north of Tehachapi division point.

of the Central Valley Project, though a little better at lower interest rates and a bit worse at higher ones. In view of the rather optimistic population forecasts which underlie estimates of urban water benefits, no discount rate lower than 5 or 6 per cent should be considered realistic, and at these or higher rates it is not economically feasible at its designed scale, embodies excessive or distinctly premature water-facilities development, and implements misallocations on the frontiers of interseasonal and interbasin transfers. It may readily be inferred from the B/C ratios that it is overscaled (with B'/C below unity); detailed examination suggests that it could have been brought into the range of economic feasibility by downscaling basic features, eliminating costly and wasteful features like the long East Branch aqueduct across the Mojave Desert, and reducing irrigation-water deliveries to the south San Joaquin.

On the basis of these analyses plus preliminary surveys of actual and proposed additions to the projects analyzed we conclude that in the federal-state sphere or Central Valley water development the first best project

TABLE 9

BENEFIT-COST AND REVENUE-COST RATIOS FOR THE FEATHER RIVER PROJECT,
CALCULATED FROM 1964 ESTIMATES OF 1960 PRESENT VALUES OF PROJECT BENEFITS,
REVENUES, AND COSTS *

	Time Period	Rate of Discount per Annum			
		3%	4%	5%	6%
R/C—Revenue-Cost Ratios †	50 years	0.95	0.83	0.72	0.63
	80 years	1.12	0.99	0.80	0.68
B/C—Benefit-Cost Ratios with Benefits Based on Marginal Values	50 years	0.78	0.68	0.54	0.51
	80 years	0.95	0.86	0.62	0.56
B'/C—Benefit-Cost Ratios with Benefits Based on Average Values	50 years	1.09	0.94	0.80	0.69
	80 years	1.32	1.11	0.90	0.75

* Source: Bain, Caves, Margolis (1966).

† The revenues entering these ratios are calculated from uniform average annual equivalent contract prices. If cash-flow revenues reflecting anticipated prepayments and deferred payments are used instead, the R/C ratios are altered slightly, as follows for 80 years: 3%—1.07; 4%—0.97; 5%—0.82; 6%—0.72.

opportunities were submarginal, involving the overinvestment and misallocations mentioned, and that the future of progressive development does not look as bright.

Conclusion

Overlooking the fact that a number of the findings presented above are unlikely to gain 100 per cent acceptance without challenge or argument, we might conclude by returning to the hypothesis implied above that a late-arriving federal or state agency which attempts multipurpose river-basin development in a basin which is already pretty well settled and developed encounters multiple legal and physical disabilities which deter it from approximating its theoretical potential. In addition, it finds a good deal of the cream skimmed from water-development opportunities, so that it is induced to undertake suboptimal and frequently submarginal additions to an existing water-facilities system. A corollary of this hypothesis is that by far the best case for comprehensive river-basin development by a central agency is made in a vacuum—a vacuum in particular of appreciable settlement and prior water development—where it can exploit a virgin opportunity full-force, internalizing externalities to the hilt and coordinating everything. (The only possible trouble with this is that local interests are in general unlikely to leave attractive vacuums lying around.)

This hypothesis seems to draw some sustenance from the bureau's experience in the Central Valley, wherein the "disabilities" argument can be documented in considerable detail. It also draws sustenance from any dispassionate preliminary appraisal of those scheduled future features of the California Water Plan which emphasize a large augmentation of irrigation-water supply in the Central Valley, not to mention the separate appraisal of the irrigation features of the Feather River Project. As to the other major features of the FRP, they do not serve to test the hypothesis mentioned, but raise extremely serious questions (exaggerated greatly when pulling Columbia River water into Arizona is seriously suggested) concerning an ongoing tendency toward uneconomic real estate promotion in arid regions.

It has been suggested that flood-control benefits should be appraised with reference not only to the losses averted to people inhabiting highly floodable lands, but also with reference to the net benefits of having people inhabit those lands at all. Any firm believer in the nonexistence of secondary and tertiary benefits may ask a comparable question about the wisdom of subsidizing the development or growth of urban centers in the midst of deserts.

REFERENCES

Bain, Joe S., Richard E. Caves, and Julius Margolis
    1966 Northern California's water industry. In Water research. Johns Hopkins Press, Baltimore, Md.
California Department of Water Resources
    1963 Dams within jurisdiction of the state of California, January, 1962. Bulletin No. 17. Sacramento.

III

THE ECONOMICS OF
AGRICULTURAL WATER USE

Gardner Brown

Introduction

Iᴛ is fitting that one paper in this series be devoted to the economics of irrigation, quantitatively the most important use of fresh water from streams in the United States, especially in the West and the Pacific Northwest (Mackinchan and Kammerer, 1961). In the United States in 1960 water used for irrigation amounted to about 45 per cent of total out-of-stream water use. Not surprisingly, the comparable figure for the Northwest was much higher, close to 90 per cent, in round numbers. Historically, irrigation always has been the most dominant use, although it is reasonable to suppose that its importance will decline relatively to rural, municipal, and industrial uses in the future.

Prior to 1910, surface-water sources accounted for at least 90 per cent of water withdrawals. The picture changed sharply when new discoveries in well drilling and pump technology brought ground-water sources within the economic reach of prospective irrigators. After 1920, ground-water withdrawals became increasingly important and have accounted for more than 63 per cent of total public and private irrigation development in the seventeen western states since 1940 (U.S. Senate, 1960).

In the absence of further breakthroughs in pumping and well-drilling technology, it is doubtful that the growth of irrigated acreage will continue at its recent pace, because much of the past expansion has been due to ground-water mining; that is, pumping at rates which exceed the annual natural replenishment.

Gardner Brown is assistant professor of economics at the University of Washington.

In the United States, about 39 million acres are irrigated annually. Approximately 43 per cent of these acres are located in California, Texas, and New Mexico. The Pacific Northwest accounts for 15 per cent and the rest is distributed over the remaining thirteen western states. There is very little irrigated acreage east of the Mississippi River, most of which is supplemental. Perhaps this overview provides some feeling for the physical dimensions of the problem.

The Simple Economics of Demand for Water for Irrigation

In general it is true that water is just another input or factor of production which the firm, the farmer, uses to produce some output or combination of outputs. Although water shares certain very important characteristics of other inputs, such as fertilizer, seeds, and harvest labor, which make it amenable to conventional textbook analysis, it also possesses other salient physical, economic, and institutional attributes which make the practical economic analysis of water for irrigation use an exciting but formidable subject. Some of the more important complicating factors will be discussed in a later section.

Imagine a very simple situation. If a farmer producing one output—alfalfa, for example—is offered any amount of water he chooses to purchase at a given price, how much does he purchase? If he always prefers more wealth rather than less, he purchases successive amounts of water, until the last unit of water purchased makes a contribution to his total sale of alfalfa just equal to the cost of the last unit of water. We might observe that he chooses ultimately six units of water which cost him a total of six dollars. Under these conditions, the marginal unit of water costs him one dollar and if it results in his total alfalfa output increasing in value by just one dollar, he would be happy. He would not purchase more water because then he has to pay out a dollar but gets less than a dollar's worth of alfalfa in return. In short, buy additional amounts of water as long as it pays to. When the added costs exceed the added revenues, stop buying water. It is nothing but the old "marginal revenue equals marginal cost" efficiency equilibrium rule that economists derive for their students and for others who happen to be within earshot. It is a sensible prescription under the circumstances.

Though simple, this is a very important condition. There is more to the efficient use of water, but the other conditions bear a close resemblance to the first one. Farmers typically produce more than alfalfa. Suppose our farmer produces alfalfa and cantaloupes, under the conditions specified above. How much water should he purchase? First he performs the same calculation for cantaloupes as he does for alfalfa. If he has purchased the correct amounts of water for both crops, the following is true. He cannot improve his profit by a reallocation of water between crops. If he removes one unit of water from his alfalfa-growing activity and puts it into his cantaloupe activity, the result is a decrease in his profit.

In this simple world, our farmer must perform one other calculation to see if he is on the correct path to efficiency to the maximization of his wealth. So far our farmer has not calculated whether he gains a bit by giving up some water and purchasing more of another input. To make sure he has the right, the efficient, quantities of fertilizer, seeds, labor, and other output-increasing factors, he must abide by the following rule of thumb. Take away a dollar's worth of fertilizer and add a dollar's worth of water. If he gets more than a dollar's worth of additional output, he keeps performing this factor reallocation process until it is no longer profitable to do so, until shifting a dollar's worth of expenditures from one input to another no longer improves his total sales figure.

It is about now that one's values may become troublesome, because a decision must be made about who should get a given amount of the scarce resource, water. Should Farmer A or Farmer B get it? If each farmer behaves in the fashion we have described above, and there is not enough water to go around, then efficiency rules tell us that water should be sold to the farmer who will pay the most for it. This is conceptually no different from the rationing rule which took place between alfalfa and cantaloupes—except now it is applied to farmers, not food and fiber. To achieve allocative efficiency, the price of water should be raised until the amount of water available just equals the amount which Farmer A and Farmer B will take at that price. In general, both farmers will get some water, but not as much as each would like at a lower price.

Two issues are lurking in the background and now must be taken up. The first problem is the determination of the price of water. Why was it one dollar in our example? One must use scarce resources to develop water. Why should a firm, public or private, spend two dollars' worth of scarce resources to provide a unit of water worth only a dollar? What does a two-dollar bundle of cement, power, labor, and so forth, mean? It means simply that these resources can contribute at least two dollars' worth of value if they are put to use elsewhere in the economy. Similarly, if a bundle of resources valued at a dollar is used to develop a unit of water, that unit ought to fetch a dollar, or we as a country are wasting our resources.

So far, it has been assumed that the economy is directed toward one purpose only, efficiency. Now that there are two farmers, there may be an equity problem, a problem of how the productive value of water should be distributed. In many cases, it is possible to consider the two issues, efficiency and equity, separately. It is usually possible to devise a set of water policies which induce water to be allocated in an efficient fashion, and then use other policies to achieve the distributive objectives a collective decision-making organization would like to see fulfilled. A concrete example follows involving two farmers, one producing alfalfa, the other producing cantaloupes.

Suppose a public irrigation district supplied ground water to owners of two large farms. For some reason only 100 acre-feet of water are available per year. Now if the water price is $3.50 an acre-foot, it is likely in contemporary western United States that each farmer would want at least 100 acre-feet. Who should get the 100 acre-feet? If efficient allocation of water is the goal, then the district should raise the price until, together, the two farmers just want the available 100 acre-feet. It may be that the market clearing price is $20.00 an acre-foot and that the cantaloupe farmer gets 80 percent of the available water. Under these circumstances the district would receive $2,000 from its sale of water. We might reasonably suppose that its pumping and other costs are only $500. Its profit is therefore $1,500. Having achieved the efficient allocation of water by charging the market clearing price, the district can then try to solve the equity or distributive justice problem by choosing an appropriate policy to distribute the public irrigation district's profit to the owners, in this case the two farmers.

Selling water at a price low enough such that no profit is made does not allocate the water efficiently. It does not allocate the water to those who can make the greatest productive use of it, as measured by their willingness to pay. At the lower price, there is an excess demand for water and some nonscarcity price-rationing rule would have to be used.

Why the Economics of Demand Is Not So Simple

The economist's confidence in his prescriptive rules for efficient water resource use depends fundamentally on the accuracy of the assumptions implicit in the account just presented. The simple analysis works best, if there are many buyers and many sellers of water, each acting independently; if there are no important market imperfections; if there are no external effects; and if techniques of water development are technically and economically efficient when they come in small package sizes. Further, economic analysis is most successful if the resource is well defined, in both a physical and legal sense.

For some economists water is an intriguing resource to study because none of the above conditions are met very well. Few problem areas therefore offer as great a challenge to the analyst's imagination and ingenuity as does water resources economics. Only a fragmented account of these complications, their interconnections, and the steps which are being taken to overcome them can be presented in this paper.

There is no resource more completely managed by public entities than water for irrigation use. This implies that water is developed, managed, and exchanged, not in the private but in the public market place. In the United States and in California, where 8 million acres are irrigated annually, profit-seeking firms supply only 3 per cent of the water for irrigation use. It may be noted that the figure is not much different for industrial and domestic water use—5 per cent and 11 per cent, respectively (Ciriacy-Wantrup, 1960).

The early history of private irrigation water development is a sad one, marked by fraud, extreme ignorance, shortsightedness, exploitation, and bankruptcy.* Moreover, irrigation projects by and large do not come in small packages. Because there are substantial economies inherent in large-scale projects it has always paid, in general, to construct very large irrigation projects. Finally, irrigation projects past and present are capital intensive, and capital markets are not perfect. For these reasons it is no surprise that federal agencies, large public water districts, and more recently state agencies have played dominant roles in irrigation development. In addition, public institutions have multiple goals and face different constraints than their private counterparts. For the moment the practical consequence of this difference may be noted: observed irrigation water prices reflect efficiency prices, modified by the sacrifices in efficiency that public decision-makers are willing to make in order to achieve other goals.

While all these considerations distinguish water from other factors of production, the phenomenon of externalities is perhaps the most vital and essential demarcating characteristic. External effects arise when an individual's actions confer a benefit or place a cost on someone else that is not just offset by an equivalent payment (either positive or negative). In other words, an economic action entails a symmetric exchange. When an externality exists, the reciprocal nature of the exchange process breaks down.

The following is a very important example of an irrigation externality. In

---

* See, for example, Adams (1916), Brewer (1961), California Conservation Commission (1912), Hall (1886), U.S. Department of Agriculture (1901).

the production of alfalfa, the input, alfalfa seed, becomes "embodied" in the final output. This is not quite true for irrigation water because water is *used,* not *consumed* or embodied. In regions supplied by Bureau of Reclamation water, a diversion of 4 acre-feet of water per acre of alfalfa is typical. The farmer uses directly perhaps 2 acre-feet and the rest is lost to *him* through evapotranspiration, surface runoff, spilling, and percolation below the subsoil. To simplify the problem, assume there is no loss to the atmosphere. Thus about one half the original quantity of water is available for reuse. It can and often happens that Farmer A purchases the 4 acre-feet, and a different farmer, Mr. B, uses the 2 acre-feet residual. The externality arises because we have not devised an effective apparatus which enables Mr. A to charge Mr. B for this fugitive 2 acre-feet of water. As a result of Farmer A's actions, a Farmer B receives a direct benefit. With irrigation efficiencies as low as 50 per cent, one can readily see that the size of this externality is extremely substantial. Note that this externality does not terminate with Mr. B. There may be a third farmer below Mr. B who gets half of the 2 acre-feet, and so forth. Economists at Colorado State University have explicitly specified this important externality in some studies (Hartman and Seastone, 1965).

There has been a quite heated controversy regarding the economic efficiency of western water law (Gaffney, 1961; Trelease, 1961). Observing the high legal cost of water rights adjudication proceedings, many economists conclude that the present system of water law is extremely inefficient. Their conclusion may be questioned. Western water law permits all those affected by the exchange of a water right to participate in the adjudication process. The second farmer, in the example just given, has arranged his whole farm enterprise around the availability of half of the first farmer's water. When the first farmer sells his water to someone outside the immediate water basin, the second farmer and subsequent farmers would incur substantial losses in their farming enterprise. High legal costs simply reflect, in part, the fact that nature and institutions are complex organisms, not that water law is necessarily inefficient.

If this problem is economically important and has a long history, why have we not devised a suitable apparatus to handle the externality effectively? In some cases the development of public irrigation districts serve such a purpose. This organizational arrangement makes the external or third-party effects of individual action internal to all the members of the district. However, there is a very real identification problem. Mr. B exists conceptually, but identifying him as the beneficiary of Mr. A's actions and estimating the magnitude of the resulting externality is extremely difficult, given our present knowledge about the surface and subsurface flow of water.

The Development of the Bureau of Reclamation Pricing Policy

Let us turn to a consideration of the policies of the most important public water agency, the Bureau of Reclamation. Today's federal pricing policy for irrigation water is in no sense independent of past events. Publics and public policy do not exist in a timeless vacuum, but are creatures with an historical legacy, whose features at a moment in time are sculpted out of the momentum of past events. Accordingly, a thumbnail sketch of recent history is a necessary prerequisite for an understanding of contemporary policy.

The federal government became formally engaged in public irrigation projects with the passage of the Reclamation Act of 1902. The legal justification for this responsibility was built on the loose construction of the Commerce Clause in the Constitution. The Federal Reclamation Act was a natural extension of the government's activities in the public lands disposal programs.

The main objectives of federal water policy were threefold: to develop the arid lands of the West, to achieve a wide distribution of benefits, and to create a proper social environment. I have been unable to find an unambiguous reference to efficiency as the overwhelming public goal at that time or since.

From my reading of this portion of history, it is clear that the public servants, living in a different era, differed significantly from the bureau's civil servants of today. Their values, their devils real or imagined, and their lexicon were distinctive. Water was believed to be a necessary condition, perhaps even a sufficient condition, for western economic development. They believed that development should exhibit a certain character consistent with America's cherished values; namely, that the proper social environment would be preserved by the establishment of small family-farm communities.

As a forerunner to the classic Arvin-Dinuba study (Goldschmidt, 1947), the father of the 1902 Reclamation Act, Elmwood Mead, contrasted the social conditions between a small farm area in Utah and the Sacramento Valley where farms were ten times as large and declared, "The irrigable lands of California are no place for bonanza farms" (U.S. Department of Agriculture, 1901:28–29). The 1912 California Conservation Commission study (1912:8–18) asserted:

> Everybody believes that land would be better used for the public good if it is
> in the private ownership in small areas. The benefits from water which

originally belonged to the public, should accrue to the public, serve the public and not enrich a few monopolies. They [underdeveloped power sites] should be preserved and held for the benefit of all people and should not be surrendered to private interests.

To achieve desired outcomes a water policy was developed, shored up when loopholes were discovered, and preserved for over sixty years (Wertheimer, 1944). With a few exceptions users of water from federally financed water projects can own no more than 320 acres. Three other policies are important because of their economic effects. Irrigationists do not pay interest charges on the project capital costs attributed to irrigation. Second, there is a lapse of at least ten years between the time when water is first delivered and contracted payments are first made. Finally, excess revenues from other project purposes, notably power, are used to reduce agriculture's repayment obligations. As a result of these policies and others not mentioned, according to one estimate, farmers pay one-third of the cost of producing an acre-foot of water—about $3.50 or less as compared to $10.00 an acre-foot.

It is as if when a young man begins to look at houses, his father-in-law, anxious that his daughter continue to live in the style to which she has been accustomed, says he is prepared to pay, for the benefit to him, all the interest cost portion of the mortgage, and perhaps one-third of the monthly payments which, in any event, do not begin until 1975.

How does the economist view this set of policies and its consequences? Well, the $10.00 is the efficiency price of water, the charge which reflects the scarcity value of the resources used to develop the water for irrigation. The difference between the real cost and the actual price, $6.50 in this example, times the number of acre-feet delivered to agriculture, the economist concludes, must be the value which our public decision-makers place on the other public goals, in particular the goal of developing the arid West. It is the sacrifice in efficiency which the decision-makers are willing to forego in order to achieve the welfare or distribution (from society to irrigationists) goals implicit in a project. In our house analogy, the difference between the true cost of the house and the price which the young man pays is just equal to the subjective benefit that the father-in-law receives from knowing that his daughter will live in a superior environment.

Consider two questions. Are the nonefficiency goals legitimate? If so, are there lower-cost policy alternatives for achieving the same goal?

Contemporary economists refuse to pass judgment on the legitimacy of public goals. However, even if it were granted that the public goal of developing the arid West was a meritorious one sixty years ago, it is doubtful if this goal is as urgent today, when, for example, California is the most populous state. When the value of a public objective declines through time, public policies should be adjusted to reflect the changed valuation. To illustrate: Suppose some industrialists proposed to build a new railroad linking the East with the West. How many would seriously believe that the new railroad was so important to the growth of the West today that we as a nation should grant them a title to over 46 million acres, as we did in the case of the Northern Pacific?

One might argue that to induce western development we should be willing to grant to this proposed railroad, title to a million acres of land. Perhaps this would cost 100 million dollars. But how much additional western growth would this particular policy generate? There are a whole set of policies costing 100 million dollars, and associated with each policy is, in principle, an incremental regional growth rate. What we really want to do, given the goal "develop the West," is choose that policy which is most efficient, which gives us the most incremental regional growth for a given expenditure. It should be very clear that departures from the efficiency criterion do not diminish the productivity of the economist's analytical tools. But nonefficiency goals must be carefully specified for the economist or he must construct them before the economic analysis of policies can be undertaken.

Finally, the contemporary federal irrigation pricing policy brings about substantial repercussion effects affecting the entire pattern of resource allocation throughout the whole country. Taking an efficient water-pricing policy as the standard, a number of these effects may be mentioned.

First, for any given multiple-purpose project, the other beneficial uses are systematically discriminated against because more water for irrigation is desired at the lower nonefficiency price. Hence a greater fraction of the project resources are devoted to this use. Second, water projects are oversized because less water would be taken at the higher efficiency price. Agricultural output within the project service area is greater than it otherwise would have been, implying that the agricultural sector purchases a relatively greater quantity of other scarce resources such as chemicals, machinery, and research talent. Because the quantitative demand for these resources is relatively greater, other economic sectors using these resources must pay higher prices.

The repercussion effects of charging nonefficiency prices for irrigation are forcefully illustrated by the following question: if the Pacific Southwest farmers were required to pay the efficiency price for the 5 to 10 million acre-feet of water proposed to be supplied to them by the Bureau of Reclamation, would there be any serious talk about the need to divert water from the Northwest to the Southwest?

Economizing Tendencies—A Comparative Analysis of the California Water Project

Economists have been criticized occasionally from within their profession but most often from without on the matter of ascribing maximizing behavior to economic agents. It has been argued quite persuasively, for example, that individuals or firms simply do not have the wits to maximize. Rather, they "satisfize." As an analytical device, the maximization assumption has proved extremely useful. As a matter of fact, the assumption (as it is operationally defined) is optimistic at best.

Max Weber carefully avoided the charge of impossible goal ascription. In what some students of Weber regard as his intellectually most significant contribution, *Wirtschaft und Gesellschaft,* Weber spoke of and analyzed economizing tendencies, thus avoiding "the fallacy of misplaced concreteness." It is helpful to set efficiency as one standard against which we can talk usefully about economizing tendencies. The merit of such a concept can be illustrated by way of a comparative analysis. After a brief description of the pricing policies associated with the California State Water Project there will be enough background to make a comparison between the practices of two important water agencies, the Bureau of Reclamation and the California Department of Water Resources.

The department—California Department of Water Resources—had its own set of historical legacies which greatly differed from the bureau's. In brief, it did not have the social objectives that the bureau had or has. The California state project was designed to serve a part of the state, and it was a plan, unlike the bureau's, which all the voters could directly accept or reject by popular referendum on a bond issue. With a little more time it could be shown persuasively that for the bond issue to pass, the department had to devise a set of policies which contained precious little subsidy.*

Second, for various reasons, the possibility of an acreage-limitations policy was out of the question. It is substantially correct to say that the state offered to sell as much water to anyone as long as the contractor would pay the price. The state set the price of water equal to the cost of the resources required to

* For a defense of this proposition and a more complete treatment of ideas mentioned in the following paragraphs, see Brown (1964).

develop and transport the water. If a contractor was close to the source of water he paid less because it will cost less to deliver water one hundred miles as compared to five hundred miles.

No definite cost was established in the contracts. Rather a pricing formula was given to the contractors. This feature is necessary because water projects are such long-lived affairs that future costs cannot be known today with a high degree of accuracy. Whatever the future costs are, the contractors will have to pay them.

The contrast between the bureau's and the state's water-pricing policies is striking. It may be true that the aqueduct was not located in the precise economically optimal location. It may be true that certain accounting procedures obscured the achievement of the optimally efficient price at every point of diversion along the aqueduct. But is it clear, I think, that California's water-pricing policies show a marked economizing tendency.

They did not prohibit the more productively efficient large-scale farmers from purchasing water. They avoided the most serious problem of windfall gains accruing to some individuals as a result of a public investment decision, by selling water according to the willingness to pay principle. The real costs of the project were used in the determination of price; that is, the price paid for water was determined on the same basis that mortgage payments are calculated. Both public agencies realized that agriculture should not have to make payments during the initial period of development. *But,* unlike the bureau, if agriculture delays its repayment obligations to the state it must make up these payments in the future and pay compound-interest charges on the earlier postponed obligations.

I have proposed two measures for evaluating economizing tendencies of water projects. The first is the project reimbursability ratio—the ratio of total project repayment obligations to total project costs. Second is the contractor reimbursability ratio, the ratio of a contractor's repayment obligations to the total project costs attributed to that contractor. The most economic projects would have ratios of 1 in each case.

The state project (aqueduct) reimbursability ratio is 97 per cent according to my estimates. The closest comparison I can draw is that of the Bureau of Reclamation's Central Valley Project where, again according to my calculations, the project reimbursability ratio is about 69 per cent. Alternatively, the project reimbursability ratio of the earlier and comparable State Water Plan of 1930 was about 77 per cent.

The agricultural contractors for state water have a reimbursability ratio of about 90 per cent. In contrast, the highest conceivable ratio attributable to irrigation districts receiving water from the Central Valley Project is 28 per cent. In my view, these estimates suggest that not only does the California State Water Project exhibit economizing tendencies when compared to alternative large-scale public water projects, but also the tendency is a very marked one.

Time and the Value of Water

The advent of computers has greatly increased our ability to build models which more closely mimic actual irrigation enterprise activity. We are able, in short, to carry out much more realistic analyses. A few illustrations follow.

In the past it was common to assume that a given crop required a given amount of water and a given amount of other inputs. It was assumed that this water was applied in a rigid irrigation pattern. Lands of different soil characteristics were explicitly considered but only in terms of their effect on product yields.

It is presently possible, and a few optimality studies exist, to consider alternative quantities of water, applied during different time intervals, on lands with different soil characteristics, for the production of alternative cropping combinations (Moore and Hedges, 1963). The economically optimum timing of water application and water values associated with such an optimum have been estimated for limited circumstances. There is at least one study in which alternative farm sizes, several policy restrictions reflecting various federal agricultural programs, and the other variables just mentioned were introduced into a program which determined the economic demand for water for irrigation (Moore and Hedges, 1963). Some of these efforts constitute more than a flexing of the computer's muscles. It is reasonable to suppose that the optimum amount of water used to produce alfalfa changes as the price of water changes or as the other variables take on alternative values. We are beginning to get quantitative measures of these changes. Experimental evidence shows that the timing of water application to achieve optimum physical output differs significantly from the economically optimum time and economically optimum water-quantity application. To reiterate, empirical evidence indicates that the best time to irrigate and the best quantity of water to apply is very sensitive to the price of water.

Conclusion

There is growing public concern at the district, county, state, regional, and national level about desirable water development, pricing, and management programs. Since all agencies are not likely to have the same objectives, nor be willing to trade an increment of improvement in one objective for losses in another at the same rate, growing conflict over rival programs may be expected. Irrigation pricing policies necessarily will be included in the public debate. Under these circumstances, there is an urgent need for careful and imaginative economic analyses. Only when a much greater effort is made to estimate the magnitude and distribution of costs and benefits associated with competing policy choices, can the participants rank and then select the preferable alternative. Poor decisions are costly because water-development schemes in general, and irrigation schemes in particular, are long-lived and seem to be growing in size. Concomitantly, the rewards can be large for better economic analyses.

REFERENCES

Adams, Frank
    1916 Irrigation districts in California, 1887–1915. California Department of Engineering, Bulletin No. 21. Sacramento.
Brewer, Michael
    1961 Water pricing and allocation with particular reference to California irrigation districts. University of California Agricultural Experiment Station, Report No. 456.
Brown, Gardner, Jr.
    1964 Distribution of benefits and costs from public water development: A case study of the San Joaquin Valley—Southern California aqueduct system. Unpublished doctoral dissertation, University of California.
California Conservation Commission
    1912 Report of the Conservation Commission of the State of California. Sacramento.
Ciriacy-Wantrup, S. V.
    1960 Projections of water requirements in the economics of water policy. Giannini Foundation Paper No. 193, University of California.
Gaffney, Mason
    1961 Diseconomies inherent in western water laws: A California case study. In Water and range resources and economic development of the west. Report No. 9, Conference Proceedings of the Western Agricultural Economic Research Council, January, pp. 55–80.
Goldschmidt, Walter R.
    1947 As you sow. Harcourt, Brace & World, New York.
Hall, William
    1886 Irrigation development. Part I: The introductory part of the report of the State Engineer of California on irrigation questions. Sacramento.

Hartman, L. M., and D. A. Seastone
  1965 Efficiency criteria for market transfers of water. Water Resources Research, 1:165–71.
Mackinchan, K. A., and U. C. Kammerer
  1961 Estimated use of water in the United States, 1960. U.S. Geological Survey Circular No. 456.
Moore, Charles V., and Trimble R. Hedges
  1963 Economics of on-farm irrigation water availability and costs, and related farm adjustments. Part III: Some aggregate aspects of farmer demand for irrigation water and production response on the San Joaquin Valley Eastside. University of California Agricultural Experiment Station, Report No. 261.
Trelease, Frank
  1961 Water law and economic transfers of water. Journal of Farm Economics, 43:1147–52.
U.S. Department of Agriculture, Office of Experiment Stations
  1901 Report of irrigation investigation in California. Bulletin No. 100. Washington, D.C.
U.S. Senate, Select Committee on National Water Resources
  1960 Water resources activities in the United States, future needs for reclamation in the western states. Committee Print No. 14. Washington, D.C.
Wertheimer, Ralph B.
  1944 Legislative and administrative history of acreage limitations and control of speculation on federal reclamation projects. In Central Valley Project studies, a report on Problem 19, acreage limitation in the Central Valley.

IV

BENEFIT-COST ANALYSIS: A CRITERION FOR SOCIAL INVESTMENT

Robert C. Lind

Introduction

SINCE World War II benefit-cost analysis has increasingly commanded the attention of professional economists and government administrators. The general idea that the potential benefits of a public project ought to be measured and compared with its costs was well established in the thirties, but it was not until the postwar period that the idea was systematically explored and developed in detail, in connection with an attempt to establish criteria by which to evaluate public investments in the field of water resources. A close connection between the development of benefit-cost analysis and the general field of water resource management is reflected by the fact that many of the best statements of the rationale of benefit-cost analysis are contained in works which address various aspects of the design of water resource systems (Eckstein, 1958; Maass, 1962; McKean, 1958). This connection is also apparent in documents prepared by agencies of the United States Government which set forth principles and procedures for use in formulating and evaluating water-related programs (U.S. Congress, Senate, 1962; U.S. Inter-Agency Committee on Water Resources, 1958).

Despite its historical connections with the analysis of water projects, the benefit-cost framework is completely general and can be used to evaluate a broad class of investment programs. During the past few years there has been a resurgence of interest in benefit-cost techniques because of large public investments in transportation, urban renewal, education, and public health.

Robert C. Lind is assistant professor in the Department of Engineering-Economics Systems at Stanford University.

In all these areas the benefit-cost approach has been used to evaluate alternative programs.*

The objective in undertaking a social investment is, in some broad sense, to increase social welfare; to make correct choices among alternative investment opportunities one must have a criterion by which to rank the available alternatives in accordance with this objective. It is generally accepted that social welfare, or a change in social welfare, is a function of a number of variables among which economic efficiency, the distribution of income, regional development, and national defense are most often included. Ideally one would define an objective function on the relevant variables and design a model which would predict the effect of each alternative investment program on these variables, thereby obtaining a complete ranking of the alternatives. In practice this ideal is seldom attainable, and the economic analyst is content to present an incomplete display of the effects of each alternative on the important variables, leaving the problem of how to weigh the various consequences to some decision-maker.

There is, however, a class of public investments where economic efficiency may be presumed to be the primary objective, and in other cases the problem of choosing between alternative investments may be so structured that the choice can again be made solely on the basis of some criterion of efficiency. Such might be the case where regional budgets for investment in public works are given in advance, the problem then being to select the most efficient set of projects consistent with these budget constraints. Where increased economic efficiency is the prime objective of a program of social investment, benefit-cost analysis can be used to obtain a ranking of alternative investments and to determine whether a particular investment is efficient.

This paper outlines the general procedure of benefit-cost analysis and explains the rationale behind the procedure. The desired measure of benefits and costs is discussed, as are the conditions under which market prices can be used in measuring benefits and costs. At this point in the paper the relationship between the benefit-cost criterion and economic efficiency is brought out, clarifying the exact meaning of economic efficiency in this context. In addition the benefit-cost criterion is compared with the profitability criterion, as the latter is used to select among alternative investments in private capital markets. It will be seen that a very close parallel exists between the benefit-cost approach and those profitability considerations which determine choices

---

* For a survey of the literature on benefit-cost analysis, see Prest and Turvey (1965).

among alternative investments in the private sector of the economy; however, some notable differences stem from the special nature of investments generally undertaken by some public agency. The special characteristics of this social investment are then discussed, as are the difficulties and special conditions that these characteristics create for the measurement of benefits and costs. In any investment decision an exceedingly important consideration is the way that risk is incorporated into the decision rule, and the case of social investment is no exception. This problem is discussed in connection with the social rate of discount, and several alternative positions on the issue are presented. Finally, the last section of the paper discusses conditions under which benefit-cost analysis may be applied and points out several important cases where market imperfections may complicate the problem of measuring costs and benefits.

The General Benefit-Cost Approach

An investment is the allocation of current resources to an activity which will produce future goods and services, and the value of these goods and services represents the benefits derived from making the investment. The cost of an investment is the value of the goods and services that could have been produced had these resources been allocated to some alternative productive activity. Assuming that the costs and benefits are correctly measured, an investment is justified if the benefits which will accrue as its consequence are greater than the costs incurred. This proposition is simply a straightforward statement of an efficiency condition for any productive activity. Similarly, if two mutually exclusive investments are being considered, the choice should be made so as to maximize the value of net benefits—i.e., benefits minus costs. This summarizes the basic principle underlying the benefit-cost approach to investment decisions.

Several very difficult conceptual problems remain to be solved, however, before the framework outlined above may be used in selecting among alternative investment opportunities. The most important obstacle involves the measurement of benefits and costs at a given point in time and the weighing of these cost and benefit measures when they exist at different points in time.

Abstract from the problem of making commensurable those benefits and costs which accrue at different points in time by assuming, for the moment, that all benefits and costs occur at a given point in time. We then measure the benefits as the maximum amount of money that the recipients of these benefits would willingly pay for them, and we measure the cost of operating the activity which produced these benefits as the minimum amount of money required to fully compensate the owners of the resources allocated to this activity. Denote the total benefit by B and the total cost by C, and suppose that $B - C > 0$. In this case the beneficiaries of the productive activity can fully compensate (by paying the full resource costs) those individuals who initially bear the costs and still be better off than if the activity were not in operation. If in addition we assume that the beneficiaries of this activity would willingly forego the goods and services which make up the benefits for a sum of money equal to B, then it follows that, if $B - C > 0$, the beneficiaries could not be made as well off by a lump-sum payment of C dollars as they would be if this activity were put in operation and the benefits were received free of charge. Therefore, the benefit-cost criterion is essentially a compensation criterion. If this criterion is satisfied along with the above assumption, it follows that beneficiaries can fully compensate those who incur the costs of the project and still be better off than they were initially; in addition they could not have been made as well off by a payment of a sum less than or equal to the cost of the project. Therefore, the benefit-cost criterion tells us whether a project is economically efficient in the specific sense outlined above.

Given the assumption that the beneficiaries are indifferent between receiving the benefits, for which they would willingly pay B dollars, or receiving a payment of B dollars, then the benefit-cost criterion can be used to arrive at a consistent ordering of alternative projects and to separate all projects into two classes, efficient and inefficient (Marglin, 1962). In most cases the above assumption is a very reasonable one and is explicitly or implicitly made in all benefit-cost studies.

This discussion may be further clarified by considering the following example. The project under consideration is a reservoir and distribution system which will irrigate a certain area. The farmers in this area will gain benefits from the use of water to increase production on their farms. The maximum amount that they would willingly pay for this water will equal the total increase in net farm incomes in the area, which therefore measures the benefit of the project. The cost of the project is the amount of money required to pay for construction and maintenance of the system. If benefits exceed costs, then the farmers as a group can pay for the irrigation system out of increased incomes and still have higher net incomes than before the project was constructed. Suppose, instead, that the government wishes to subsidize farmers in the area and increase their net incomes by an amount B, and that the choice of policies is either to give the farmers a direct subsidy of

B dollars or to build the irrigation project which would provide a certain amount of water free of charge. Suppose, in addition, that $B - C > 0$ where *C* is the cost of the project. Clearly, the government could achieve its objective more efficiently by building the irrigation project for *C* dollars rather than paying a subsidy equal to *B*. On the other hand if $B - C < 0$, the converse would be true.

It is in the dual sense just outlined that a project is said to be efficient if net benefits are positive (i.e., $V = B - C > 0$) and inefficient if $V < 0$. A similar line of reasoning can be carried out to show that if there are two alternative, mutually exclusive projects, the one which yields the higher net benefits is preferable in terms of the definition of efficiency just outlined. In general, where alternative investment programs are considered under a variety of technical and financial constraints, the alternative programs can be ranked on efficiency grounds according to the value of their net benefits. The benefit-cost criterion dictates that the investment program be chosen which maximizes net benefits, subject to the constraint that net benefits are positive.

Time Preference and Discounting

To this point the discussion of measurement has been simplified by assuming that all benefits and costs occur at one point in time. The essence of investment, however, is that benefits and costs are spread over time. Therefore, one of the central problems in benefit-cost analysis is how to make commensurable the values of benefits and costs which occur at different times. It follows that if we are to add up the benefits and costs in each period, we must have some rule for assigning weights according to time of occurrence. One procedure would be to ignore the time factor and to weigh benefits and costs in each period equally. In this case the value of total benefits would be given by

$$B = \sum_{t=0}^{T} b_t$$

and value of total costs by

$$C = \sum_{t=0}^{T} c_t ,$$

where b_t and c_t are the value of benefits and costs, respectively, which accrue in period *t*, and where *T* is the life span of the investment.

This procedure is, however, unsatisfactory because individuals have time preference and are not, in general, indifferent to having an additional dollar of income at different points in time. Suppose that an individual is indifferent to trading a dollar of income today for $(1 + \xi_t)$ dollars of income at time t; then 1 dollar at time t is worth $(\frac{1}{1+\xi_t})$ dollars today. The value today, measured in dollars, of a dollar at time t is said to be its present value and ξ_t is said to be the marginal rate of time preference relating income in period t with income today. ξ_t is not fixed and is in general dependent on the time profile of an individual's income and also upon his desired consumption at different points in time. It is reasonable to assume that as an individual trades more and more income today for income in period t, the marginal rate of time preference will rise, i.e., he will require more future income for each dollar of present income foregone.

To make this more clear consider a case where there are only two periods and where the individual receives an income of y_1 and y_2 at the beginning of periods 1 and 2 respectively. Given this distribution of income payments over time and the individual's desired consumption over time, suppose that the individual is indifferent to trading 1 dollar of income in period 1 for $(1 + \xi)$ dollars in period 2. In this example it is clearly conceivable that $\xi < 0$, i.e., the individual would be willing to trade 1 dollar in period 1 for less than 1 dollar in period 2. This might be the case if the individual's income were large in period 1 and small in period 2 relative to his needs. However, as the individual trades more and more of income in period 1 for income in period 2 the value of his marginal rate of time preference rises and, in most cases, will become positive at some point.

Now suppose the individual is given the opportunity to borrow or invest at a fixed rate of interest r. Then, given the marginal rate of time preference associated with his initial distribution of income over time, he will invest money if $r > \xi$ and borrow money if $r < \xi$. He will continue to borrow or to invest up to the point where $\xi = r$, i.e., he will continue to alter the time pattern of his income stream until the rate at which he can trade a dollar of income in period 1 for a dollar of income in period 2 is just equal to the rate at which he is indifferent to making such a trade. If $r > 0$, then his marginal rate of time preference is also positive at the point where he reaches an equilibrium.

Now the concept of present value can be used to make commensurate benefits and costs which accrue at different points in time. Suppose that benefits to a given individual are $b_0, b_1, \ldots, b_t$. Then the present value of these benefits to this individual is

$$B = \sum_{t=0}^{T} \frac{b_t}{(1 + \xi_t)},$$

where ξ_t is the marginal rate of time preference relating time t with time zero. Clearly, $\xi_0 = 0$. In the same way a stream of costs can be discounted to their present value which is given by

$$C = \sum_{t=0}^{T} \frac{c_t}{(1 + \xi_t)}.$$

It is assumed for simplicity that ξ_t remains constant over changes of the magnitude of b_t and c_t. The present value of net benefits is given by

$$V = B - C = \sum_{t=0}^{T} \frac{b_t - c_t}{(1 + \xi_t)}.$$

From the foregoing discussion it is clear that the benefits and costs accruing to a given individual can be put in terms of present dollars by discounting them to their present value using $1/(1 + \xi_t)$ as the discount factor for benefits and costs accruing at time t. Therefore, to get the correct measure of the total value of net benefits in terms of present dollars, one would need to calculate the benefits and costs accruing to each individual; discount them to their present value using discount factors based on that individual's marginal rate of time preference; and then sum over-all individuals.

This procedure presents some practical difficulties. First, even if benefits and costs accruing to each individual can be identified, there is the problem of knowing what discount factors to use in the calculation of present values. Second, benefits and costs cannot always be measured for each individual, and in such cases there is the problem of determining the correct discount factor for the aggregate of benefits and costs accruing at time t. In this case some weighted average of the individual discount factors is appropriate; however, the correct weights cannot be determined without knowing the percentage of total benefits and costs accruing to each individual. There is one case, however, where this is not a problem. If the marginal rates of time preference are the same for all individuals, then the discount factor applicable to total benefits and costs in any period is the discount factor applicable for any individual. The problem of measuring the correct discount factors is one facet of the more general problem of measuring benefits and costs. The following section of this paper examines the conditions under which market prices and the market rate of interest can be employed in benefit-cost studies as measures of benefits and in determining the marginal rates of time preference.

The Use of Market Prices in Benefit-Cost Measurements

Suppose that the conditions of a perfectly competitive economy prevail and that the economy is in equilibrium. From well-known theorems in economics it follows that each individual is indifferent between having an additional unit of any commodity and paying the equilibrium price of that commodity. Therefore, the equilibrium price measures the maximum amount of money that the individual would pay for the marginal unit of any commodity. In addition he would willingly give up a unit of this commodity for an amount equal to its price, since he is indifferent on the margin. Furthermore, given competitive equilibrium, the marginal cost of producing an additional unit of a commodity equals its price. Therefore, it follows that costs and benefits as previously defined can be measured in terms of market prices.

A perfectly competitive market affords perfect capital markets where everyone has the same opportunities to borrow and to invest. In competitive equilibrium a single market rate of interest exists at which all individuals can borrow and lend. For simplicity suppose that the rate of interest remains constant over time. Then 1 dollar invested today, which along with the earned interest is reinvested each year, is worth $(1 + r)^t$ at time t. By a similar line of reasoning, 1 dollar at time t is worth $1/(1 + r)^t$ dollars today. Therefore, each individual in competitive equilibrium will have adjusted his income by borrowing and lending so that $(1 + \xi_t) = (1 + r)^t$. In other words the appropriate discount factor for time t is $1/(1 + r)^t$ for every individual and therefore for the aggregate as well. Note that if imperfect capital markets deprive individuals of equal opportunities to invest and borrow, then the marginal rates of time preference will, in general, differ among individuals, which, as we have seen, creates difficulties of measurement.

To summarize, if we assume that conditions in the economy approximate those of a perfectly competitive economy, then market prices and the market rate of interest can be used to measure benefits and costs and in determining the appropriate discount factors. While this makes the problem of measurement more manageable, it by no means resolves all difficulties. For example, it is still necessary to forecast future prices, and such forecasts are at best tentative. In addition the special nature of social investment greatly complicates the problem of measurement.

Profitability and the Benefit-Cost Criterion

Before proceeding to discuss the special nature of social investment, it is instructive to consider the profitability criterion used by private investors in light of the previous discussion. An investment in the private sector of the economy will produce a stream of output which is sold at prevailing market prices. Associated with this productive activity is also a stream of inputs which the entrepreneur buys at market prices. Therefore, the entrepreneur must choose among investments which yield various streams of revenues and costs. Given the market rate of interest, a profit-maximizing entrepreneur will choose those investments which maximize the present value of net revenues where the market rate of interest is used as the discount factor. If the present value of an investment is positive, given the market rate of interest, it is profitable and will be undertaken. It is clear from the previous discussion that an investor in a perfectly competitive economy makes the same calculation and follows the same decision rules as if he were using the benefit-cost approach to investment decisions. There is, however, one significant difference. The private entrepreneur actually sells the output and buys his inputs in the market. Therefore those who receive the benefits of the investment actually pay the costs incurred. On the other hand, the general benefit-cost approach does not require that the beneficiaries pay any or all of the costs—i.e., it requires only a hypothetical test of whether such compensation could be carried out and still leave the beneficiaries better off than they previously were. Therefore, benefit-cost analysis can be looked upon as an extension of the profitability criterion used in the private sector of the economy. In the case of social investments it may be either undesirable or impracticable to require that the persons who receive the benefits pay the full cost. A wide range of financial arrangements is available. In many cases the beneficiaries pay some, but not all, of the costs of a given project, the balance being borne by the general public through taxes.

The Special Nature of Social Investment

The preceding discussion addresses the general question of investment criteria without specific reference to the special nature of social investments. At this point it is important to consider the circumstances under which it may be necessary or desirable to undertake some investments socially rather than privately and also to examine the measurement problems associated with social investments. The consideration of the special nature of social investment is given added importance when we note that the profitability criterion used by private investors in a perfectly competitive economy is virtually identical to the benefit-cost criterion. Why, then, not leave all investment to private investors?

It is necessary for the operation of markets that the goods and services bought and sold be readily identifiable and appropriable, in the sense that the good or service can be supplied to some individuals and withheld from others. Where this is possible, individual producers can sell their products to persons willing to pay the market price, while others who choose not to purchase this product do not enjoy its use. Food, clothing, furniture, and so forth, are examples of appropriable commodities. For goods and services of this sort, the private entrepreneur can capture the full value of the benefits and similarly must pay the full value of costs. There is, however, an important class of goods, called public goods, which are not appropriable. Goods in this class are such that if one individual enjoys their use all may do the same. An investment which produces a good of this type yields benefits to everyone, whether or not they make any payment whatsoever. As a result, it is not in general possible for a private entrepreneur to capture the value of such benefits through user charges; consequently, it will not be profitable for him to undertake the investment. An example of a public good in the water field is structural flood control. A system of dams and reservoirs which protects one piece of property in the flood plain also protects all other property there, regardless of whether the property owners make any payment. Air-pollution abatement is another type of investment which produces a public good, as everyone is free to enjoy the resultant clean air.

It is clear from these examples that public goods may be of immense value and that if each individual were accurately to reveal the value to him of having this good, total benefits would far exceed costs. However, if an individual knows that this good may be made available whether or not he contributes an amount equal to the benefit he receives, he is likely to withhold payment in the expectation that others will purchase this good and that he will receive the benefits free of charge. This strategy consideration makes it impossible for an entrepreneur to capture the benefits through voluntary payments; therefore, if the investment is to be made it must be made by the government. Through its power of taxation, the government—wishing to recapture the value of benefits from the beneficiary— can levy compulsory taxes on him and thus circumvent the withholding of voluntary payments. In another case, the government may wish to undertake an investment without recapturing all or part of the benefits, as from a social point of view the redistribution of income which results may be desirable. To summarize, in the case of public goods socially desirable investments will in general have to be undertaken socially rather than privately because the nature of these goods causes a divergence between the benefit captured by the entrepreneur (or private benefit) and the correct measure of total benefit (which will be referred to as social benefit).

The case of public goods is a very important special case of a more general phenomenon known as external effects, or spillover effects. External effects exist whenever there is a divergence between private benefit and social benefit or between private cost and social cost. External costs are levied, for example, when a pulp mill dumping waste into the water and air imposes a resultant cost on people adversely affected by the pollution. In this case the pulp mill, not having to pay these costs, makes investment and operating decisions which do not maximize the net value of social benefits. A second example is investment in facilities to immunize people against contagious diseases. Here the benefits are partially appropriable. The individual immunized receives a benefit which can be withheld. However, the public at large receives a benefit in the form of improved community health and a lower probability of exposure to contagious disease. Many areas of public concern, including education, involve a product which has some of the characteristics of both a private and a public good.

The existence of externalities does not necessarily require or justify the public's owning and operating the activities which generate external effects. In a great number of cases these effects may be relatively insignificant and can be ignored; in other cases it may be possible to eliminate the divergence between private and social costs and benefits through a system of taxes and subsidies. For example, in the case of the pulp mill dumping pollutants, a tax on effluent which is designed to reflect the external costs of pollution can make private costs identical with social costs. Such an effluent charge, which directs the operating decisions of the pulp mill, is probably a more desirable alternative than public ownership of the pulp and paper industry. In still other cases, however, the externalities are so extensive and significant that public ownership may prove necessary. This is the situation in the case of multipurpose river-basin development, where it is more simple and more practical for the government to step in and plan an entire development, taking prior account of external effects, than it would be to develop a system of market incentives capable of directing the combined efforts of private investors to the optimal system.

Thus, the degree and the extent of externalities largely determine whether a given investment should be in the private or the public domain. It is a matter in part of empirical evidence and in part of value judgment to decide when external effects justify direct social control of a productive activity.

There is another circumstance under which it may be desirable to have a productive activity operated by the government. Where large economies of scale may be realized, it is not technically efficient for a large number of competitive firms to produce a given product, since the cost per unit is minimized if the entire output is produced by one firm or production unit. While it would be technically efficient to have in operation only one firm, the danger of monopoly exploitation would then be present. To achieve the economies of scale without incurring problems associated with monopolistic behavior, it may be advisable for society to undertake the operation of this activity collectively.

An example of this is the distribution system for a municipal water supply. Clearly, it would be inefficient to have a number of competitive firms selling water, each with its own system of pipes, meters, and so forth. On the other hand, to have the supply of water controlled by a single private firm would run great risks of monopoly exploitation. For this reason most municipal systems are publicly owned and operated.

It should be pointed out, however, that public regulation of a private monopoly is an alternative method of securing the gains from economies of scale without incurring the disadvantages of monopolistic output and pricing policies. An example of such a regulated monopoly is the American telephone industry. Which method of control is preferable where large economies of scale exist is partly a matter of value judgment and partly an empirical question concerning the effectiveness of public regulation and the relative technical efficiency of private and public monopolies.

Special Problems in Measuring Benefits and Costs

It has been demonstrated that under competitive conditions market prices can be used to measure benefits and costs. However, in the case of a public good there is no market price, because the nature of such a good precludes its being traded in the market; therefore it is necessary to impute the value of benefits from other information. Since the benefit to any individual is the maximum amount of money he would willingly pay for a given amount of the public good, it follows that this value must be imputed for each individual. While it is true that in the case of a public good everyone enjoys the same amount and quality of the good, it does not follow that its value will be the same for every individual. This clearly complicates the problem of benefit measurement, which is perhaps the most troublesome technical difficulty arising in the application of benefit-cost analysis. There is no general method for overcoming this difficulty, and methods of imputing benefits vary with the nature of the good in question.

The case of flood control provides a good example. When a system of dams, levees, and storage reservoirs is constructed, losses from flooding are reduced. If it is assumed that individuals and firms would willingly pay for flood protection an amount up to the value of the reduction in their property losses, then a measure of the benefits can be obtained by estimating this reduction in flood losses. Note that the benefit which accrues to different individuals will differ according to the nature and value of the property they have exposed to the hazard of flooding. While the estimation of flood losses is not a trivial problem, the existence of this surrogate for the value of benefits greatly facilitates such estimation. In the case of some public goods, such as national defense, the measurement of benefits is a practical impossibility.

In the general case of externalities, market prices do not accurately represent social benefits and costs. As in the case of public goods, relevant external benefits and costs have to be imputed from other information. Again depending on the particular case, this can be exceedingly difficult. For example, imagine the problem of measuring the external costs associated with the discomfort and the health hazards caused by polluted air. In recent years much of the work related to benefit-cost analysis has addressed problems of this type associated with a wide range of public programs. While a survey of such work would lead well beyond the scope of this paper, its importance for public investment decisions is clear (Dorfman, 1965).

A second type of measurement problem arises when either a new good is introduced or the price of some existing good changes as the result of a public investment. When this happens, a consumer's surplus is created. The concept of consumer's surplus can best be illustrated by example. Suppose that as the result of a hydroelectric project electricity is made available in an area which previously was without electric power. Further, suppose that this power is sold for a price, P, per kwh which equals the marginal cost of producing an additional kwh of power. The demand schedule for power is represented in Figure 1; given the price P, the residents of the area will purchase q units of power at a price P. The total market value of the benefits produced by the project is pq; however, the market value understates the true value of the benefits.

This differential occurs because the market price represents the amount of money the consumer will willingly pay for the marginal, or last, unit purchased. In general he would willingly pay an amount greater than the market price for the first kwh, the second, and so forth. The fact that he has to pay only the market price means that he receives a surplus of value equal to the difference between what he would willingly have paid for the power he buys and what he does in fact pay in the market. This is called the consumer's surplus. An individual would clearly be willingly to pay a lump sum equal to his consumer's surplus for the opportunity to purchase any amount of electric power at a price of p dollars per kwh. From the definition of the measure of project benefits, it follows that the correct measure of benefits is the sum of their market value and the consumer's surplus.

Some difficult conceptual questions arising in connection with the consum-

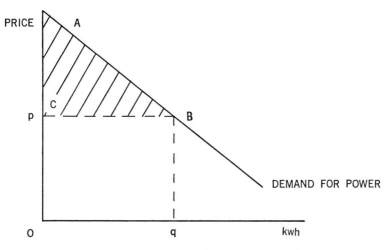

Figure 1. Assumed price-demand relationship

er's surplus are beyond the scope of this paper and, in addition, there are several different theoretical measures of this concept. However, given the appropriate assumptions, the total consumer's surplus can be measured by the shaded area of the triangle ABC in Figure 1. As a practical matter, the measurement of consumer's surplus is a difficult task even under the best of circumstances, for example, where available data permit the accurate estimation of the demand for the good or service in question.

There is, however, a situation where a simple rule of thumb can be used to estimate the value of benefits which include some consumer's surplus. Consider the following example. Suppose electric power is being supplied to a region at a price p, and a quantity q is purchased at that price. Now introduce a hydroelectric plant, increasing the supply of power to the area, and reduce the price to p', $p' < p$. At this new price an amount q is consumed, as illustrated in Figure 2.

The total benefit from the production of electricity, including consumer's surplus, is represented by the quadrilateral $OADF$. However, before the introduction of the new project the benefits were equal to the area of the figure $OABE$. Thus, the net increase in the benefits from power production equals the area of $EBDF$ which in turn equals $\frac{1}{2}(p + p')(q' - q)$. In other words, to measure the benefit of the project we multiply the increase in output by the average of the prices that obtain before and after the introduction of the project. This procedure depends on the fact that the demand

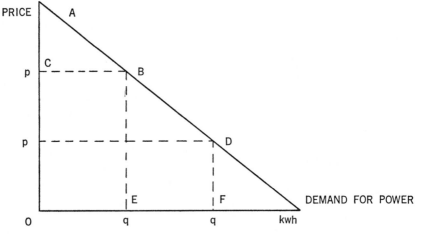

Figure 2. Assumed price-demand relationship

curve is assumed to be linear; in cases where the price change accompanying the introduction of the new facilities is not too large, the demand curve can be assumed to be approximately linear in the region under consideration, and this method of measuring the increments in benefits can be used with reasonable confidence.

The above example brings out an additional point of particular importance for developing the correct measure of benefits. Suppose that the new hydroelectric project completely displaces previously existing facilities, in the sense that these are taken out of operation and the entire output is produced by the new facilities. It is tempting to consider the benefits from the new project as the entire area $OADF$. However, this is incorrect, since a part of these benefits would have been produced whether or not the new facilities had been constructed. In cases such as this, only the incremental benefits should be counted. The new facilities may effect a saving in operating costs, and this must be taken into account in making the benefit-cost calculation. However, it cannot be emphasized too strongly that unless care is taken to count only the increment in benefits which results from a project, the benefits may be vastly overstated.*

When the introduction of a project results in a number of price changes, the theoretical measure of the consumer's surplus becomes more complex and the problems of measurement virtually insurmountable. It follows that for the benefits and costs of a given project to be measurable in practice, its impact must not cause large price changes throughout the economy. In general, a particular project, such as a dam or power plant, is extremely small in comparison to the total national economy even though its size may be great in terms of some absolute scale. As a result, the impact of such a project on prices determined in national markets is generally insignificant, even while it may have a pronounced effect on local prices or on the price of its primary output—as in the case of a hydroelectric plant. Where price changes occur, efforts must be made to measure both the consumer's surplus and the producer's surplus, the latter being an analogous concept pertaining to the supply side of the market. A rule of thumb for measuring the value of goods that undergo price changes is to use the average of prices obtaining before and after the project is introduced. As was seen in Figure 2, this procedure takes the surplus into account.

Conditions under Which the Benefit-Cost Technique Is Applicable

When a public investment program results in major structural changes in the national economy or some regional economy, and when, as a consequence, significant changes occur in the price structure, benefit-cost analysis is not applicable. The benefit-cost approach is in essence a partial equilibrium technique for evaluating marginal changes in the economy. When programs involving greater than marginal changes are being considered, a general equilibrium model is required in which interrelationships between the investment program and the important economic variables in the system are explicitly incorporated into the analysis. Almost all public investments have a significant impact on some locality, and from the point of view of a given locality a project may represent a major change. Whether the use of the benefit-cost framework is appropriate in evaluating any given project is largely a matter for judgment. It is clear that for small public-works projects

---

* For a case study in which displacement effects are critical to the evaluation of benefits, see Krutilla (1967).

the benefit-cost approach is applicable; however, in the case of a major water-diversion program having widespread effects on the economies of several large regions, the usefulness of this approach is less clear. In the latter case the benefits and costs are so widespread that it may not be possible in practice to identify them or to solve the problems of measurement.

To summarize much of the preceding discussion, benefit-cost analysis is a technique for evaluating investment programs that result in marginal changes in the economy. As a practical matter, the implementation of benefit-cost analysis requires a situation where most costs and benefits can be measured in terms of market prices. This can be done if the conditions of competitive equilibrium are satisfied. In a large number of markets one would expect competitive forces to produce conditions corresponding closely to those of the competitive model; however, in other markets it is apparent that existing conditions do not fit the model of perfect competition. Because of these market imperfections, the prices of some commodities may not accurately reflect their social value, and benefits and costs must then be computed on the basis of other information.

The Case of Unemployed Resources

There are two situations of particular importance where the existence of market imperfections requires a modification of procedures for measuring benefits and costs. The first is where available productive resources are unemployed. Suppose that a project utilizes resources which in the absence of the project would be unemployed. In this case the cost of employing these resources is zero in terms of alternative uses foregone. Therefore, zero is the correct measure of the social cost even though the actual amount paid for these resources is positive.

To exemplify this situation, consider a region where there is widespread unemployment among construction workers. In addition, suppose that the union wage rate is $2.50 per hour and that labor in the region is immobile. Then if a water project is constructed in this region which draws its labor from the ranks of the unemployed, the cost of using this labor in terms of alternatives foregone is zero even though the actual wage bill may be large.

Great care must be taken in applying this principle, however, as seldom do productive resources have no alternative uses. In some cases resources are temporarily unemployed but will be re-employed as individuals and firms adjust to market conditions. In the previous example, workers may in the absence of the local water project migrate to areas where they can find employment. In this case the opportunity cost of using the unemployed labor on a local project is the production foregone elsewhere because they did not move. Even in the case where unemployed resources are completely immobile it does not inevitably follow that the cost of these resources should be set at zero in making benefit-cost calculations. Suppose the government is considering a number of projects in a region with unemployed resources. In addition suppose that if all the projects under consideration are constructed, resource requirements will then exceed the quantity unemployed. In this case the opportunity cost of using unemployed labor on one project equals the benefits foregone by not using this labor on the best alternative project. A serious understatement of costs might occur if the benefit-cost calculation for each project were made on the assumption that unemployed resources would remain unused in the absence of that particular project. In cases such as the one outlined above, the opportunity cost of using unemployed resources can often be obtained as shadow prices by the use of the techniques of mathematical programming.

The Choice of the Correct Rate of Discount

There is a second situation where imperfections in the market may necessitate modification of the procedure which could have been followed had all conditions of the perfectly competitive model been satisfied. Under conditions of the competitive model one market rate of interest, *r*, obtains in equilibrium, and *r* equals the marginal rate of time preference for each individual as well as the rate of return on the marginal investment. Under these conditions, *r* is clearly the correct rate of discount. However, in the real world we observe many rates of interest, differing among individuals and among varied types of securities. For example, we observe different rates on savings and loan accounts, government bonds, and various private notes; and the rate of interest paid by borrowers to consumer loan companies and to banks may differ substantially. As a result, the question of the appropriate discount rate cannot be solved simply by using the market-determined rate of interest.

Two explanations are frequently offered for the fact that a multiplicity of rates of interest exists in the capital market. The first is that differences in the observed rates merely reflect variation in the riskiness of different investments. Under this hypothesis, the rates paid by alternative investments are identical except for adjustments for risk. In this case the rate of return on a risk-free security would represent the marginal rate of time preference for every individual. The second explanation of these differential rates is that various imperfections in the capital market afford individuals different opportunities to borrow and to invest. As a result, each individual will borrow or lend to the point where his marginal rate of time preference equals the rate of return on his marginal investment opportunity—or the rate of interest at which he can borrow. Since these opportunities differ among individuals, different rates will be observed in equilibrium.

These two explanations are not mutually exclusive; in fact both differences in riskiness and imperfections in the capital market probably contribute to the observed differences in interest rates. However, the two explanations have very different implications for the choice of a social rate of discount and for the financing of public projects.

Suppose that the differences in rates paid on different securities are due solely to differences in riskiness among investments. Then clearly the correct social rate of discount for the evaluation of a public investment with a certain payoff is the rate paid on a risk-free security, such as a long-term government bond. However, most public investments do involve risk, and there are two points of view within the economics profession as to how this risk should be handled. One suggests that for each public investment we find a similar investment in the private sector and that the rate of return on this private investment be taken as applicable to the corresponding public investment. This in effect means that society at large discounts risk in exactly the same way that private entrepreneurs discount it. There are, however, several reasons to believe that this procedure is inappropriate and that only the expected payoff of a public investment should be considered. By this hypothesis, the benefit and cost figures should be the expected value of benefits and costs, and the rate of discount applied should be that on a risk-free security. One reason for supporting the latter position is that the government is in a better position than a private entrepreneur for coping with risk. The government undertakes a large number of projects, and because of the law of large numbers, risk is essentially eliminated. In addition, recent works have demonstrated that if the risk associated with one public investment is independent of other risks in the economy and if the project represents a small fraction of the community's resources, then the cost of risk bearing to the community as a whole is negligible. In this case the appropriate rate of discount is the rate of return on risk-free assets.

Suppose, on the other hand, that the observed differences are due solely to imperfections in the capital market such as credit restrictions and barriers to entry in certain fields of investment. Then individuals will in equilibrium have different marginal rates of time preference, and returns on marginal investments in various sectors of the economy will differ. In this case benefits and costs accruing at different points in time are weighted differently by different individuals, and the social rate of discount will have to be a weighted average of individual rates. A discussion of how to choose the appropriate weights is beyond the scope of this paper; however, an idea of some of the factors that must be taken into account can be gained by considering the implication of imperfections in the capital market for the financing of public investments.

Suppose that a public investment program is to be financed by taxation. In general the funds raised through taxation will come at the expense of both private investment and private consumption. To the extent that the public program displaces private investments, the return on the private alternative must clearly be taken into account. Therefore, it is a matter of concern that the method of financing be such that investments displaced in the private sector have a low rather than a high return.

The question of the appropriate social rate of discount remains a matter of some controversy—and one of the most difficult theoretical issues pertaining to the development of criteria for public investment decisions. While the foregoing discussion raises the major points at issue, a more complete treatment of the problem is well beyond the scope of this paper.

The foregoing discussion has outlined the benefit-cost approach to public investment decisions and has brought out the major analytical issues with which benefit-cost analysis is associated. Conceptually the benefit-cost approach is exceedingly simple and intuitively appealing. However, the application of this concept can become extremely complex because of the difficulty of measuring benefits and costs and of making commensurable those which accrue at different points in time. Because the problems of identification and measurement become practically prohibitive if an investment brings about a major change in the structure of prices, benefit-cost analysis is essentially limited to the evaluation of investments which make only marginal changes in the economy.

The usefulness of this type of analysis in evaluating public investment in any of a wide range of areas of public concern will largely depend on whether the benefits and costs can adequately be measured. Measurement problems are often specific to a particular type of investment and have to be solved for each case. Therefore it seems likely that while benefit-cost analysis will prove an exceedingly useful tool in some areas of public policy, it will be of little use in others.

Although the benefit-cost approach brings a much-needed framework of rationality to the area of public decision making, it is important to realize its limitations. One must take some care not to force the benefit-cost approach into areas where measurement problems make it inapplicable; and, just as importantly, programs of obvious worth should not be shelved simply because their potential benefits are not easily measured.

REFERENCES

Dorfman, Robert (ed.)
   1965   Measuring benefits of government investments. Brookings Institution, Washington, D.C.
Eckstein, Otto
   1958   Water resource development: The economics of project evaluation. Harvard University Press, Cambridge, Mass.
Krutilla, John V.
   1967   The Columbia River Treaty: A study in the economics of international river basin development. The Johns Hopkins Press, Baltimore, Md.
Maass, Arthur, *et al.*
   1962   Design of water-resource systems. Harvard University Press, Cambridge, Mass.
McKean, R. N.
   1958   Efficiency in government through systems analysis. John Wiley and Sons, New York.
Marglin, Stephen A.
   1962   Objectives of water-resource development: A general statement. In Design of water-resource systems, by Arthur Maass *et al.* Harvard University Press, Cambridge, Mass.
Prest, A. R., and R. Turvey
   1965   Cost-benefit analysis: A survey. Economic Journal, 75(300):683–735.
U.S. Congress, Senate
   1962   Policies, standards, and procedures in the formulation, evaluation, and review of plans for use and development of water and related land resources. Report by the President's Water Resources Council, 87th Congress, 2nd session, Senate Document 97.
U.S. Inter-Agency Committee on Water Resources, Subcommittee on Evaluation Standards
   1958   Proposed practices for economic analysis of river basin projects. Revised report. Government Printing Office, Washington, D.C.

V

PRESENT SURFACE-WATER RESEARCH
IN THE STATE OF WASHINGTON

Thomas H. Campbell

The Setting

THE state of Washington, like the neighboring lands to the north and south, is an area characterized by precipitation extremes. Its location as a maritime state on the western coast of the continent, in conjunction with its latitude, places it in the path of moist air moving eastward. Its mountain barriers cause great variation in precipitation and temperature. Some mountainous regions collect more than 20 feet of water a year; yet the arid eastern plateau includes large areas which receive less than 10 inches annually. The average yearly precipitation for the state as a whole is about 32 inches; yet the unequal distribution makes possible dense rain forests within a few hours' drive of desert wastes, parts of which only recently are being made productive by irrigation.

The great Columbia River flows down through the eastern part of the state, then turns west to empty into the ocean, forming a part of the boundary between Washington and Oregon. In this distance its flow is increased little by contributions from Washington. Most of the numerous other river systems of the state are relatively small, and flow directly to salt water in the part of the state west of the Cascade Mountains. The location and geology of these mountains are reflected in the characteristics of the streams which drain their slopes.

These surface waters are an important resource. Due to their location, dispersion, and behavior, problems arise in planning for their control or use.

Thomas H. Campbell is professor of civil engineering and director of the C. W. Harris Hydraulics Laboratory at the University of Washington.

In fact the natural laws governing the behavioral characteristics of our surface waters are still so poorly understood that economic decisions regarding their control or use often must be made on the basis of insufficient information. The need for fundamental knowledge is pressing.

In order to gain a better understanding of the temporal and spatial behavior of these surface waters, it is necessary to learn more about such natural phenomena as precipitation, snow and ice, losses due to evaporation and transpiration, soil-water relations near the soil surface, streamflow, sedimentation, reservoir mechanics, estuarine hydrology, and wave effects. Pertinent studies must be concerned with the entire history of water in the natural progression from atmospheric vapor through the streams to the sea, including those waters stored or released from storage beneath the surface of the earth. Historically, this last topic has usually been studied separately as ground water, differentiated from surface water, and is discussed in this book in the chapter by James Crosby III.

Land use has an effect on surface runoff. Urbanization, the cutting of forests, and changes in agricultural patterns influence both the amount and the time distribution of this runoff from a drainage basin. These effects are understood in a general qualitative sense, but with very few exceptions not enough is known to be able to relate or predict quantities. In some cases of proposed deforestation, it may be entirely a matter of conjecture as to whether the water yield may be increased or decreased. This is a deficiency in knowledge that will have to be rectified, because the use of land in this state is not going to remain as it is at present.

The Research Needs

Because of these considerations, it is suggested that at present the important research needs having to do with surface waters are those which: (1) develop techniques to make better use of existing information; (2) develop means of obtaining urgently needed new information; (3) optimize the use of these means of getting information; (4) develop concepts leading to better use of our water resources. The highest priority should be given to the use of modern analytical, statistical, and stochastic techniques to interpret and extend existing data regarding precipitation and streamflow for drainage areas of economic importance, and the development of new instruments for measuring accurately the flow of vapor in the air and the flow of water in small streams. The establishment of pilot-instrumented sites for hydrologic study, particularly in the mountains, should be high on the list of needed research. These projects are given high priority either because they can yield valuable results quickly and at reasonable cost, or because they are vitally needed as steppingstones to obtaining even more important information. Each of these will be discussed as they were presented to the State of Washington Water Research Center, representing urgent current research needs (Campbell, 1967).*

New Treatment for Old Data

An illustration of the power of new methods of treating existing data can be related to the Colorado River. Since 1922 several major decisions involving scheduling of storage reservoirs and an interstate compact have been made on the basis of historical records, only to be followed by an unprecedented series of dry years which would have influenced these decisions if the drought had occurred earlier (Maughan, 1965). A stochastic analysis of streamflow performance, based on methods newly developed by the "Harvard Group" and others, could have revealed that this type of dry period had a definite probability, and could have been anticipated. The lesson is that economic decisions should not be solidly based on historic streamflow records, since they will never again be repeated. The new stochastic methods can generate an endless series of hypothetical streamflows which have just as much likelihood of occurring as the series which has actually occurred on any given stream, if there is an existing record of reasonable length (for example, thirty years). This technique can provide a new perspective for economic analyses having to do with streamflow.

The benefits of this sort of treatment include better frequency analyses of floods as well as of droughts or of total runoff. Economic studies concerned with flooding are extremely sensitive to the estimated frequencies of flood stages on the given stream. These frequencies commonly are subject to an undesirable degree of indeterminateness due to the difficulty of interpreting the one or two highest flood peaks in the context of the remaining flood records. Yet the feasibility of engineering works concerned with flooding is more easily influenced by frequency values than by any other variable. A stochastic analysis usually results in a flood frequency relation in which much more confidence can be placed, as compared to the bare historic array.

In all cases where economic decisions are based on streamflow records, the stochastic treatment can give results of greatly improved quality so that these

* Since the time this paper was written, much research has been done and much progress has been made in several of these areas.

decisions can be sharpened. A tabulation of pertinent stochastic extensions of records for the important streams of the state would be of great value to all whose planning includes some consideration of the flow characteristics of these streams. These characteristics would include low flows, mean flows, and floods.

Although the statistical analysis of streamflow data can give us information of immediate economic importance at or near points of historic record, the use of this information to estimate flow relations at a site with different characteristics is open to considerable error, and gives little help in predicting the effect of weather modification. A more rational approach to the study of all the characteristics of the amounts and distribution of our water resources ultimately depends on a clear understanding of the amounts, distribution, and forms of precipitation. At present it is believed that we have a fairly good idea of precipitation characteristics in the lowland areas, but our knowledge of rainfall and snowfall amounts and intensities in the mountains is totally inadequate. In several large mountainous drainage basins, the recorded annual runoff exceeds the amount of water which can be arrived at by estimations based on all existing precipitation data. The Sultan River basin of the Cascade Mountains produces about 140 inches of runoff a year. Available meteorological data indicate an average precipitation on this basin of about 80 inches. Since the runoff from this drainage area must depend solely on its precipitation, allowance for losses leads to the necessary conclusion that the actual precipitation is about double that indicated by direct measurements.

Twenty per cent of western Washington is above 4,000 feet in elevation. This area supplies far more than its proportionate share of water, particularly the economically important summer streamflow and the damaging floods. Yet we have almost no understanding of the precipitation in this area. The truth is that we do not even have a clear picture of how much we know and how much we do not know about this precipitation.

Stochastic techniques are powerless to help our interpretation of rainfall data in the way that we can treat streamflow records, because precipitation appears to be completely random in nature. However, similar statistical manipulation of precipitation data is capable of revealing how accurately this data represents the precipitation patterns in a given region, how meaningful the averages and interpolations are, and where we should best obtain more information in order to improve our inadequate knowledge. This technique can be used to design data collecting networks, and, in some cases, to delineate important storm paths.

Our Olympic and Cascade ranges lie across the path of moist ocean air, and cause large amounts of orographically induced precipitation, about which very little is known. Operationally, the River Forecast Center at Portland, Oregon, pleads for more information on this phenomenon so they can produce flood forecasts with less guesswork and with reasonable accuracy. Scientifically, some meteorological authorities have stated that this site is so ideally situated to study orographic precipitation that it should be a duty to use it as a laboratory for the benefit of the world.

There are a host of such important areas of needed research having to do with streamflow and runoff, or directly with precipitation, which cannot be considered until we have a better knowledge of precipitation in some important geographical regions. None of this can begin, in any coordinated way, until we have a systematic inventory of what we know and what we need in respect to precipitation data. Hence statistical studies of precipitation in the state are given the highest type of priority.

New Instruments

Most meteorologists agree that existing devices for measuring precipitation are sufficiently accurate for the purpose, particularly in view of the unknown variation of precipitation with distance from the site. (There is some disagreement in this.) Also, methods of measuring the flow in large streams are well established and accurate, although expensive.

Yet the runoff characteristics of small drainage areas in many parts of the state are poorly known, and those of our mountainous areas are virtually unknown, because we have almost no records of flow from such areas. The adequacy of bridges over large rivers can be judged by any traveler, but the economic waste due to the overdesign or underdesign of thousands of culverts and small bridges is rarely evident to any but engineers of highway departments, the Forest Service, the Bureau of Public Roads, or other such offices. Forest Service facilities alone, in the winter of 1964–65 in Oregon and Washington, suffered flood damages requiring $11.9 million in repairs, a considerable portion of which could have been eliminated if more had been known about the hydrology of the geographical areas affected. The proper control of such streams and the sediments they carry is not possible until there is some means of estimating what rates and volumes are likely to be involved.

To measure the flow on a sufficient number of these streams to gain some quantitative insight into their behavior is a major effort which will require the cooperation of a number of state and federal agencies. It is a need that will have to be met. Yet, at present there is no adequate flow-metering device which can be produced, installed, and operated in numbers at a reasonable cost. Such a device would be of immediate world-wide value. It seems reasonable that a university-oriented research effort could develop such a meter.

Another device that is urgently needed is a meter for measuring the flux of atmospheric vapor. At present the losses due to evaporation and transpiration are usually evaluated as being a residual in a water-budget accounting procedure. At all but specially selected sites this is an unsatisfactory procedure due to the difficulty of measuring the transfer of water under the surface of the ground. If a vapor-flux meter could be developed, having the accuracy of the sonic anemometer, evapotranspiration could be measured directly. With a meter to measure the surface runoff from an area and with adequate precipitation gauging, the subsurface losses could be treated as the residual in a water-budget equation and our accuracy of accounting for water on a given area would be greatly increased.

The amount of water that escapes into the air from the soil, or vegetation, or reservoir is a major loss, in some areas exceeding the precipitation. Our state's evapotranspiration losses are not known within 10 per cent; yet 10 per cent of these losses represent something like 5 million acre-feet per year. A Corps of Engineers chief-of-section stated that their most noticeable gap in usable knowledge is that of the losses that make the difference between rainfall and runoff. The development of a moisture-flux meter and of a simple meter for the flow in small streams together would constitute a major breakthrough in hydrologic data-gathering ability, and promote new horizons in hydrologic analysis.

Pioneer work has been done on the principle of a moisture-flux meter, and its development as a usable tool in a reasonable time appears completely practicable.

Field Sites

The third category of high priority projects involves the locating and establishing of selected field sites for hydrologic experimentation and study. In this regard, existing laboratory facilities should be recognized, such as Forest Service, Agricultural Research Service and Experiment Station installations, and cooperative use sought if the sites can serve a purpose within the purview of the planned research effort. Some completely new sites undoubtedly would be considered. These sites should be selected with a thought of having them serve as many purposes as possible. Such a location may be a relatively compact area, or may be the hub of an extensive observational network.

It has already been stated that our knowledge of the hydrology of our Pacific Coast mountains is almost nonexistent. Yet this mountainous region is one of our most important sources of water supply and causes some of our most damaging floods. It also has an effect on the paths of damaging storms. Economic decisions regarding such water supplies or floods or storms at present must be based on information which usually consists of rough approximations at the best. Proper planning involving these factors (such as for optimum water development or changed land use) requires analyzing information which must be obtained in these mountains. Consequently some sort of a mountain hydrologic laboratory should be designed to obtain needed data. The planning for this sort of laboratory should be given high priority. It must be recognized that such an effort cannot be comprehensive in the sense of yielding all the answers, but is more likely to be a pilot study which could be expanded by collaboration with other interested governmental agencies such as the Weather Bureau and Geological Survey. Basic instrumentation for such laboratories need not be unduly expensive. The high costs are usually associated with recording equipment. Other high-priority research efforts, such as in ground water and in water quality, undoubtedly will also require similar recording facilities. For this reason a van type of recording center may be worth serious consideration. Such a center could be scheduled for best use by all Water Research Center investigators. An estimated cost would be thirty thousand dollars.

Other Research

There are a number of highly important research projects which cannot be started in a comprehensive way until the foregoing projects have produced results. For instance, an evaluation of the water budget of the state of Washington must remain in the realm of crude estimates until information is supplied by the procedures and instrumentation described above, or by similar means. However, there are significant supporting studies which can be made at present, and which have not been detailed in the foregoing statements only because they are not as crucial to our understanding of the surface waters of our state.

REFERENCES

Campbell, Thomas H.
  1967 Surface water. In Water resource research needs in the state of Washington, Donald L. Bender, comp. State of Washington Water Research Center, Pullman.
Maughan, W. D.
  1965 Major decision on the Colorado River revisited through application of stochastic hydrologic processes. American Society of Civil Engineers Water Resources Engineering Conference, Preprint 162. Mobile, Ala.

VI

PROBABILITY AND STOCHASTIC MODELS IN THE PLANNING PHASE OF WATER RESOURCES DEVELOPMENTS

John S. Gladwell

Introduction

IN the planning and design phases of water resources developments all quantitative data available is used. Traditionally the historic sequence of flow has been used because it has been the only tool readily available to engineers. More recently, however, investigations into the potentialities of generating artificial flow sequences with many of the statistical characteristics of the historical flows have developed. These will undoubtedly be tools which will increase the effectiveness of the preliminary analyses. One such study completed by T. H. Campbell and A. A. Harms (1966) of the University of Washington under a grant administered by the State of Washington Water Research Center for the Office of Water Resources Research, Department of Interior, has shown that it is possible to duplicate on a small time-period basis many of the historic statistical relationships while simultaneously producing nonhistoric computer-generated probabilistic (or stochastic) flow sequences which can then be analyzed individually. This study extended work previously done by H. A. Thomas and M. B. Fiering (1962) so that it is now possible to generate monthly flows.* Depending upon the confidence the

John S. Gladwell is associate hydraulic engineer at the R. L. Albrook Hydraulic Laboratory; associate professor of civil engineering at Washington State University, Pullman; and associate water research scientist at the State of Washington Water Research Center.

* The author wishes to give full credit for the technique of stochastic generation used in this study to Thomas and Fiering (1962). This tool has opened up an avenue of analysis which the author is sure will prove to be of great value to the engineering profession. The full cooperation of Campbell and Harms (1966), furthermore, in generating the sequences from the author's data was particularly helpful.

designer has in his ability to define the statistics based on the historic flow, we now have techniques for *creating* river flow sequences against which we can test our plans.

It is not the intention of this paper to discuss the theoretical relationships of the stochastic generation processes—for this the reader is referred to the original references. Briefly, however, the generations are based on the following statistical factors of the historical flow: (1) *mean,* the average discharge over the time unit (month, year); (2) *standard deviation,* a statistical characteristic indicating the spread of the data from the mean; (3) *first-order serial correlation coefficient,* a coefficient that indicates the tendency of the data to be predictable in one period by its value in the previous period, e.g., when the flow is high in one year there may be a tendency to have a high flow the following year. If the coefficient is 0 there would be no evident effect; if it is 1 the year following is predictable exactly by the previous year's flow.

The data are analyzed by determining the tendency for like years to follow each other and assuming that the reason extremely low-flow years may follow high-flow years, or vice versa, is explained as a "randomness" effect. Thus, our mathematical model of the river in essence includes everything that we can say we know about the river plus a factor which is probabilistic. The importance of this technique becomes evident when one realizes that the chance of getting "extreme" conditions in a short period of record is slight. By using this stochastic generation process we are extending the historical data and thus opening up the probability of encountering the more rare occurrences. In the usual design problem it is these rare occurrences which will control. These rare occurrences may be low flows, high flows, or merely critical sequences or combinations of flows. For example, in the design of a reservoir for supplying water to a city we would not want the reservoir to go dry every summer. But we would probably not accept even a slightly more infrequent failure. The use of a *long* historical sequence (in excess of 100 years) would probably give acceptable results under normal conditions, but most streams do not have long records; thus a stochastic sequence would give us a better tool for determining how often we could expect that reservoir to go dry. We could then study the size of the reservoir as a function of its frequency of failure and then, applying cost figures, arrive at an acceptable arrangement.

Let us look for a moment at a typical problem. We would like to place a reservoir on a certain river to supply water to our city, assuming for simplicity that either (1) we have already decided that this is the economic solution, or (2) we need information such as this to make comparisons. The river which will supply this reservoir has a gauged history of 50 years.

The first things that will be determined are the amounts and timing of the water required to satisfy the city's demands. The simplest procedure is to compare this demand curve with the supply curve of history (50 years). This will tell us the size of reservoir we would have needed had we been building our reservoir 50 years ago. This technique has been used for years by engineers because of its simplicity—not because they believed that history would repeat itself. An important revelation in this type of study is the interdependence of the sequential supply-and-demand curves. We find, for example, that in periods of extreme low flow some of the water that a city is using may be that which came down the river one or two years before, depending, of course, on the size of reservoir and amounts of withdrawals. But normally we are completely dependent, when using this procedure, on the historical sequence of flow. Is this significant?

Somewhere in engineering design history someone asked the question, "What if we juggled the flows around so that they occurred in different sequences?" The technique was tried and more often than not resulted in critical design conditions—in other words, the reservoir that was properly designed under historical conditions was underdesigned under the new hypothetical conditions. Unfortunately, however, the new river sequences did not always have the appearance (the statistical characteristics) of the historical. The average (mean) flow was the same and the variations from the mean (standard deviation) were identical, but the sequences were different somehow. What we had now was a purely random arrangement with the limitation that the individual events were identical to those of history. What was needed was something which would give us what we could all "see." This was the characteristic of dry years following dry years, and wet years following wet years—not all of the time but enough that it looked like the river we knew. The inclusion of the serial correlation coefficient seems to satisfy this requirement.

With the aid of electronic computers we are now able to rapidly produce these artificial, but statistically similar, river flows. We will be "creating" conditions which are not limited by history either in their sequence or in their magnitudes of flow. It is possible, then, to assume different-size reservoirs, allow a stochastic streamflow to run into them, and to draw off water according to our original demand curve. For any given size we can determine how many times in a given period that reservoir would have been underdesigned; we will be determining the *probability* of failure. Having determined the probabilities of failure, we must decide what degree of failure can be tolerated. It should be noted, furthermore, that generally the cost of an increment of protection will exceed that of the previous increment. Thus, if we were to plot a curve of failures versus cost it would show that the costs would be rising extremely rapidly as the allowable failures approached zero.

What does this mean? In the reservoir example above it would mean, simply, that to ensure, say, that 10,000 cfs would be available with *no* probability of failure—the city would *never* have a water problem, probability of failure equal to zero—would require an extremely large reservoir. The actual cost would depend on the reservoir site and runoff characteristics. But,

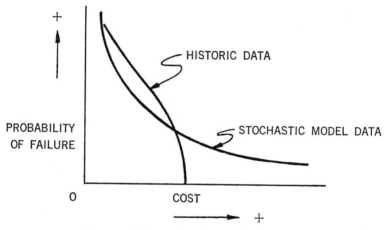

Figure 3. Difference between conclusions using
limited historical and unlimited stochastic streamflow records

as we allow the possibility of some failure, then the reservoir size can be reduced. As the size is reduced, normally the cost would also come down. With limited historical data the curve would give an indication (falsely in most cases) that the probability of failure would very quickly go to zero, whereas the enlargement of the data through stochastic processes would give a more realistic appraisal. Although the above example is limited to a reservoir design problem, there is no requirement that this technique be limited to "physical" problems. Any decision which is a function of flow, and which would be improved if we had more flow information, will benefit from stochastic flow generation. It is important, therefore, that we understand some of the implications of "probability of occurrence."

The applicability of the stochastic generation procedure is based upon three very important assumptions. These are (1) that the data available are of sufficient quality to adequately represent the historic events, (2) that the data are representative of the *total* population, and (3) that the arrangement of the statistics in the stochastic equation will produce a sequence which will with some degree of precision duplicate the statistics of the historical records. Obviously the first assumption is inapplicable if there are major diversions or regulations of the stream unless these modifications are somehow accounted for. In the study reported below the modifications have been adjusted so that the resulting bits of information are essentially what would have occurred had there been no diversion or regulation—virgin flow conditions. The second assumption requires that the record be of sufficient length. It furthermore assumes that some mathematically describable probability relationship can be established. This assumption says, in effect, that if we were to have a great deal more historical records the statistics would remain essentially the same—that the record is a representative sample of what could happen. The third assumption is perhaps obvious—the statistics of the stochastic sequence should be, on the average, essentially identical to those of the historic record. If they are not, then obviously the model is not representing accurately the physical conditions.

The Columbia River Example

Because of the importance of the Columbia River system to the Pacific Northwest and to the state of Washington in particular it was decided to use the Thomas-Fiering technique in analyzing the annual discharges. Time periods of shorter duration would have been more desirable (the Campbell-Harms variation has been shown to be acceptable to monthly units); however, because of the extreme manipulation of river flow for irrigation diversions, hydropower production, and flood peak reduction, this was not thought to be possible with any establishable degree of precision. In fact, the future holds even more drastic regulation in store, thus limiting the value of any monthly flow information at a station as low as that at The Dalles. The records at The Dalles were selected because they are of sufficiently long duration and the flows of such magnitude that minor errors in estimation of the effect of man would lose their significance statistically. Figure 4 shows the Columbia River system and indicates the drainage areas at various locations in the state of Washington. Table 10 shows the data, including the modified portion which was used in this study. The record covers 85 years of flow (to 1963) and is sufficiently long to be representative. There is no way of "proving" this statement, however, other than by comparing the results of

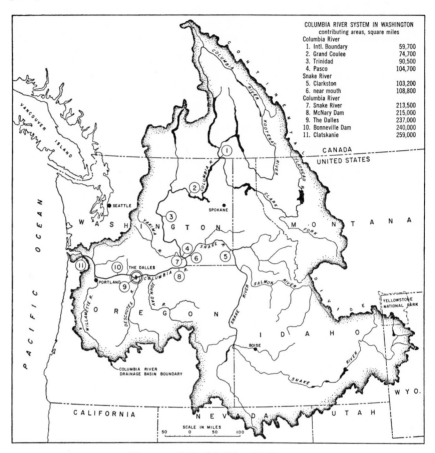

Figure 4. Columbia River Basin map

the study with future events. The analyses made in this study used only the modified flows. The results, then, it must be realized, are those that would theoretically prevail were there no effect of man on the river's flow. Later it will be shown how the effect of depletions can be reintroduced. The fact that future reservoir regulation will affect annual flow distribution as well as those of shorter duration is not considered in detail here. This, however, does not alter the fact that having made the following analyses it will be possible to know, in effect, how much runoff is being *generated* each year (on a probability basis) in the watershed above The Dalles.

The Thomas-Fiering technique had assumed a normal (Gaussian) distribution of annual discharges. To ensure that this was applicable to the Columbia River flow the modified data were plotted on four different kinds

TABLE 10

MODIFIED HISTORICAL FLOW, COLUMBIA RIVER, AT THE DALLES, 1879–1963

Year	Historical Flow * (cfs)	Modified Flow † (cfs)	Moving Averages (Modified) cfs		
			3-Year	5-Year	7-Year
1879	242000	242300	—0	—0	—0
1880	264000	264400	253033	—0	—0
1881	252000	252400	249767	240840	—0
1882	232000	232500	232500	235300	233357
1883	212000	212600	219900	225360	228857
1884	214000	214600	213967	217040	228357
1885	214000	214700	213367	222720	221143
1886	210000	210800	228800	220580	207214
1887	260000	260900	224533	204660	205000
1888	201000	201900	199267	201140	198086
1889	134000	135000	178000	192220	195900
1890	196000	197100	166100	179920	197286
1891	165000	166200	187567	183640	205057
1892	198000	199400	195367	219700	204186
1893	219000	220500	245067	219440	217900
1894	313600	315300	243867	232400	224757
1895	194000	195800	247367	241540	234200
1896	229000	231000	223967	243900	239486
1897	243000	245100	236133	228120	240357
1898	230000	232300	237933	234280	227000
1899	234000	236400	231767	232440	227600
1900	224000	226600	228267	223420	225214
1901	219000	221800	216133	219820	225257
1902	197000	200000	212033	221620	212600
1903	211000	214300	219900	205040	201843
1904	242000	245400	201133	192900	202814
1905	140000	143700	183400	199580	199786
1906	157000	161100	179400	196840	199057
1907	229000	233400	198367	186740	199586
1908	196000	200600	209633	201600	192171
1909	190000	194900	204500	208080	198629
1910	213000	218000	202133	199180	206886
1911	188000	193500	200133	202840	201200
1912	183000	188900	200433	202580	194429
1913	213000	218900	200467	189620	201629
1914	187000	193600	188567	199980	201471
1915	147000	153200	197367	205580	204100
1916	238000	245300	205133	204180	202686
1917	210000	216900	224700	201260	195000

TABLE 10 (*Cont.*)

MODIFIED HISTORICAL FLOW, COLUMBIA RIVER, AT THE DALLES, 1879–1963

Year	Historical Flow * (cfs)	Modified Flow † (cfs)	Moving Averages (Modified) cfs		
			3-Year	5-Year	7-Year
1918	205000	211900	202600	203640	201300
1919	172000	179000	185333	202120	206643
1920	157000	165100	193933	196860	198257
1921	230000	237700	197800	191800	187957
1922	183000	190600	204967	184960	187600
1923	179000	186600	174000	193820	179929
1924	137000	144800	180267	171340	187414
1925	201000	209400	159833	176720	187343
1926	118000	125300	184067	186840	180129
1927	206000	217500	193333	185900	173243
1928	231000	237200	198267	171700	170914
1929	133000	140100	171900	172340	168657
1930	131000	138400	135667	167560	180243
1931	122000	128500	153500	161400	180400
1932	186000	193600	176167	177100	172171
1933	198000	206400	206200	185340	176243
1934	211500	218600	201533	193360	176100
1935	170200	179600	188933	182120	186386
1936	158900	168600	161867	180940	181229
1937	128700	137400	168833	168720	174471
1938	190200	200500	165133	164620	164257
1939	149700	157500	172367	160320	165900
1940	148500	159100	154567	171060	173029
1941	130000	147100	165766	174660	185815
1942	178600	191100	185566	188540	180172
1943	207300	218500	212166	188920	187000
1944	119600	226900	202133	200560	193286
1945	150800	161000	197733	202960	207300
1946	196100	205300	189800	208300	207029
1947	193700	203100	217867	200760	208486
1948	235500	245200	212500	214300	209871
1949	180100	189200	221033	220560	216671
1950	217100	228700	218167	221660	214457
1951	226400	236600	224633	210580	216843
1952	198200	208600	211667	216700	208943
1953	179300	189800	206067	208940	218271
1954	209100	219800	199833	212520	214943
1955	179000	199900	221400	211880	208586
1956	243400	254500	216600	212340	210671
1957	194100	205400	217333	213020	213143

TABLE 10 (*Cont.*)

MODIFIED HISTORICAL FLOW, COLUMBIA RIVER, AT THE DALLES, 1879-1963

Year	Historical Flow * (cfs)	Modified Flow † (cfs)	Moving Averages (Modified) cfs		
			3-Year	5-Year	7-Year
1958	180700	192100	206900	216460	210457
1959	211600	223200	207467	205760	208972
1960	195300	207100	210433	200580	199243
1961	189000	201000	195866	199440	0
1962	169300	179500	188966	0	0
1963	174100	186400	0	0	0

MODIFIED FLOW
Mean: 202290
Std. Dev.: 34900
Cor. Coef.: 0.233

* Source: The U.S. Geological Survey.

† Adjusted for estimated irrigation depletions and major reservoir storage only. The minor corrections are included to show the progression only—not to indicate any presumed accuracy.

of probability paper: (1) linear-normal (usually called normal distribution), (2) log-normal, (3) linear-extreme value (Gumbel), and (4) log-extreme value. These "probability papers" are designed so that a series of data which has the designated mathematical distribution will plot as a straight line. We are, therefore, looking for the "best" straight-line plot. Based on a visual interpretation of the plots (see Figs. 5-8), there can be no doubt that the linear-normal plot forms a straight line at least as well if not better than the other three plots. A normal distribution of the annual flows was therefore assumed and the stochastic model developed along this line.

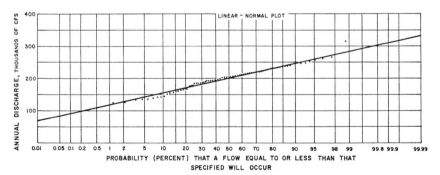

Figure 5. Modified historical data-probability analysis—
normal distribution

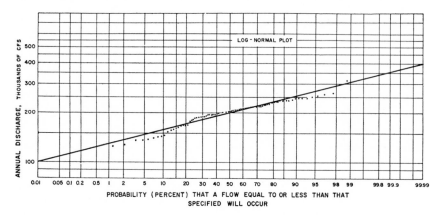

Figure 6. Modified historical data-probability analysis—
log-normal distribution

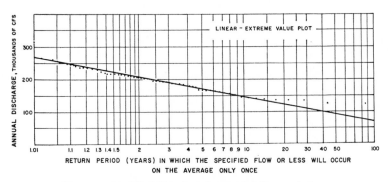

Figure 7. Modified historical data-probability analysis—
linear extreme value distribution

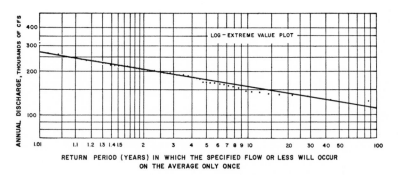

Figure 8. Modified historical data-probability analysis—
log-extreme value plot

Stochastic Generation

With the analysis of the statistical characteristics and acceptance of the *normal* distribution it is possible to proceed to the computer operation. Twenty-five 300-year stochastic sequences were generated. If necessary, it would be possible to analyze each of these sequences individually for their serial relationships. In a study involving a "project," this would probably be done in order to check the design considerations against probable flow occurrences. In fact it is really this possibility of use that makes this technique so valuable. However, in this study the statistical characteristics only were analyzed. Nevertheless, in making the study this way it is hoped that a *feeling* for the probability of flow variation can be imparted. It would be my hope that upon finishing this paper that the use of the terms "mean flow" or "100-year flow," and so forth, as though they were fixed and unequivocal values, would be eliminated. I would hope that it would be seen that even these flows have probabilities of occurrence.

Annual Discharges

Figure 9 shows the variability within the twenty-five 300-year sequences for each of the given return-period flows. It should be noted, however, before

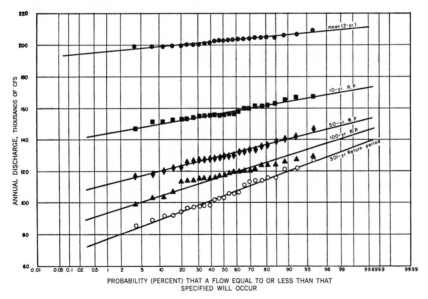

Figure 9. Variability of annual flows for varying return periods—
stochastic—Columbia River at The Dalles

proceeding, that the computer, had the runs been long enough, would have generated sequences in which the statistics were essentially identical to each other and to the modified historical data. The fact that, for example, the 301-year return-period flows varied from as high as about 125,000 cfs to as low as about 85,000 cfs should be a warning to the indiscriminate uses of *mean* values in discussing statistical characteristics. Furthermore, it is an indication that even records which would normally be considered excellent in length (the stochastic sequences are of 300 years each) may not reflect the parent population exactly. Returning to the 301-year return-period flow line of Figure 9, this may be interpreted as follows: The *apparent* mean 301-year flow (the flow that can be expected to occur on the average once every 301 years) is about 104,000 cfs, but there is a 50 per cent chance (± 25 per cent from the mean) that the *true* mean 301-year flow is between 112,000 cfs and 97,000 cfs.

Figure 9 shows the family of curves based on single-year values (not running averages). The twenty-five plotted points indicate one value from each stochastic run. These were determined by assuming that the lowest flow of each of the 300-year runs was the 301-year flow (not 300-year because of the method used, but essentially indistinguishable) and the third lowest was the 100-year flow. It would have been more correct to analyze each run independently and, using a linear fit (mathematical or otherwise), determine the flow values for the respective return period. This would have reduced the effect which is often evident in historic data and equally so in the stochastic—that of having occurrences more rare than would be indicated by the length of record. In other words, it is quite possible to have a flow of, say, 1,000-year return-period magnitude occur in a period of 25 years of record. This would not be a 26-year return-period flow, although in the simplified method used here it would seem to indicate this condition. In fact it would remain, as stated, the 1,000-year flow. Fortunately, with longer length sequences this effect is minimized. Apparently, the 100-year return-period flow on Figure 9 indicates this statistical anomaly. The line was drawn through the data, but its location was influenced to a great degree by the two bounding lines.

It will be noted that the slopes of the lines tend to flatten out with the lower return periods. Thus, at the 2-year return period (mean) the variation between the 25 sequences is considerably less than that of the 301-year return-period flows. Apparently, any attempt to extrapolate on a probability chart will get into areas of less and less precision. This is a very important point to remember and should, hopefully, make the investigator consider carefully before "extending the line."

In summary, then, the reliability of the estimated probability of occurrences depends to a great degree on the length of record. But even records which would normally be considered excellent (we used 300 years in this study) will have some variability. Furthermore, the variability will be greatest with the more rare occurrences, i.e., the degree of precision in estimating, for example, a 300-year flow will be much lower than for estimating a 10-year flow.

Running Average Discharges

Figures 10, 11, and 12 show the analyses of 3-, 5-, and 7-year running averages. These were made of the stochastic sequences in the same manner as

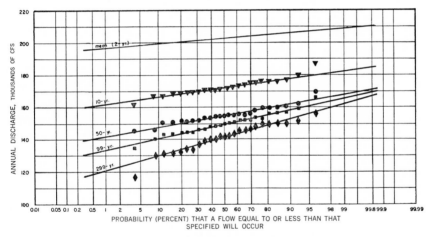

Figure 10. Variability of 3-year running averages for varying return periods—stochastic—Columbia River at The Dalles

shown for the historic data on Table 4. The analyses were conducted exactly as were those of Figure 9 (see previous paragraphs) and may be interpreted identically. Since the mean of the yearly flows is identical to the mean of the running averages only the line is reproduced from Figure 9.

The mean values from the data of Figures 9 through 12 were extracted and plotted as shown on Figure 13. Thus, the probability of occurrence of a flow of a given magnitude in any time period is shown. The historical analysis is shown plotted for the 3-, 5-, and 7-year running averages. If this system of

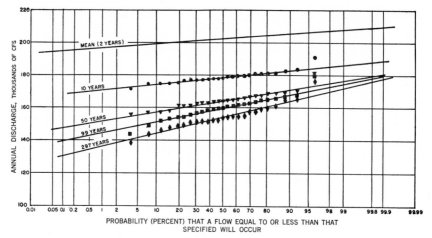

Figure 11. Variability of 5-year running averages
for varying return periods—stochastic—Columbia River at The Dalles

stochastic generation can be accepted as representing the historical, but over a longer time period, then it would appear to indicate that the Columbia River at The Dalles may have been experiencing some prolonged low-flow periods which are perhaps of somewhat rarer occurrence than would be indicated by the length of record. Because of the almost exact duplication of the annual flow probabilities the historic data is not plotted—the reader may compare this plot with that of Figure 5 for his own satisfaction.

Figure 14 is essentially an extension of Figure 13 to indicate the flattening of the lines as the running-average periods become longer. The three-hun-

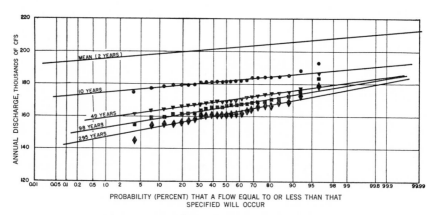

Figure 12. Variability of 7-year running averages
for varying return periods—stochastic—Columbia River at The Dalles

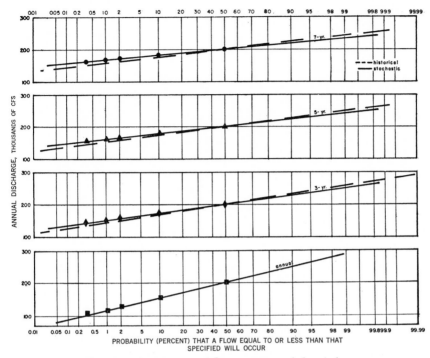

Figure 13. Average annual flows over extended periods—
stochastic and modified historical—Columbia River at The Dalles

dred year running average will, of course, be recognized as also being the
mean (two-year) plot of Figure 9.

Sequential Relationships

Unquestionably one of the most important uses of the generated sequences
is the serial relationship analyses made possible. Figure 15 shows the plot of
the modified historical annual and the seven-year running-average flows.
Compare this with Figure 16 which is a portion of only one of the twenty-

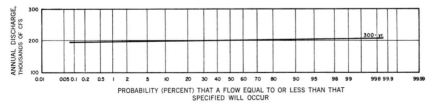

Figure 14. Average annual flows for 300-year periods—
stochastic—Columbia River at The Dalles

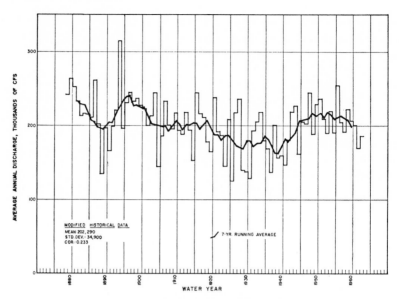

Figure 15. Columbia River modified historical hydrograph,
1879–1963, at The Dalles

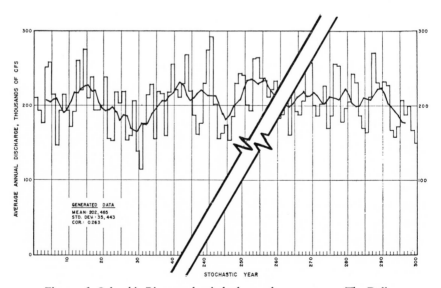

Figure 16. Columbia River stochastic hydrograph, 300 years, at The Dalles

five three-hundred-year computer generations produced in this study. If the serial relationship of flows is important to the design, then, quite obviously, the longer sequences would be extremely valuable.

No detailed study has been made to compare the *apparent* cyclic tendencies which are evident in both the historic and stochastic annual flow hydrographs. It is obvious, however, that the statistics used in the stochastic model of annual flow do cause variations from the mean which would *seem* to be representative of the historical variations.

Depleted Flow Conditions

The results of this study and another (State of Washington, 1967) completed at the State of Washington Water Research Center, concerning the undepleted flow conditions at The Dalles and historic and projected depletions resulting from irrigation, may be superposed. As stated previously, the stochastic generations are based on undepleted (termed "modified" in this study) river flows. Thus, these probability analyses are basic or primary and are not a function of time, and the mean, then, must remain about 202,000 cfs (undepleted flow conditions) irrespective of what the actual flow conditions are at any time in the future. Figure 17 is taken from the previously mentioned report (State of Washington, 1967) and shows the estimated flow depletions by irrigation as far into the future as A.D. 2020. This information, in addition to other data available on maximum potential irrigable land and subsequent water depletions, was used to prepare the curves of Figure 18. This shows what the effect would be at any time in the future as a result of flow-depletion conditions *at that time*. It should be recalled, however, that this family of curves is for the "mean" conditions only. Referring back to Figures 9 through 12 it will be noted that there is a definite probability that the actual values will be higher or lower than the *apparent* means.

Figure 18 has had the flow units converted to millions of acre-feet, the mean being about 146 million acre-feet. It should be noted that each line has been designated a certain year "condition." This is, of course, based on the forecast shown in Figure 17; however, at *any time* in the future in which the depletions equal one of the forecast conditions, that curve will control. This chart should not be accepted too literally, however. Obviously, under conditions of extreme drought (such as might be explained by a 1 per cent or lower probability occurrence) reservoir manipulation and irrigation curtailment will be administered in an attempt to offset the low-flow conditions. The flow requirements of other users (such as fisheries, power, pollution control, municipalities, industries, and recreation, to name a few) would become

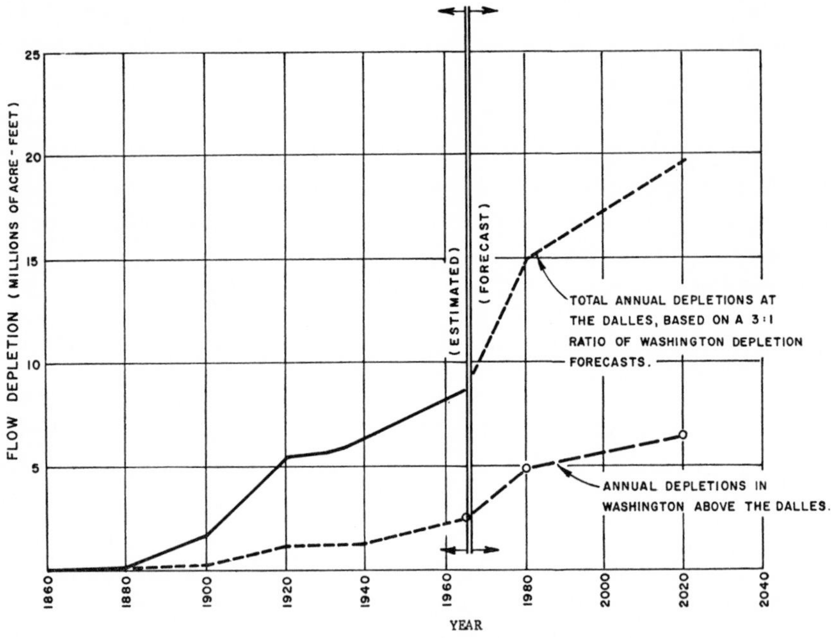

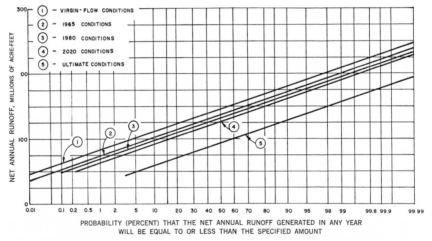

Figure 17. Estimated annual Columbia River flow depletions
by irrigation (to The Dalles, Oregon)

Figure 18. Probability curves for current and future conditions of the Columbia River
system to The Dalles as a result of forecast irrigation depletions only (assumes constant
depletions; for extreme low-flow years this is excessive, since irrigation will probably be
curtailed under those conditions)

extremely critical. Thus, the curves of Figure 18 would probably, in reality, be forced to curve more flatly to the left to indicate the inacceptability and unquestioned regulation which would prevail should extremely low natural flows occur. The minimum level below which further consumptive use would not be tolerated has, however, not been determined—nor is it a simple task. It will be noted in Figure 18 that the flows are given as runoff generated *to* The Dalles rather than flow *at* The Dalles. This was purposely done to reflect the changes which are rapidly occurring with regard to reservoir storage in the Upper Columbia River system. Although the actual flows at The Dalles may change in the future, the amount of water generated in the watershed above that point will have essentially the same characteristics as before.

The task of maintaining minimum flows is made even more complex when it is realized that Figure 18 represents single-year occurrences. If multiple-year drought conditions should prevail, and that probability is indicated to a degree by Figure 13, the manipulation of reservoirs for low-flow augmentation becomes more difficult. The problem, of course, is that having modulated the first year's low-flow condition, the reservoir levels may be precariously low and surplus water unavailable for further assistence during the second or third years. It is for these circumstances that the stochastic sequences became of primary value during the design phases. It is possible, however, to use these probability charts in conjunction with a simple mass-diagram technique to derive a roughly approximate answer as to the total amount of usable storage availability necessary to affect any given degree of regulation. In this last regard, however, the approximation will be closely associated with the demand curve used, and on a system as large as that of the Columbia River this is a large task in itself. It would be of much greater value to use the sequential generations to compare against the expected demand curves. It is in this manner that the greatest potential of the stochastic series is realized.

REFERENCES

Campbell, T. H., and A. A. Harms
  1966 Computer generation of stochastic streamflow. C. W. Harris Hydraulics Laboratory Technical Report No. 20. Department of Civil Engineering, College of Engineering, University of Washington.
  1967 An extension to the Thomas-Fiering model for the sequential generation of streamflow. Water Resources Research, 3(3):653–61.

State of Washington Water Research Center

  1967 An initial study of the water resources of the state of Washington. Pullman.

Thomas, H. A., and M. B. Fiering

  1962 Mathematical synthesis of streamflow sequences for the analysis of river basin simulation. Chap. xii of Design of water-resource systems, by Arthur Maass *et al.* Harvard University Press, Cambridge, Mass.

VII

GROUND-WATER HYDROLOGY OF THE PULLMAN-MOSCOW BASIN, WASHINGTON

James W. Crosby III

Introduction

Perhaps before undertaking a discussion of ground-water hydrology it might be well to answer some basic questions about ground water and put the subject in an appropriate frame of reference. The nonprofessional may ask, "Why do we make such a big fuss about ground water?" or "Where does ground water fit in the over-all water picture?"

Fresh water contained in ground-water storage in the United States far exceeds the capacity of all surface reservoirs, including the Great Lakes. It is estimated that the total usable ground-water body is equivalent to ten years of annual precipitation or to thirty-five years of annual runoff (Thomas, 1955). Although these are rather well-known and often-quoted figures, it may come as a surprise to learn that 26 per cent of all public supply in Washington is derived from ground waters which sustain a third of the state's population. In fact, over 15 per cent of all water withdrawals, exclusive of power generation, are from ground water. And this is in Washington where we reputedly have such a surplus of surface water that California is going to help us use it.

Ground water is a desirable commodity for other than sheer magnitude of the resource. Unlike surface-water reservoirs, ground water is little subject to evaporation. Its temperature is little affected by seasonal change. Its chemistry remains essentially constant over long periods of time, and it is generally free of pollution by chemicals, bacteria, or particulate matter. Perhaps most

---

James W. Crosby III is a geologist and lecturer in geology at Washington State University, Pullman.

important, many areas of the world must rely solely on ground water as the only available source of fresh water.

The development and use of ground waters date from the ancients. Prior to the seventeenth century most of the knowledge of the accumulation and movement of ground waters was bound up in mythology and superstition. By the end of the seventeenth century a rudimentary, but essentially correct, knowledge of the hydrologic cycle had been acquired and supported by measurements. During the eighteenth century fundamental geologic influences on ground-water hydraulics were established. Henry Darcy, in 1856, set forth the relation governing the flow of water through porous media which we now know as Darcy's Law. In the last half of the nineteenth century and first part of the twentieth century our knowledge of ground-water hydraulics expanded rapidly. During this period numerous investigators derived methods for describing the steady-state flow of water toward a well. In 1935 C. V. Theis presented a solution to the equation for unsteady flow to a well and made possible predictions of future changes in ground-water levels resulting from pumping. Still more recent studies have been directed to special applications of the Theis formula.

Unquestionably we have made great advances in our knowledge of ground water since the ancient Greek philosophers reasoned that springs must be derived from sea waters passing through subterranean caverns, being purified, and raised to the surface. We no longer have to base our ground-water laws upon such tenets as "percolating water moves in a mysterious manner, in courses unknown or unknowable." Still our knowledge is pitifully limited. Because of the ever-increasing demands on the available water supply we find our technology further behind our needs than at any other time in history.

Research Needs

In 1965 I completed a study (Crosby, 1967) of ground-water research needs in the state of Washington. In the course of this study I had the opportunity to discuss needed research with many of the scientists involved in ground-water studies in the Northwest and to review the current status of our accomplishments. After evaluating the consensus, I was forced to conclude that we do not know how much ground water we have in Washington, how much will be needed in the future, or to what extent consumptive use is offset by recharge. To make matters even worse our tools for deriving the necessary answers are inadequate, expensive, and overly time consuming.

Primary research interest, therefore, centers around improved inventory techniques and the development of new methodology for quantifying the results of our studies.

Areal ground-water investigations in the past have attempted to describe qualitatively the features of the ground-water environment. Occasionally the results of several pump tests present some widely divergent transmissivities and storativities which are, nevertheless, an attempt at quantifying aquifer characteristics. The boldest investigators may sometimes venture a guess that the safe yield of an aquifer has been exceeded or that a given supply is adequate for the immediate future. Such information, however, is of little value to the Lincoln County farmer considering a $60,000 investment for a well to irrigate his 2,000 acres. He needs to know how much water he can pump and what the effect of pumping will be. He also needs to know how his operation will be affected when his neighbors follow his example. The ground-water scientist must, in the future, be prepared to predict the number of acre-feet of water that can be withdrawn per foot of water-level change. Incomplete analyses of past performance projected into the future will not suffice. Research must provide the methodology which will allow accurate assessments within the hydrologist's time and monetary budget.

Typical of needed research in methodology is the aquifer evaluation test as applied to basaltic aquifers. Analysis of time-drawdown or distance-drawdown pump-test data utilizing the Theis nonequilibrium formula is a technique we use routinely, but it is of questionable value. The coefficients so obtained are sensibly meaningless because basaltic aquifers depart materially from the basic conditions required by the Theis method, and it is not likely that modifying assumptions can correct all the shortcomings. It becomes the responsibility of the ground-water researcher to redefine the pump test for basaltic aquifer evaluation or to devise entirely new techniques.

Description of the Study Area

During the last several years we have been conducting research studies in the Pullman-Moscow ground-water basin of eastern Washington. Continually declining ground-water levels in this area have generated intense interest in the problem and funds have been made available to explore several advanced techniques.

The Pullman-Moscow basin is situated near the eastern margin of the Columbia Plateau, straddling the Washington-Idaho state line. The ground-water basin is horseshoe-shaped, opening westerly or southwesterly. In pre-

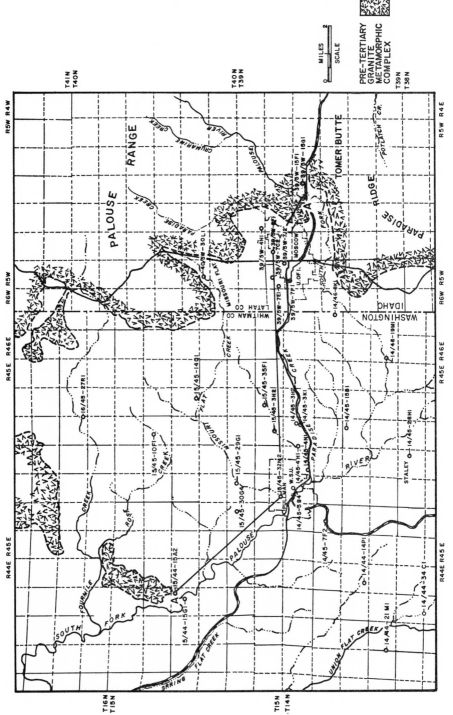

Figure 19. Map of the Pullman-Moscow area showing well locations

Miocene times the area was mountainous with a relief of over 4,000 feet. Pre-Cambrian sedimentary and metamorphic rocks and Cretaceous granitics, which now constitute the basement rocks, were exposed at the surface. During the Miocene epoch basalt flows advancing from the west invaded the well-established drainage system, damming the streams and creating numerous lakes. These lakes were especially common in the eastern, or Moscow, portion of the basin. Clays, sands, and gravels derived from the deeply weathered pre-Tertiary rocks accumulated rapidly in the lakes. Subsequent burial of the lacustrine deposits by renewed basaltic eruptions triggered a repetition of the cycle.

Following cessation of the igneous activity at the close of the Miocene, the basalts and lacustrine deposits were subjected to moderate erosion. The erosion surface so developed was then capped by the Pleistocene Palouse loess which has since been sculptured into the characteristic rolling-hill topography of the region.

The resulting stratigraphic sections show interlayered basalts and terres-

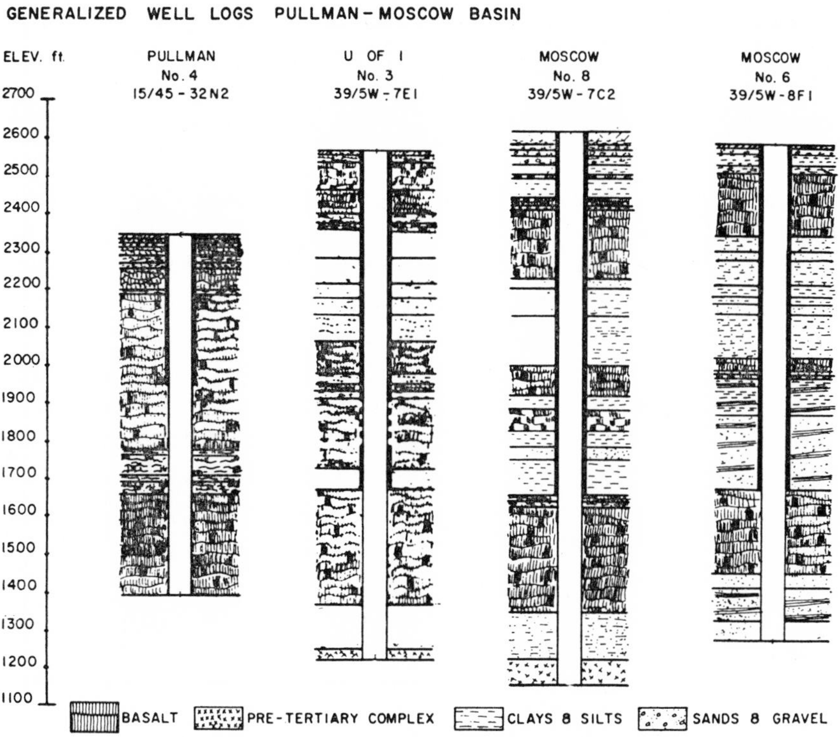

Figure 20. Generalized well logs, Pullman-Moscow basin

trial sediments resting on the pre-Tertiary complex and covered by up to 150 feet of loess. In the Moscow portion of the basin, sediments may constitute as much as 70 per cent of the section whereas in the Pullman area basalts account for 98 per cent of the stratigraphic column.

Seismic Studies

Our first intensive study of the basin was started in the Moscow area in 1959 when we undertook a series of seismic soundings utilizing high-resolution reflection techniques. At that time the deepest wells in the Moscow subbasin were about 500 feet deep, were highly charged with iron, and water levels were falling at a rate of several feet per year. I must admit that we were apprehensive about seismic reflection methods because of the nearly universal lack of success in basaltic areas. Refraction methods we had ruled out for other than near-surface work because of the numerous velocity reversals in the section.

Following many days of unsuccessful shooting we finally managed to develop techniques which gave us occasional usable reflection records. Though our ratio of usable to unusable records was poor we were able to piece together a picture of basalt and sediment distribution and to outline a crude representation of the pre-Tertiary topography. Our findings indicated the basin to be much deeper than previously estimated, with an unanticipated basalt horizon at depth. On this basis we recommended deep exploratory drilling to tap the lower basalt horizon and to investigate the pre-Tertiary—Tertiary contact.

Three highly productive wells, essentially iron-free, have tapped the lower basalt sequence. The deep aquifers apparently are not hydraulically connected with the upper aquifers and are truly artesian. Static water levels are around 150 feet lower than those of the upper aquifers. The seismic interpretations have proved to be substantially correct. However, because it was necessary to estimate a velocity for the deep section, we interpreted the basement as being deeper than subsequent drilling has indicated.

We have recently finished and reported on further seismic studies in the drainage basin of the South Fork of the Palouse River (Cavin and Crosby, 1966). We hope to obtain additional information on the nature of the pre-Tertiary—Tertiary contact in the outcrop area and its possible function in ground-water recharge. One of my graduate students is working on essentially the same problem. By detailed geologic mapping of the contact area and of the basalts he is attempting to determine the principle geologic controls on infiltration processes.

Carbon-14 Dating of Ground Waters

For the past two years we have been studying the value of water-dating techniques for ground-water inventory and recharge assessment. I readily admit that we do not have all the answers at hand after completing the first phase of this work. Frankly, we are not unshakable in the conclusions we have reached and solicit comments and criticism. We do believe that C^{14} dating of ground waters is a powerful new tool which may ultimately provide us with ready answers to many ground-water problems which are difficult or impossible to approach by other methods. Although some of our C^{14} results are fogged by inadequate supplementary data, we believe that we have established many of the parameters requiring definition to optimize results.

Several tritium dates which were also obtained in the study served only to verify certain recent dates obtained by C^{14} methods. Other tritium values proved to be below detection limits.

The value of the C^{14} technique for the dating of ground waters is dependent upon the formation in the soil zone of CO_2 derived from biogenic sources such as plant respiration and the decay of plant material. This organically derived CO_2 will have a C^{14} content essentially identical with living plant material.

As the biogenic CO_2 dissolves in the soil water, it reacts with calcium carbonates of the ground-water recharge area to produce bicarbonates according to the reaction:

$$CaCO_3 + H_2O + CO_2 \rightarrow 2HCO_3 + Ca^{++}$$

The resulting bicarbonate should have a C^{14} content essentially half that of living plant material, providing the $CaCO_3$ source contains only dead carbon. Such would be true of a pure marine limestone reactant. However, soil-forming processes may act to modify the original C^{14} content of rocks in the outcrop area. Waters percolating through such soils may actually be contacting $CaCO_3$ sources containing considerable amounts of C^{14}. Additional complications are presented by the ready availability of biogenic CO_2 in the soil zone which permits further isotopic exchange to take place between C^{12} and C^{14}. Ultimately the C^{14} content of the bicarbonate may vary between 50 and 100 per cent of that of recent plant material.

Below the zone of active humus decay in the soil (considered by agronomists to be only a few meters), seepage waters cannot exchange additional

C^{14} and the apparent C^{14} age of a given ground water is controlled primarily by radioactive decay.

Ingerson and Pearson (1964) have shown that in the relationship:

$$CO_2 + H_2O + CaCO_3 \rightarrow Ca^{++} + 2HCO_3^-$$

the measured C^{14} activity of a water must be referred to that portion of the total carbonate derived from the soil air. Because there is frequently insufficient $CaCO_3$ present in the recharge area or because equilibrium has not been established, carbonate species in a ground water may include both H_2CO_3 and HCO_3^-. The water activity, referred to the original soil air, will then be related to water composition as:

$$(\text{C initial}) = (H_2CO_3) + \tfrac{1}{2}(HCO_3^-)$$

and a correction factor P' determined as:

$$P' = \frac{(H_2CO_3) + \tfrac{1}{2}(HCO_3^-)}{(H_2CO_3) + (HCO_3^-)}$$

may be applied to the measured water activity. This relationship is applicable, however, only to waters whose pH is a function of the carbonate buffer system and in which CO_3 is not present in significant amounts. Therefore, a more general relationship would be valuable and complement the information derived from carbonate chemistry.

Münnich and Vogel (1959), Vogel and Ehhalt (1963), and Pearson (1965) have shown that in certain circumstances the C^{13} value of the carbonate in a water can be used to estimate the proportion of carbon derived from an average marine limestone ($\delta C^{13} \approx 0\%o$) and that derived from soil air ($\delta C^{13} \approx -25\%o$). Ingerson and Pearson (1964) have proposed a correction factor

$$P = \frac{\delta C^{13}\,\text{sample} - \delta C^{13}\,\text{limestone}}{\delta C^{13}\,\text{plants} - \delta C^{13}\,\text{limestone}}$$

which when applied to C^{14} water ages compensates for the original C^{14} content of the water. Ideally, the δC^{13} values for the plant material and limestone should be determined on samples from the aquifer recharge area. However, average values may be employed with some sacrifice of accuracy.

The C^{14} dating technique for waters has, on occasion, been questioned because of possible isotopic exchange of C^{14} for C^{12} within the aquifer. The stable isotope ratio does not appear to support this contention. However, Erickson (1962) has suggested a mechanism by which the C^{13}/C^{12} ratio could remain constant and still permit C^{14}—C^{12} exchange. Field studies conducted by several investigators in varying geological environments strongly suggest that C^{14}—C^{12} exchange does not actually take place to any appreciable extent. Results obtained by researchers using the C^{14} technique for dating ground waters are proving to be entirely rational and in keeping with the findings of standard hydrological techniques.

Carbon-14 Studies in the Pullman-Moscow Basin

The study of the Pullman-Moscow basin is one of the most comprehensive yet undertaken. Some 50 water samples have been collected from a 120-square-mile area and analyzed for carbon-14 or tritium. The raw data, as derived from this study, are thought to be reasonably accurate because ground waters of the basin are characteristically of the calcium bicarbonate type. The C^{14} ages are, therefore, related primarily to the original C^{14} content of the water as it left the soil zone. Ordinarily, then, application of correction factors based upon water chemistry and confirmed by utilizing the stable isotope ratio C^{13}/C^{12} would remove most of the age uncertainty of the dates. However, an unusual situation apparently exists in the Pullman-Moscow area which materially affects the carbonate chemistry of the ground waters.

The "nonbiogenic" carbonate of the Pullman-Moscow area must be derived primarily from soil carbonates such as caliche. Because such material cannot be assumed to be a dead C^{14} source, a further complicating factor is presented if any attempt is made to evaluate the initial C^{14} content of the ground water. (Measured radiocarbon dates on caliches from nearby areas actually show such material to be near the half-life of C^{14}.) Measurement of C^{14} values and of C^{13}/C^{12} ratios on soil samples might be utilized in conjunction with C^{13}/C^{12} measurements of living plant materials of the area to provide information on the initial biogenic carbonates of the ground water.

It is thought, however, that such a method might produce inconsistent and erratic results. A better approach might be based upon shallow ground-water bodies occurring at the base of the Palouse loess section and perched upon the basalt bedrock. Such shallow ground waters in the Pullman-Moscow area have consistently given raw data ages which correspond to modern (95 per cent National Bureau of Standard oxalic acid standard). These results indicate that isotopic exchange between biogenic CO_2 and $CaCO_3$ has been complete, has been an enrichment process (assuming caliche-like soil minerals to be an active C^{14} source) through repetitive reactions, or has been a combination of both mechanisms. Regardless, the bicarbonates in these perched ground-water bodies could be expected to have C^{13}/C^{12} ratios typical of local vegetation, or of about $-25\%o$ if referred to marine limestone. Measured values have, however, proved to be $-13.4\%o$ relative to NBS-20 standard limestone. I cannot offer a totally satisfactory explanation for this anomalous condition. I would suggest, however, that it is closely allied to caliche formation, solution, and redeposition. In the Pullman-Moscow area the total absence of limestone requires that biogenically produced CO_2 form bicarbonates through reaction with caliche or siltlike particles of calcite in the soil. Another possible mode of bicarbonate formation is by decomposition of primary minerals typified by such generalized reactions as:

$$CaAl_2Si_2O_3 + H_2O + 2CO_2 \rightarrow Ca^{++} + 2HCO_3^- + Al_2O_3 + 2SiO_2$$
$$3CaMg(SiO_3)_2 + 5H_2O +$$
$$6CO_2 \rightarrow 3Ca^{++} + 6HCO_3^- + H_4Mg_3Si_2O_9 + 4SiO_2$$

Finally, bicarbonates can be produced by cation exchange reactions with the soil colloidal complex.

Repetitive reactions of the types mentioned may well tend to enrich soil waters in C^{14} while simultaneously maintaining C^{13}/C^{12} ratios between those of marine limestone and modern plant material. However, little is yet known about C^{13} values of caliches or of the soil in the Pullman-Moscow area.

Although these relationships are unclear, the value of C^{14} water-dating in the Pullman-Moscow area is in no way impaired. Because all waters are of the calcium bicarbonate type and in the pH range 6.8 to 7.2, they should be unaffected by outside influences. The fact that δC^{13} values are identical in recent perched waters and in ancient deep waters strongly suggests that isotopic exchange does not occur in the aquifer. Water ages should therefore be actual and controlled only by radioactive decay.

Sample Collection

Water samples were collected from selected wells in the basin with due consideration given to well location, well depth, and casing schedule (see Fig. 19). Every effort was made to sample wells in which the productive zone was known or fixed by casing and which were not complicated by more than one aquifer. This was not always possible, however, especially in those wells tapping the deep productive zone. As an example, Pullman well No. 4 (15/45-32N2), though cased to a depth of 399 feet, is known to have limited hydraulic connection with the shallow aquifers. To further complicate matters the number of productive zones below the 399-foot level is unknown. It was, nevertheless, necessary to sample this well because it is the only deep well in the Pullman subbasin.

Carbon for C^{14} analysis was obtained from the well waters by exchanging bicarbonates on strongly basic anion exchange resins, according to methods described by Crosby and Chatters (1965a). These methods have been questioned as possibly permitting isotopic fractionation processes to take place. However, recent work by Crosby and Chatters (1965b) has shown that (1) bicarbonate extraction is quantitative, (2) the C^{14} content is identical with that obtained on a duplicate water sample extracted by the U.S. Geological Survey method of Hanshaw,* and (3) the ratio C^{13}/C^{12} is identical with a duplicate sample treated by the USGS method. Although Crosby and Chatters (1965a) originally used both a weak- and a strong-base anion exchanger arranged in series, recent practice has been to use only the strong-base resin in greater quantity. This modification simplifies the process without introducing undesirable side effects and eliminates dangers of isotopic fractionation in the weak-base exchanger.

Analysis of Results

Figure 21 presents the C^{14} ages of ground waters of the Pullman-Moscow basin plotted against the elevation of the respective productive zones. Although some of the productive zones are well known and can be accurately portrayed, others are obscure and can only be shown as the total uncased, or perforated, portions of the borehole. The data can readily be divided into three envelopes comprising (1) the upper waters of the Moscow subbasin, (2) the upper waters of the Pullman subbasin, and (3) the lower waters which are probably common to both basins.

Clearly, the ground waters are distinctly stratified with an inverse relationship between elevation of productive zone and water age. It should be noted, as shown in the figure, that a given well sampled at different times may give slightly different water ages. The changes appear to be systematic in that a well sampled after the pumping season advances gives a greater age than it does during the period of low pumpage. This is what might be expected from purely hydraulic considerations, i.e., more of the water is drawn from deeper levels as the cone of pressure relief expands.

It is strongly suggested by the data that the deep ground-water system may have been essentially full by the close of the Wisconsin glacial stage and that the upper system was in the process of filling. The argument is even more

---

* Private communication with B. B. Hanshaw, 1965.

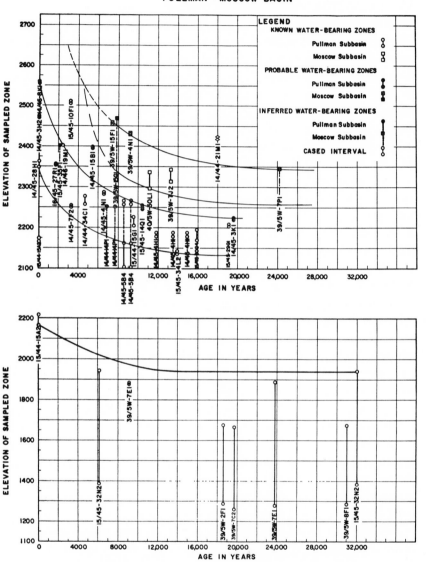

Figure 21. Aquifer elevation–age relationship, Pullman-Moscow basin

conclusive if we disregard the youngest ages obtained from wells 15/45–32N2 and 39/5W–7E1. The sample from well 15/45–32N2 was collected during the low pumping season. It could well be influenced by younger upper waters which are under greater potentials than the lower aquifers and known to have some degree of hydraulic interconnection with the deep system here. The sample from well 39/5W–7E1 was collected by an in-well sampling technique following completion of drilling and after the well had remained idle for several months. It is entirely possible that the sample was contaminated. Should the samples, in effect, be correct the dates may indicate some recharge to the upper layers of the deep system. Such recharge might occur by infiltration along the weathered pre-Tertiary surface as suggested by the extension of the envelope line of the lower system to include well 15/44–15A2 (see Fig. 21).

The deep artesian zone is thought to be common to both Pullman and Moscow subbasins. C^{14} age-depth relationships tend to support this thesis but are yet too limited in scope and too dependent upon assumptions as to productive zone location. All deep wells, however, have essentially common static water levels and appear to be currently near static equilibrium. Wells in the deep system have much higher specific capacities than those of the shallow zone and the water is of superior quality. As the indicated thickness of the productive zone is greater, a much larger reserve is postulated. Recharge potentials are entirely unknown and will probably remain so until pumping has continued long enough to produce dynamic changes.

Further analysis of Figure 21 suggests relatively static conditions in the reservoirs until the "thermal maximum" about 6,500 years ago. With the advent of cooler, moister conditions, and continuing to the present, the reservoirs have been filling at increasing rates. Data suggest that recent accumulation rates for the Pullman subbasin are about 0.5 inch of saturated rock per year.

The absence of recent waters in the Moscow basin indicates accumulation to an elevation of, perhaps, 2,500 to 2,550 feet, after which clays of the uppermost Latah formation limited further additions to storage. Subsequent incident precipitation on the Moscow subbasin has evidently been carried off by surface runoff, by underflow through sand horizons in the uppermost Latah formation, or by "spillage" into the Pullman subbasin.

The upper waters of the Moscow subbasin are restricted from continued downward percolation by the impermeable clays of the underlying Latah formation. Whether by subsidence through loading or by past erosional processes, these clays are essentially bowl-shaped. Infiltrating precipitation collecting in this depression apparently was restricted from moving westward into the Pullman subbasin by a ground-water mound near the state line. This mound is associated with a distinct structural high on the basalt surface, possibly representing the final basalt dam across the westward opening of the Moscow subbasin. At the time static water levels at Moscow rose above the ground water, mound-pressure gradients were reversed and waters moved westward into the Pullman area. This mechanism probably accounts for the anomalous age-elevation relationship of wells 14/45–15B1 and 15/45–10F1 shown in Figure 21.

Although the sample density in the Moscow subbasin is not high enough to state unequivocally that recent waters do not exist, the inference can be made that little, if any, recharge is occurring in the upper aquifer system. Certainly the limited catchment area coupled with an unmeasurable accumulation rate could hardly be expected to keep pace with heavy pumpage. It may well be that recharge conditions have changed materially from a period of seven thousand years ago, which corresponds to the age of the youngest sampled waters.

The pattern of water ages in the Pullman subbasin is somewhat different. Although no recent waters are known in the area of heavy pumpage, some recharge appears to be occurring at the margins of the cone of depression. The conditions for recharge are much improved over the Moscow area because the upper permeable basalt zone is exposed at the surface at many places and is elsewhere covered only by the Palouse silt-loam. The permeability of the Palouse is unquestionably much higher than that of the Latah clays.

The upper waters of the Pullman subbasin are separated from the deep zone by a horizon of impermeable basalts. These are at a lower elevation than the corresponding impermeable Latah clays of the Moscow area. The relationships are shown diagrammatically in Figure 22. Geological controls coupled with a much greater catchment area serve to explain the slower decline of the piezometric surface at Pullman than at Moscow.

If we can assume that present average recharge rates are similar to those indicated in the past, if we assume an average basalt porosity of 5 per cent, and if we assume that drainage of the aquifers is occurring, we can estimate average annual recharge. The Pullman subbasin encompasses about 250 square miles. At an annual accumulation rate of 0.5 inches of saturated rock the indicated recharge would be 108 million gallons per year. This is only one-tenth of the present pumpage rate in the basin. The recharge in the Moscow portion of the basin would be correspondingly less and still farther out of balance with pumping rates. Though these rates are well below estimates based on hydrologic considerations, they may be more in keeping with known water level declines. Any use of average values for accumula-

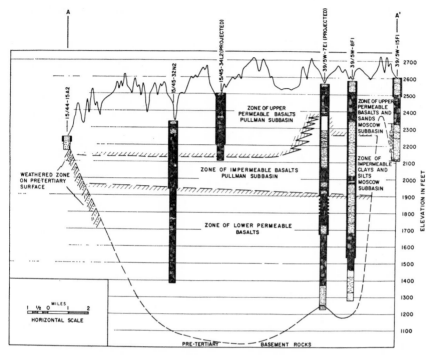

Figure 22. Idealized cross section through the
Pullman-Moscow ground-water basin

tion or decline rates must be tempered by a realization that individual stratigraphic horizons can vary greatly in effective porosities.

Future Studies

The information derived from the study of the Pullman-Moscow basin points out some basic shortcomings which should be remedied in future C^{14} research in basaltic terranes. Drilling logs are seldom of sufficient accuracy or detail to permit positive definition of water-bearing zones within narrow limits. In many instances more than one such zone are present in a well and tend to make the C^{14} age less meaningful.

It is an established fact that potentials of Pullman-Moscow basin aquifers generally decline with increasing aquifer depth. Therefore in wells tapping more than one zone flow will be established from the upper zone into the lower zone.

To overcome these problems it is suggested that all wells, prior to C^{14}

sampling, be geophysically logged. A logging combination including spontaneous potential, resistivity, gamma, and neutron logs will probably provide the required information. Subsequent sampling should then be directed, where practical, only to those wells tapping a single, vertically limited aquifer. In the Pullman-Moscow area or other areas where C^{14} water studies are undertaken it would be highly desirable to establish several C^{14} observation wells. Monthly or even semiannual sampling of these wells could be undertaken to study C^{14} variations in time as well as space.

Conclusions

The C^{14} method of water dating in basaltic terranes offers much promise both as a research technique into basic fundamentals of ground-water movement and as an inventory procedure. Much additional study of the method in other environments utilizing the suggested improvements is needed. The method should be tried in the Columbia Basin area for studying the relationship between recent irrigation waters and the pre-existing ground-water regime. It may also serve as a valuable tool in inventorying ground-water supplies in the area adjacent to the Columbia Basin project.

As applied to the Pullman-Moscow ground-water basin, C^{14} studies indicate that the upper water-producing zones are being depleted at rates well in excess of recharge. Limited recharge is occurring in the Pullman subbasin, but recharge in recent times is not demonstrable in the Moscow subbasin. The conclusion regarding the Moscow subbasin may be attributable, in part, to inadequate sampling density. However, infiltrating stream and precipitation waters may recharge only sand and gravel horizons in the uppermost Latah formation and may not be reaching the primary basaltic aquifers. Recharge to the Latah sands may be carried from the basin as underflow or may be effluent to streams like Paradise Creek and the South Fork of the Palouse River.

Future municipal drilling in the basin should be directed to the deep artesian zone. This largely untapped resource is expected to contain greater reserves than the shallow system and should meet the increased pumping needs for at least a decade. The fact should not be overlooked, however, that this is essentially a stored body of water and pumping may not induce significant amounts of recharge. Because both Pullman and Moscow will probably be pumping from the same system, effects of withdrawals could be magnified. An analysis of the performance of the deep system must wait until pumpage has continued long enough to produce some measurable effects.

REFERENCES

Cavin, R. E., and James W. Crosby III
   1966   Supplemental seismic studies for the city of Moscow, Idaho. College of Engineering Research Report 66/9–19, January.
Crosby, J. W. III
   1967   Ground water. In Water resource research needs in the state of Washington, Donald L. Bender, comp. State of Washington Water Research Center, Pullman.
Crosby, J. W. III, and R. M. Chatters
   1965a   New techniques of water sampling for carbon-14 analysis. Journal of Geophysical Research, 70(12)2839–44.
   1965b   Water-dating techniques as applied to the Pullman-Moscow ground-water basin. Technical Extension Bulletin No. 296, Washington State University, Pullman.
Erickson, E.
   1962   Application of isotope techniques in hydrology. Technical Report Series, No. 11, International Atomic Energy Agency, Vienna (reprint of panel, Vienna, 1961).
Ingerson, E., and F. J. Pearson, Jr.
   1964   Estimation of age and rate of motion of ground-water by the C^{14} method. Pp. 263–83 in Recent researches in the fields of hydrosphere, atmosphere and nuclear geochemistry (Sugawara festival volume). Maruzen Company, Tokyo.
Münnich, K. O., and J. C. Vogel
   1959 C^{14}—Alterbestimmung von susswasser—kalkablagerungen. Naturwissenschaften, 46.
Pearson, F. J., Jr.
   1965   Use of C—13/C—12 ratios to correct radio-carbon ages of materials initially diluted by limestone. Proceedings of the International C^{14} and H^{3} Dating Conference.
Thomas, H. E.
   1955   Water, in The Yearbook of Agriculture 1955, 62. U.S. Department of Agriculture.
Vogel, J. C., and D. Ehhalt
   1963   The use of carbon isotopes in ground water studies. Pp. 383–95 in Radioisotopes in hydrology. International Atomic Energy Agency, Vienna.

VIII

METHODOLOGY IN ESTABLISHING
WATER-QUALITY STANDARDS

Robert O. Sylvester
and Carl A. Rambow

IN recent years it has become apparent throughout the nation that previous methods of water-quality management have been ineffective in far too many instances. When effective, they were frequently so only because the development of the region had not yet reached the stage where the dilution capacity of the receiving water was overtaxed. These methods generally established receiving water-quality standards at a minimal level but at a level that would permit enjoyment of several or all beneficial uses. The water quality would then be allowed to degrade to these limits.

Standards set with these objectives are technologically and economically defensible, but in reality they are frequently not attained or maintained. They are in fact low water-quality standards. In a developing area, pollution loads, in many instances, are imposed on the adjacent waters more rapidly than pollution-control measures can be instituted. When a stream water

Material for this paper was taken from a study by the authors on *Water Quality,* Volume IV of "An Initial Study of the Water Resources of the State of Washington" (Pullman, Wash.: Washington Water Research Center, 1967). Half of the study cost was funded by the Washington State Legislature through the Department of Conservation and the remaining half was divided equally between funds provided by the University of Washington and Washington State University.

Robert O. Sylvester is professor of civil engineering at the University of Washington. At the time this paper was prepared, Carl A. Rambow was research associate professor of civil engineering at the University of Washington. He is now president of Montgomery Research, Inc., Pasadena, California.

quality reaches this minimum tolerable level and a municipality or a new industry then wishes to discharge an additional load, the regulatory agency is faced with forbidding the new discharge or requiring all other waste dis- chargers to upgrade their treatment. Usually the latter prevails, and the stream quality deteriorates because of the long time involved in negotiations, design, financing, and construction for all parties concerned. This can be a never-ending process in which the desired water-quality control is not achieved and beneficial uses are often harmed. It is analogous to automobile highway construction in a rapidly developing area where the vehicles in- crease faster than highways are built for them. Other solutions are necessary.

Further, it is, with our present state of knowledge, practically impossible to set water-quality standards at these minimal values. Considering stream biota alone, there are hundreds of substances that may be introduced that would affect their growth and survival. Tolerance to these substances varies with each species, age of the species, water temperature, dissolved oxygen content, presence of synergistic or antagonistic substances, and so forth. This situation produces never-ending arguments on just what level of even a single pollu- tant can be tolerated before severe damage results. These levels are not established for most substances. A policy of clean water with high standards permits the setting of these standards in a straightforward fashion subject only to the arguments of those who believe that water is a resource whose ability to accept pollutants should be exploited to its fullest capacity. If all of the costs, both primary and secondary, of high water quality versus minimal water quality are projected into the future, it is the contention of the authors that it is to the over-all advantage of society to have a policy for high standards.

Water-quality control problems have generally been associated with mu- nicipal and industrial waste-water discharges. Land use is also becoming increasingly important in its relationship to water quality. In many instances, the effect on water quality caused by irrigation return flows, erosion, and diversion far transcend the effects of municipal and industrial waste water. A new philosophy of approach is needed for control of land use as it relates to water quality and quantity. This particular subject is not specifically dealt with in this paper because of space limitations.

There is now a clear trend away from the policy of "controlled degrada- tion" and from the premise that dispersion and dilution of effluents is a "beneficial" use of receiving waters. This trend is made most evident by recent national legislation and by the general awakening of the public to water pollution and its effect on our environment. The attitude that accepts water pollution as a necessary consequence of modern life is rapidly changing.

Basic Premises

As part of a study by the authors (1967) on water quality in the state of Washington, it was necessary to propose a set of water-quality parameters and values as a reference. The basic premises underlying the water-quality standards and goals presented here are as follows:

1. The objective ideal is to achieve or maintain clean water. Clean water is defined as water that approaches its natural state of purity and permits uninterrupted present and future beneficial uses.

2. The right to pollute water and damage other uses does not exist.

3. The dispersion and assimilation of pollutants into a body of water is not a beneficial use of water. It is, however, a necessary use since economics, present technology, and multiple-purpose usage do not permit the complete elimination of water-quality degrading materials.

4. All waste-water discharges, no matter what their volume or location, should receive as a minimum degree of treatment the removal of settleable and floatable solids and the removal or neutralization of toxic substances. Additional treatment would depend upon the location, volume, and characteristics of the waste-water discharge.

5. The assimilation by receiving waters of these residues from effective waste-water treatment processes must be apportioned on an equitable basis. A particular municipality or industry does not have the right of the unilateral exploitation of this assimilative capacity (difference between natural water quality and stream standards).

The Approach

Three basic principles may be considered in developing an approach to the reference criteria presented.

1. *Maintain original water quality.* As an ideal, it would be desirable to restore surface waters to near their condition before the impact of civilization caused quality impairment.

2. *Maintain the value of each quality parameter at that point dictated by the most critical use of the water in question.* This approach permits changes from the original water quality but permits no interference with beneficial uses of the water.

3. *Set requirements more restrictive than necessary to serve beneficial uses,*

to assure high water quality with expanded usage in the future. Portions of all three of the above are incorporated into the proposed reference criteria. The second element provides the starting point in establishing each limit, with the other two used as guides in developing the final values.

A problem in taking this approach (particularly with the second element) is that the optimum limits of a parameter for a particular beneficial use may not be known precisely or may be sufficiently elastic to require the application of considerable judgment in the selection of a value for protection of that beneficial use. For example, the U.S. Public Health Service (1962) prescribes a turbidity limit of 5 units for drinking water. The ideal value would be zero. In this case, the safety of the water for drinking is not at issue; the limit is imposed purely as an esthetic matter. It may be argued that the Public Health Service drinking-water standards, generally accepted as reasonably conservative, are sufficiently restrictive that the turbidity limit proposed therein can be accepted without modification. On the other hand, it may also be argued that these standards represent limits which water-quality values should never exceed. Then it would be reasonable to set water-quality goals, if not standards themselves, at more restrictive levels than those which are intended to be grounds for acceptance or rejection of a water supply for drinking. It is likely that future standards will be more restrictive.

Goals and Standards

In order to apply water-quality control measures intelligently, it is necessary to have water-quality objectives toward which control efforts can be directed. In general, these objectives can be represented as standards and goals of water quality.

1. *Goals* may be defined as desirable values of water-quality parameters, which may or may not be realistic, either now or within the foreseeable future. If a goal is not now realistic, it may be because the technology does not presently exist for achieving it or because the technology exists, but that the economics of the situation preclude applying it. A water-quality goal, if carefully selected, has value as a point of reference, to which standards and abatement procedures can be compared.

2. *Standards.* Standards of water quality may be identical to the corresponding goals or may be more lenient. A standard is proposed as an objective to be achieved or maintained immediately or within a short period from the time of its establishment. Setting of a standard implies consideration of the present limiting factors of technology, economics, and public policy. Thus, while the meeting of a water-quality standard may be of a

lower order than achievement of the corresponding goal, the standard nevertheless fulfills a purpose by accomplishing what is realistically achievable at a particular time. Presumably, a water presently meeting the "goal" criteria would not be allowed to degrade to the "standard" criteria.

3. *Derived values.* With this distinction in mind, a set of water-quality goals and standards can be developed.

It is considered desirable and practicable to maintain virtually all fresh surface waters in a condition well suited for all or most beneficial uses, including those uses with the most restrictive water-quality requirements; i.e., domestic raw-water supply, fish propagation, and contact recreation. Most fresh waters now have, or can be expected to have, these uses. The values proposed for each pollution parameter, presented in Table 11, presuppose effective effluent dispersion in the area of discharge. Water-quality monitoring in its time and space relationships together with allowable percentage and frequency deviations from these values, however, is of course a function of the regulating agencies.

Values are presented in Table 11 for salt water but are omitted for estuaries, which contain changing mixtures of fresh and salt water. Estuarial water quality may be evaluated by using a combination of fresh- and salt-water values as appropriate.

Rationale

The goals and standards were developed from the experience of the authors and from the work of many investigators, as summarized in the principal treatises on the subject available to the authors of this study (U.S. Public Health Service, 1962; McKee and Wolf, 1963). The detailed descriptions of the rationale followed for each of the fifty-five quality parameters considered is far too lengthy for inclusion in this paper, but is published in our previously mentioned study (Rambow and Sylvester, 1967).

In most cases, the proposed standards are more restrictive than the published criteria for threshold values of possible undesirable effects. These values are given in consideration of cases where the present water quality of a stream may be substantially higher than the most restrictive requirements would necessitate, where introduction of increasing quantities of a specific pollutant might imply concomitant introduction of other, more serious pollution, and where future economic developments (e.g., establishment of certain industries) might unavoidably result in increased discharge of the pollutant in question. In the latter case, the strict limitation on the pollutant might be relaxed at some future time if found to be desirable and necessary. Other-

TABLE 11

Summary of Surface Water-Quality Limit Proposals, State of Washington

(All Values in mg./l Unless Otherwise Specified)

Parameters	Fresh Water		Salt Water	
	Goal	Standard	Goal	Standard
Alkalinity (Phenolphthalein)	*	*	*	*
Alkalinity (total)	*	*	*	*
Ammonia nitrogen	0.3	0.5	0.0025	0.003
Arsenic	0.003	0.005	0.003	0.004
Bacteria	†	†	†	†
Barium	0.01	0.05	0.05	0.06
Bicarbonate	‡	‡	‡	‡
BOD	1.0	2.0	1.0	2.0
Boron	0.1	0.3	4.7	5.5
Bottom deposits from waste-water discharge	None	None	None	None
Cadmium	0.0005	0.001	0.00011	0.00013
Calcium	§	§	§	§
Carbonate	§	§	§	§
CCE (carbon Chloroform Extract)	0.00	0.10	0.05	0.10
Chloride	10	20	Natural	120% of natural
Chromium	Trace	0.01	0.0005	0.00006
Chemical Oxygen Demand	#	#	#	#
Coliforms—domestic sewage origin	50/100 ml.	240/100 ml.	50/100 ml.	240/100 ml.
Color	5 units	5 units over natural	None	5 units
Conductivity	110% of natural	125% of natural	Natural	120% of natural
Copper	0.05	0.02 above background	0.05	0.06
Cyanide	0.005	0.01	None	0.01
DO (Dissolved Oxygen)	95% Saturation	85% Saturation	95% Saturation	85% Saturation
Fecal streptococci	**	**	**	**
Floating solids	None	None	None	None

TABLE 11 (*Cont.*)

Summary of Surface Water-Quality Limit Proposals, State of Washington

(All Values in mg./l Unless Otherwise Specified)

Parameters	Fresh Water		Salt Water	
	Goal	Standard	Goal	Standard
Fluoride	0.5	1.0	1.3	1.5
Hardness	20–75 as CaCO₃	20–125 as CaCO₃	—	—
Hydroxide	None	None	None	None
Iron	0.0 above natural	0.1 above natural	0.01 above natural	0.2
Lead	Limit of detectability	0.02	Limit of detectability	0.004
Magnesium	††	††	††	††
Manganese	Trace	0.01	0.002	0.04
Nitrate	0.1 above natural	0.4 above natural	0.6	0.6
Nitrogen (total)	0.4 above natural	1.0 above natural	0.5	0.6
Odor	1.0 (Threshold odor no.)	3 (Threshold odor no.)	1.0 (Threshold no.)	3 (Threshold no.)
Oil and tars	None	None for coverage herein	None	None
Pesticides	Insufficient data			
pH	7.0–8.0 units	6.5–8.5 units	7.5–8.4 units	7.5–8.4 units
Phenol	Limit of detectability	0.0005	0.04	0.05
Phosphate (total)	0.03	0.15	0.3	0.4
Potassium	2.5	5.0	380	450
Radioactivity	None	‡‡	None	‡‡
Selenium	Limit of detectability	0.002	0.004	0.005
Silica	§§	§§	§§	§§
Silver	Limit of detectability	0.003	0.0003	0.0004
Sodium	10 over natural	35 over natural	10,500	12,500

TABLE 11 (Cont.)

Summary of Surface Water-Quality Limit Proposals, State of Washington

(All Values in mg./l Unless Otherwise Specified)

Parameters	Fresh Water Goal	Fresh Water Standard	Salt Water Goal	Salt Water Standard
Spent Sulfite Liquor	Effect covered by	other parameters		
Sulfate	15†	30	2700	3200
Surfactants	Trace (LAS)‡	0.10 (LAS)	Trace (LAS)	0.10 (LAS)
Temperature	Natural temp. + 1° C	Natural temp. + 2° C	Natural temp. + 1° C	Natural temp. + 2° C
Total Dissolved Solids	‖‖	‖‖	‖‖	‖‖
Toxicants, Miscellaneous	None detectable	None detectable	None detectable	None detectable
Turbidity	5 units§		3 units	5 units
Viruses	None proposed at present	Natural present		
Zinc	Limit of detectability	Limit of detectability	0.01	0.012

(For discussion of the derivation and significance of these proposed limits, see Ref. 3.)

* No specific limits. A waste discharge is not to increase the natural total alkalinity by more than 10 per cent. A waste discharge is not to impart phenolphthalein (CO_3 and OH^-) alkalinity to a receiving water.

† No limit specified—*see* Coliforms.

‡ No limit specified—relates to Conductivity and pH.

§ No limit specified—*see* Hardness.

‖ Although carbonate itself in moderate concentrations is not particularly detrimental, it is associated with high pH values (greater than 8.3). Any carbonate discharge is not to be detectable below the point of discharge.

Since the chemical oxygen demand is related to the BOD, DO, and CCE and is not a determination in the basic data program, it has no limit specified here. It may be desirable to add limits at a later date.

** Fecal bacteria are represented by the coliform group standard.

†† Controlled by hardness content; no limit specified.

‡‡ As proposed in the U.S. Public Health Service *Drinking Water Standards*.

§§ No standard proposed. Turbidity will include colloidal silica.

‖‖ No standard proposed. Conductivity standards are related.

wise, the first few developments in an area would tend to discharge pollutants in such quantities as to shortly bring the stream to the brink of unsatisfactory content of that material. This would then probably produce the undesirable piecemeal abatement approach. In other words, high standards are proposed in an attempt to preserve the high quality of rivers at least long enough for the assimilative capacity and waste transport capacity to be more effectively distributed among the maximum number of users.

The Guidelines for Establishing Water Quality Standards for Interstate Waters, promulgated by the Secretary of the Interior upon transfer of the Federal Water Pollution Control Administration from the Department of Health, Education and Welfare to the Department of the Interior on May 10, 1966, indicates some of the basic philosophy by which state water-quality standards will be judged when submitted to the FWPCA for review. Among other criteria for acceptance, the *Guidelines* states, "In no case will standards providing for less than existing water quality be acceptable." This guideline must be construed to apply to water now receiving a near maximum of tolerable pollutants and not to natural waters. If interpreted literally, along with the assumption that any increase in concentration of a potential pollutant constitutes a degradation of water quality, this statement would mean that without complete waste-water processing, virtually no increase in population or agricultural irrigation could be permitted, especially the latter, and would impose a serious limit on the growth of industrial operations. This is the case because virtually any beneficial use of water involving withdrawal results in an increase of dissolved minerals in the returned waste streams. It is questionable whether this criterion can be satisfied, at least under present conditions of development of technology and economic conditions. This is particularly true in the case of irrigated agriculture, where in many cases the return flows are not even susceptible to interception, much less demineralization treatment. It must be assumed, therefore, that the criterion will of necessity be administered more broadly or that threshold concentrations for specific minerals (and possible other materials) will be established, below which any increase will not be considered to constitute quality degradation.

It should be emphasized that values presented here were adopted for the purpose of a specific study (Rambow and Sylvester, 1967) but enjoy no official recognition. They hopefully will serve as guidelines for water-quality control practices and procedures in the future. They are not necessarily intended to be rigid but subject to changes with increasing information on effluents, local natural water qualities, technological improvements, and so forth.

Application of Goals and Standards

Three conditions may exist when applying these values to specific waters: (1) present quality exceeds goal values, (2) present quality is below goal values but exceeds standard values, or (3) present quality is below standard values.

In those instances where natural-water-quality parameters fall below the goal or standard values throughout the year, it would be advisable at this time to set the standard at the level of natural quality. The goal values, however, should continue as objectives. In many instances these natural values may be greatly improved in the future through better land-management practices, stream channeling, and so forth. Standards could then be raised for that particular water body. With this interpretation, the following assumptions as to potential application of our criteria may be considered for the three conditions defined above.

Case 1. Present quality exceeds goal values. The standard values were selected so that if water quality just met them, no (or negligible) impairment of any present or foreseeable beneficial uses would result. The goal values are more restrictive, and it may be said that water quality meeting the goal values would be of better quality than required to support such beneficial uses without adverse effects. It would therefore be reasonable to allow degradations in quality, in Case 1 instances, to goal values of quality so that orderly development of a region may be permitted. This is not to imply that unbridled pollutant discharges should be permitted merely because such discharges would not decrease the resulting quality to below the goal values. On the contrary, treatment of waste discharges should still be required, in order that the maximum volume of discharge, and number of dischargers, could be accommodated before quality deteriorates to the goal values.

This approach is in conformance with the FWPCA *Guidelines* (1966), which states, "No standard will be approved which allows any wastes amenable to treatment or control to be discharged into any interstate water without treatment or control regardless of the water quality criteria and water use or uses adopted." It is assumed, therefore, that standards for streams in which the natural quality exceeds the goal values would be set at the goal values rather than at the existing values.

Case 2. Present quality is below goal values but exceeds standard values. It is assumed in this case, using the philosophy outlined under Case 1 above, that the quality values adopted for regulatory purposes would be those values existing in the water in its present condition. Again, treatment of all wastes is presupposed. However, in the future, it may be necessary in some instances to relax these quality requirements somewhat, possibly to as low as the standard values. This results from the inescapable fact that dissolved mineral salts are not *readily* susceptible to removal from large waste streams, such as irrigation return flows. Their presence in water at levels established by the standard values does not decrease the suitability of water significantly, if at all, for beneficial use. Such acceptance of the need for possible adjustment, therefore, is merely a recognition of the fact that this change may occur and cannot at this time be prevented without stifling development within the watershed. It should not be viewed as a retreat from the quality objectives defined by the goals, and, where and when possible, standards should be adjusted upward toward the goals.

Case 3. Present quality is below standard values. In these instances, improved waste-water treatment is necessary. Waste-water processing or control should aim at achieving values well above the standards to permit continued area development without the constant necessity for each discharger to be in a state of ever-changing demands on treatment facilities.

Original (Natural) Water Quality

In setting values for water-quality goals and standards it is most helpful to have, as a point of reference, an approximation of minimal water-quality values that existed prior to the advent of man. These may be termed original or natural quality values. Their determination in stream reaches largely unaffected by man is of course relatively easy. Where man has affected the natural water quality, it is necessary to approximate values by calculation using known pollutional inputs, by comparison with a similar stream, or by examination of quality values in unaffected upstream reaches.

The lowest or minimum natural quality occurs for nearly all parameters during periods of minimum flow which in the Pacific Northwest lies close to the period of maximum water temperatures for most waters. Turbidity and color will usually be greatest during periods of heavy runoff. Since water-quality data have been collected in a systematic and comprehensive manner on most waters only in recent years, it is necessary to approximate by calculation these minimum values for a low-flow year unless a low-flow year has fortuitously occurred very recently when corresponding quality data were taken.

After a low-flow year has been selected for reference purposes, the ionic constituents can be approximated through their correlation values with conductivity. Conductivity is plotted against stream flow for a particular year and with a log-log plot, the resulting graph is essentially a straight line. This line may then be extrapolated to the low-flow value desired and the conductivity determined for that low flow. Multiplying this conductivity value by its ratio to ionic constituents then gives an approximation of that constituent under low-flow conditions.

Color and turbidity values should be near minimal with low flow in most streams and there is little reason to suppose that pH values would not be normal for natural waters. BOD values should be very low or insignificant in the absence of man's activities and DO values should relate to the low-flow temperature estimate. For a more detailed description of this methodology, see Sylvester and Rambow, 1967.

Conclusions

The methodology for establishing water-quality criteria as presented here was done for the state of Washington where most waters do not suffer from damaging pollution. Some aspects of the methodology may be more difficult to apply in regions where most waters are more severely damaged by pollution. The authors believe, however, that the basic philosophy and rationale is applicable to all waters, although this involves a profound change in most present practices for water-quality control. They further believe that this approach is the only practicable method of achieving or maintaining high-quality water for all to use and enjoy.

A comparison of the goal and standard values, presented in Table 11, with present water quality and minimum recorded water quality in forty principal stream reaches in the state of Washington gave the following results for nine selected parameters: In the case of present quality, about 92 per cent exceeded goal values, 6 per cent lay between goal and standard values, and 2 per cent fell below standard values. In the case of minimum recorded water quality, about 73 per cent fell above goal values, 11 per cent between goal and standard values, and 16 per cent below standard values.

REFERENCES

McKee, J. E., and H. W. Wolf (eds.)
　1963　Water quality criteria. 2nd ed. Prepared with assistance from the Division of Water Supply and Pollution Control; U.S. Public Health Service, Department of Health, Education and Welfare; the Resources Agency of California, State Water Quality Control Board Publication No. 3–A.

Public Health Service, Department of Health, Education and Welfare
1962 Drinking water standards. Title 42, chap. i, Part 72. Interstate Quarantine Federal Register 2152.
Rambow, C. A., and R. O. Sylvester
1967 Water quality. Volume IV of An initial study of the water resources of the state of Washington. Washington Water Research Center, Washington State University. Pullman.

IX

MUNICIPAL AND INDUSTRIAL NEEDS FOR WATER QUALITY

Dale A. Carlson and
Robert O. Sylvester

WATER quality is an aspect of the nation's water resource that is obtaining ever-increasing attention as the need for water becomes greater and as water users begin to realize that the acceptability and adequacy of a water supply is governed by quality as well as by quantity. While critical water problems are besetting the eastern portion of the United States, water-quality problems are especially important in the western states, where water quality is the restrictive feature in further regional development. This aspect of water can become a serious problem in interstate relations involving mutual dependency or sequential use of waters. Also such problems can be international in nature, as has been witnessed in Europe and to some degree on this continent in relations with Mexico.

Water quality is the sum of the physical, biological, chemical, and aesthetic properties of water. Water quality is concerned with the environmental conditions of water. Because water incorporates, to some degree, everything with which it comes in contact, its every use, whether natural, industrial, or commercial, has some effect on its constituents. The consideration of water use thus becomes an important aspect of water quality.

The many uses of water each make certain requirements on the condition of the water being used. The water quality desired varies widely among the various users. Consider, for example, the water to be used for making

Dale A. Carlson and Robert O. Sylvester are professors of civil engineering at the University of Washington.

colorless soft drinks such as soda water as opposed to water being used by ships as a navigational vehicle.

Water is used as a transportation system for a variety of products from prime high-value materials to unusable wastes. The premium items normally are extracted from water with great care, leaving only those residuals not economically feasible to remove, while the waste products often are added to water in as high a concentration as is practicably possible when water can serve as a cheap means of disposal or as a means of transporting wastes away from any given location. These added wastes then exist as a potential water-quality problem to downstream water users.

Land use and land and urban development affect water quality. Construction can affect waters on a temporary basis such as in sloughing or depositing of fill materials, or erosion of areas exposed by excavation, or on an extended basis in the erection of facilities such as dams, revetments, or diversion structures.

Water, as an environment for living systems, can undergo major quality changes with time or with movement as a result of the biological activity of the inhabitants of the water itself or of its surrounding environs. The atmosphere too has been shown to be a contributor of water constituents both natural and man-made. Atmospheric gases will dissolve into adjacent waters, and particulate matter in air streams is deposited on water surfaces below.

Water quality, then, as expressed in this project, is concerned with the physical, chemical, biological, and aesthetic properties of water; with the health factors associated with the water environment; with water uses; and with municipal, industrial, and agricultural water needs and waste waters. Integrated into this area is the treatment of waters and waste water and the disposal of waste-water constituents, the development of techniques and methods for water analyses and evaluation, facilities design and construction, and water resource development and control.

National and Regional Aspects of the Research Needs

Water quality, as described above, is an area of intense and vigorous research activity by industrial, governmental, university, and private research personnel. The efforts in this area have been expanded and developed because of the urgency and the magnitude of the problems involved. Community, industrial, regional, national, and world-wide development rest on the need for water of the proper quality. This research has also been accelerated by a growing awareness of the effects of improper use of water resources and by the need for establishing proper responsibility as well as rights in water use.

In many sections of the United States, water quality has deteriorated to such an extent that valuable fisheries and other water uses have been lost. Many streams glowingly described as beautiful tributaries in early American literature are today repulsive in appearance. In other areas, the availability of acceptable water is restricted and ground-water storage is further depleted with each passing year.

In the area of health, the concern associated with water pollution has been expanded from identification and prevention of bacterial water-borne diseases and metal toxicity to evaluation of the significance of viruses, nematodes and other organisms in water supplies. The enhancement of medicinal, therapeutic, and other beneficial health values of water by addition of additives such as fluorides and other compounds is under investigation. Gradual evolvement of information on the cumulative effects of water constituents on humans needs further involvement by more researchers.

In responsible industry, water use is reaching a position of major concern. No longer an easily available debris catcher and tote-boy, water now must be considered an integral part of the raw-materials stockpile. Also, when industry is finished with water in a process system, the return flow must be of acceptable quality before return to the environment. But industry is not alone. Agricultural return flows, domestic waste waters, and other water activities also place responsibilities on the water user. All these water users, quite often unrestricted in the past in the availability or handling of water, are reaching the position of having to seriously consider their water needs and their water uses and disposal methods in relation to whether they can maintain their present or future activities.

Special Characteristics of the State of Washington

The use and misuse of water in many areas of the country have reached a state where reasonable water-quality goals seem almost impossible to reach at the present time under present regulatory conditions. Areas of the arid West have reached the point where the waters presently available are of unsuitable quality to allow significant future development, and suggestions are being voiced on the long-haul transport of acceptable water from water-sufficient areas to satisfy the ever-increasing demands for water.

Washington state along with other parts of the Pacific Northwest enjoys the position of having sufficient water for her present and foreseeable future development. In addition, the developing industrial activities in the state have not reached the complexity or the magnitude of much of the midwestern and eastern areas so that it is still possible here to maintain suitable water quality in Washington's streams, lakes, and tidal waters. Washington state is not without severe water-quality problems but they have not compounded yet to the point where restoration of reasonable water quality seems completely unfeasible.

The mantle of responsibility rests on the state, however, to assure its citizens of legitimate and proper water use coupled with adequate treatment and waste disposal so that the highest feasible water quality is maintained. The state must, as well, establish its water needs and rights in relation to water-poor areas of the country so that state and regional development and natural water value and beauty are not impaired by exportation of water to other regions to the detriment of future Washington citizens.

Summary of Research Needs for the State of Washington

In the fields of water quality and municipal and industrial waters, the need for research has been recognized for many years. The magnitude of the problems in these areas is attested to by the great variety of projects and large time-money allocations currently invested in these fields. Not all the important research areas can be listed in this report. In general, however, research needs could be classified under some general headings as listed below.

Studies on the Factors and Conditions That Influence Water Quality

This area has been under considerable study for several years, but there are yet many factors of major concern which have not been adequately assessed. More research is still needed on such topics as:

1. What controls stream constituents? What are the physical, chemical, environmental, and biological forces affecting the uptake or deposition of stream constituents?

2. What are the factors affecting, triggering, and sustaining growth in streams?

3. What are the effects of aeration on water quality in regard to stratification, dissolved oxygen, nutrient distribution, ice formation, and evaporation losses?

4. What are the effects of impoundments on streams in regard to heat balances, sediment transport, and sediment coagulation of radionuclides?

5. What is the fate of radionuclides in rivers and receiving waters?

6. What are the effects of land use on water quality for such operations as construction, agriculture, logging, reforestation, and irrigation?

7. What are the effects of storm-water runoff and urbanization on receiving water quality especially as regards silt, pesticides, fertilizers, and fisheries?

8. What are the effects of disposal of wastes in marine and estuarial waters?

9. What are the contamination problems in ground waters associated with irrigation and with urban and industrial development? What troublesome organisms exist in ground water? Where and why do they occur and how can they be controlled?

10. What is the fate of refractory compounds in receiving waters?

Studies on How to Control Water Quality

The need exists for the development of adequate means of determining and controlling water quality. For some aspects of water quality, it is possible that we are not adequately measuring or controlling certain water-quality parameters and hence may be accepting deleterious materials in water because not enough is known to assay the long-term effects of such constituents in water. The development of adequate water-quality assay and control methods is a major need in all major industrial areas of the United States.

Studies on What Our Water-Quality Needs Are

One of the most pressing current needs in the water field today is the determination of what the water-quality needs are for the various uses of water in the state of Washington and to what ultimate limits we can go in water use and water export before we have reached the boundaries of feasibility. Even if our water use and reuse could be greatly increased, is it advisable to tax the carrying capacity of water systems to the ultimate, and can we successfully monitor our water systems to be always certain that we are within the acceptable quality standards?

Anticipated Future Changes in Water Quality
and Their Influence on Water Demand and Use Practices

In assessing the total development of the water resources of the state of Washington, one of the major areas of concern is the anticipated uses of water for the future and how these uses will affect water quality and water demands. Such studies will need to be integrated with evaluations of future population and industrial growth, with the public awareness of its responsibility in maintaining desirable levels of water quality, and with technological advances which may help to better ascertain the desirable tolerance limits for water constituents. Such a water study will be an essential aspect to evaluation of Washington state water needs.

X

ECONOMIC ANALYSIS IN WATER-QUALITY MANAGEMENT

James A. Crutchfield

Introduction

Dramatic developments in the magnitude of water-quality problems and their impact on human lives in the past few years have brought the subject to the attention of the American people as never before. Worry begets interest, and both may—hopefully—produce some increase in real understanding of a most difficult issue in public policy. Willingness to take the necessary steps—financial, research, and administrative—to deal effectively with water quality automatically brings with it increasing awareness of the complexity of the decisions to be made, and this is a vital step toward workable solutions.

On the one hand, there is increasing recognition that the management of water quality is only one aspect of the broader problem of water allocation and development in general. The degradation of water quality represents a diminishing of available supply, and its prevention (or the reuse of degraded water) represents one of several alternative elements of "the current available supply." In addition, many of the problems of water quality can be dealt with, wholly or in part, by dilution, which, in turn, requires a direct drain on current water supplies or, at very least, alteration of temporal flow patterns. Once we come to grips with the problem of pollution and its control, it becomes painfully evident that to improve the quality of water, or to prevent its degradation, is costly; and the higher we set our sights, the greater the expenditures that must be undertaken.

James A. Crutchfield is professor of economics at the University of Washington.

Role of Economic Analysis

It is at this point that economic analysis offers the possibility of a major contribution—not as a substitute for the research and program development activities of engineers and physical scientists, but rather as a natural complement to their efforts. The general view that the term "economics" connotes something materialistic and somehow divorced from considerations that relate to the quality of life misstates the content of the discipline entirely. Economics is, above all, a methodical basis for registering and efficiently implementing human choices regarding the allocation of scarce resources to competing ends. The emphasis is on measurable evidences of people's collective desires, as evidenced by their willingness to pay for various types of goods and services. But underlying the dollar dimensions of demand are a host of considerations, intellectual and aesthetic as well as strictly utilitarian. The orderly and accurate measurement of willingness to pay constitutes a most useful measure of the intensity of the collective desire for one alternative as compared to another when evaluating competing resource uses.

In brief, economics is a theory of social choice; and it provides us with at least rough quantitative measures in a sense that no other study of human behavior can offer. It does not provide all answers to the alternatives involved in weighing different degrees of water quality against the costs of obtaining them, or of measuring pollution-abatement costs against the value of other production reduced or foreclosed by poor water quality. It does, however, give us a wonderfully useful economizing device that focuses attention on the key issues and provides a basis for quantifying the parameters that determine the most efficient of those alternatives that pass the first test of technical feasibility.

Let me repeat that economic analysis of the alternatives involved in water-quality management cannot be undertaken independent of the physical and engineering aspects of these alternatives. Though much progress has been made in recent decades, there still remains a frighteningly large array of open questions as to the physical determinants of water quality, the effects of various types and levels of degradation, and the operating parameters of various physical systems involved in changing or maintaining given quality standards. Obviously, each of these is part of the essential raw material from which economic analysis must begin. In one sense, then, the most difficult part of the research effort required for rational water-quality management lies in the physical relations that determine water quality and the effects of the innumerable environmental changes brought about by human utilization of land and water. But the fact remains that many key policy decisions cannot be made on the basis of these physical relations alone, regardless of the precision of our knowledge. There is no begging the fact that improved water quality costs money. It is not automatically "good," and the degree of social benefit from better water quality cannot be defined except by reference to costs of improvement and dollar values of additional output (or reduced production costs elsewhere) that result. Waste disposal, to put the matter another way, is one of the benefits that can be provided by flowing water and by estuarial and salt water. The essential problem is not one of pure water versus impure water, but of balancing alternative use patterns to obtain the lowest possible cost of waste disposal, taking into account all actual and potential users of the water supplies involved, and including non-water-disposal alternatives.

This paper is concerned with the principals underlying optimal and suboptimal systems of water-quality management. In most practical situations, of course, neither the availability of data nor the complex administrative problems associated with water-quality policies will permit optimal situations to be realized. Nevertheless, there is every justification for seeking a definition of region-wide water-utilization patterns that are optimal before analyzing in detail the economic effects of the inevitable retreats from optimality that are forced upon the policy-maker.

To simplify the analysis, the following assumptions are made initially. (1) There exists a region-wide authority capable of weighing and deciding all alternatives with respect to water utilization and water-quality management. (2) It is possible to value all uses of water in monetary terms. (3) Accurate projections of the level and composition of regional economic growth and the resulting structure of demands for water can be made and are used as a basis for planning water allocation and development.

Under these assumptions, there are four key questions to which the economist can contribute significantly for the formulation of efficient water-quality programs. (1) What constitutes an optimal system of waste disposal in economic terms, i.e., one that minimizes aggregate real costs of waste disposal? (We include not only treatment of waste and water but alternatives that reduce the production of waste or that do not require the use of water for disposal.) (2) How should costs of treatment and prevention of degradation be distributed, not only in terms of equity but also in terms of incentives for business and government units, in their own interest, to develop efficient waste-disposal policies and to minimize the amount of waste generated? (3) Are there technical economies that call for treatment systems involving larger-scale operations than would be available to any single decision-making unit within the region? (4) How should we design suboptimal systems to deal with three types of constraints: gaps in our knowledge of the physical effects of water quality on alternative users, inability to assign economic values to water uses abridged or foreclosed by pollution, and inability to make region-wide policies effective because of legal and jurisdictional limitations?

Effects of Divergence of Private and Social Cost

From the standpoint of the economist, the prime cause of pollution lies in the divergence of private and social costs and benefits in water use. No rational municipality or business concern would inflict on itself costs in excess of those required to prevent a reduction in the quality of water used in its own operations. If the costs are inflicted on others, however, and no offsetting charge is levied against the polluter, it is perfectly possible that a wide range of decisions that maximize the economic position of the waste discharger will result in a net loss of economic benefits to the community as a whole. (The word "benefits" is used here in the broadest sense to include aspects of water that are not measurable in dollars; for example, degradation in the taste, smell, or visual appearance of water clearly reduces the benefits from several types of water usage.)

The resulting impact on economic welfare has four dimensions. (1) The polluter's *private* costs, since he is not required to bear the full *social* cost of his actions, are too low. Consequently, he produces too much. (2) For the same reasons, turned upside down, production of goods and services involving water uses adversely affected is too low since private costs of these products are overstated by the costs properly attributable to the polluter. (3) If the polluting unit is not required to bear its full social costs, it has far less incentive to find production functions that minimize waste generation. (4) In similar fashion, the recipients of degraded water are denied the use of more efficient production methods that would be available if they did not face the cost of renovating or substituting poorer-quality water.

It should be noted that these diseconomies resulting from failure to account for and assess the full cost of using water for waste disposal are not simply transfers from one firm or individual to others. They are real costs to society in the sense that total economic output is reduced, partly because waste-disposal costs are higher than they need be, and partly because both sets of firms and households are induced to use economically inferior techniques.

The implication of this view of pollution with respect to amelioration is obvious. One essential step in the direction of a more rational water-quality policy is to identify all sources of degradation and to find, wherever possible, means of levying charges on those responsible. This is not merely a matter of equity, however important that might be, since cost-sharing arrangements can be dealt with apart from the matter of economic efficiency. The more important gain is the effect of such charges on incentives for those who use water for waste disposal to find other means of disposal or to shift to productive techniques that generate smaller amounts of waste. In some respects the real key to major and relatively costless reduction in aggregate costs of waste disposal is to harness the ingenuity of the individual manager, whether of a business concern or a municipality, to the search for methods of lowering both private and social costs. Water standards and zoning presumably have the same objective, but impose equally severe burdens in terms of information plus administrative costs, and both are inherently less flexible and probably less efficient over time.

Economies of Scale

The economist is also concerned with the complications introduced by technological economies of scale in waste disposal. Under most circumstances, the minimum aggregate cost of waste disposal cannot be realized by minimizing separately the costs of individual dischargers of waste. Increasingly, modern technology makes possible economic waste treatment only at scales beyond the capacity of individual business or governmental units, and frequently beyond the political jurisdiction of the public agencies directly concerned.

The experience of the Seattle Metro system provides an excellent illustration. Quite apart from the beneficial effects of this program on the quality of Lake Washington water, it is apparently highly successful as a cost-saving device by concentrating treatment and collection into a single system capable of operating at fully efficient scale. Similarly, the frequent opportunities for incremental water storage for low-flow augmentation as part of a general water-development program can be used to economic advantage, but only on a basis quite beyond the capabilities of the individual users affected. (In fact, the location of such storage facilities is, almost of necessity, both spatially and economically separated from those who benefit from low-flow augmentation.)

From a still broader point of view, an ideal waste-disposal system can only be defined in terms of minimizing *all* costs involved in waste disposal. The alternatives that would have to be considered would include all methods of treatment, all methods of reducing pollution loads, all direct costs of rectification, and the opportunity costs of benefits foregone if degradation of water quality is not prevented. The optimal mix is one in which no change can be made that will result in lower aggregate monetary value of costs of water-quality control plus production opportunities lost through degradation of water quality. This implies that in most, if not all, practical cases *pure* water could never be the right solution.

Water Quality as an Element of Water Supply

The relation of water-quality management to over-all water supply systems will vary widely in different parts of the United States. In the more humid areas, where aggregate water supply is not a major problem, the optimization of water quality may be considered as a problem in itself. In the arid West, however (and apparently in substantial parts of the Northeast as well), water is a really scarce economic good, and no system of water quality can be optimized without reference to the broader problem of water supply as a whole. For example, storage of water for low-flow augmentation may have either adverse or favorable effects on recreational usage of water on power generation, and on total supplies available for consumptive uses downstream. This interrelation is likely to assume real significance in cases where seasonal variations in water flows, water demands, or both are involved. Ideally, an optimal water-quality system would therefore involve not only an equilibrium situation in which no further gains can be realized from trade-offs between types of water treatment, waste-production control, and costs imposed on water users, but also equilization of values involved in trading marginal changes in water quality against resulting incremental changes in quantities available.

Economic Effects of Uncertainty

Another area in which economic analysis is directly relevant to water-quality management is the handling of risk and uncertainty. In general, there has been a strong tendency in the United States to build water structures to handle extreme values where there exists considerable uncertainty as to variance around modal figures. From the standpoint of economic efficiency, this will usually produce distinctly inferior results with respect to both water quality and over-all water supply. For example, it is highly likely that there exist more efficient alternatives to the construction of storage facilities sufficient to supply enough water to augment low-flow situations under all possible conditions. A system designed to meet modal possibilities could be supplemented by relatively high-cost procedures that would be needed to deal with infrequent periods of severe loss of quality as a result of abnormally low flows. What is involved is a comparison of the aggregate economic costs of excess capacity—that is, relatively high fixed costs in excess of those actually needed most of the time—with much lower fixed investment and relatively high variable costs of supplementary systems which would be used only infrequently.

Both on a priori grounds and on the basis of empirical investigation of some actual situations, it seems virtually certain that greater economy can be realized, with complete effectiveness in a physical sense, by dealing with the low-flow aspects of pollution in the latter fashion. The major reason for failure to consider the high-variable-cost, short-run alternatives is frequently the fact that they fall outside the jurisdiction of major federal water agencies, whose means of dealing with pollution are limited to low-flow augmentation and construction of the necessary water structures. Since the choice of a federal agency approach frequently offers the local government an opportunity to shift part of the cost of abatement, the structural approach may be preferred even where it is known to be less efficient.

As indicated above, this particular type of problem may also be reduced in magnitude from the standpoint of public policy by harnessing the ingenuity of individual users of the waste-disposal capacity of moving water. For example, varying charges to impose heavier burdens during periods when the pollution threat is severe (on advance notice) would provide a real incentive for the polluter to seek out cheaper alternatives to which he can turn during the occasional low-flow period, or to find production techniques that will minimize both peak and average waste loads.

Measurement of Economic Values

One of the most exasperating aspects of the water-pollution problem is the extent to which the uses impaired by water-quality degradation are of the types most difficult to measure in economic terms. Much of the preceding analysis presupposes at least the potential ability to convert costs and benefits foregone into a common monetary denominator. But this is impossible at the present time in several major areas affected. In one instance—that involving the adverse affects of discoloration, smell, and littered banks on the contribution of water resources to esthetic enjoyment—the difficulty is inherent.

Though they may be reflected in real estate values, for example, it is virtually impossible to quantify in economic terms the satisfactions derived from the general environmental attributes of a clear, uncluttered water course.

Another major problem area involves recreational use of water, including but not limited to hunting, fishing, swimming, boating, and water-skiing. In this case the difficulty of assigning economic values to the water services in question is not inherent but reflects the strong (and basically irrational) American attitude that outdoor recreation, particularly on public lands and waters and supported by public investment, should be free or subject only to a nominal charge. As a result it is exceptionally difficult to price outdoor recreation services in the normal fashion, although they are economic goods that stand on all fours with other resource-using physical and intangible economic outputs.

In some cases we are able to simulate demand functions for outdoor recreation through the use of travel time and cost as a proxy for a fee, but at best such studies are very specific in application, rapidly outdated, and expensive to carry out. The problems of measuring the relative value of outdoor recreation are by no means limited to the field of water-quality management, but nowhere are they more frustrating.

Economics of Suboptimal Water-Quality Systems

These measurement difficulties, coupled with the wide areas of incomplete knowledge of highly variable physical parameters, suggest that water-quality management must in practice be limited to suboptimal systems designed to minimize aggregate waste-disposal costs subject to one or more constraints. One such constraint is obviously the inability to measure accurately even the physical effects of water-quality degradation on fish, wildlife, and human beings. In such cases, economic analysis still has much to offer by providing a tested set of techniques for minimization of costs subject to a more or less arbitrary determination of absolutely "safe" standards. We may not know precisely what water quality is required for minimal protection of fish life, for example, but it is possible to specify standards at which, beyond any reasonable doubt, the fish population is protected, and to evaluate the technically feasible ways of achieving those standards.

Such suboptimal systems are obviously useful in themselves. In addition, the very design of a suboptimal system subject to constraints points up dramatically the types of additional data required and thus can be of great assistance in determining research priorities and in supporting the case for research funds.

Cost-minimizing waste-disposal systems may also be subject to constraints rising out of political boundaries that do not encompass the range of decisions that must be considered in the formulation of a fully optimal system. The essential procedure would be the same: that is, to define a suboptimal program subject to the requirement that the relevant alternatives considered be within the authority of the political agency involved. Again, as in the data constraint, the virtue of such procedures lies not only in their inherent usefulness, but in the pressure they generate for development of wider and more appropriate administrative arrangements.

It should also be pointed out that constraints of the types mentioned above need not be regarded as a permanent feature of the planning environment. It is perfectly possible, for example, to vary receiving water standards on an experimental basis to determine how much degradation of quality can be tolerated before perceptible losses began to appear. Virtually every type of water-treatment or waste-treatment procedure involves rapidly accelerating marginal costs, and even moderate reductions in permissible quality standards may result in very substantial savings. The conversion of parameters into variables is an essential part of the research process leading to more economic solutions of the waste-disposal problem.

Conclusion

As Kneese and others have pointed out repeatedly, the most common argument against the economic approach to the waste-disposal problem—the amount of factual and statistical information required—is not really valid. Attempts to deal with these problems through inferior types of solutions—zoning and the establishment of absolute water-quality standards, for example—do not resolve the data collection problem; they simply sweep it under the rug. These are even more clearly suboptimal approaches, and for a given degree of economic efficiency they would require as much or more information than the approach outlined above.

In conclusion, it would appear that economic analysis can contribute significantly to the effectiveness of research and policy formation in the field of water-quality management. It is no substitute for research in the physical and engineering fields, but rather builds on them and serves to point up, in some cases dramatically, the gaps in our knowledge of the physical determinants of water quality and the physical effects of varying degrees of degradation of water quality. In this sense, economic analysis can contribute significantly to improvement of the allocation and financing of research effort in the water-quality field. It also suggests the urgent need for broader decision-making units and for people trained to operate water-quality systems on the basis of a multidisciplinary approach. The time has passed—if it ever existed—when we should settle for anything less than a wide-ranging, long-term approach to the water-quality problem that does full justice to its major importance in the over-all pattern of water utilization in a growing economy.

XI

WATER-QUALITY MANAGEMENT AND LAKE EUTROPHICATION: THE LAKE WASHINGTON CASE

W. Thomas Edmondson

Introduction

THE work on Lake Washington to be reported in the present paper has been done without specific reference to problems of water-quality management. I am interested in lakes from a biological point of view, and the Lake Washington situation has provided me and my associates with a valuable opportunity for research on the general problem of the relation of the biological productivity of lakes to the income of nutrients. Nevertheless, the condition of Lake Washington is of considerable public interest, and some of the results of the work we have done have been of use for explanation of changes in the lake that have been noticed by the public and for prediction of the future condition of the lake (Clark, 1967). Furthermore, many lakes in the world have had the same kind of public relations as has Lake Washington, and limnologists have found themselves confronted with situations in which their scientific work had to be considered in a context of economic and political implications and consequences. This kind of activity will probably increase in the future. The purpose of this paper is to present a statement of the biological aspects of the pollution problem of Lake Washington, to review the limnological background of other lakes, to show how these problems are connected with certain kinds of water resources management problems, and to provide information of use in evaluating these problems.

My major interest is in the general problem of biological productivity in aquatic communities. Some lakes are very productive of living things, while others seem almost sterile. I want to know what controls productivity and

---

W. Thomas Edmondson is professor of zoology at the University of Washington.

how that productivity translates itself into the quantity of organisms that we see in lakes. Why do some lakes produce so many more organisms than others? What controls the large changes in abundance that take place during the year in any lake?

The term productivity has a fairly definite meaning in ecology. In general, productivity means the rate of formation of organisms or the rate of formation of organic matter. Thus, the meaning of the term productivity is very different from that of abundance or population density or organisms. But for a full assessment of productivity we need to know the size of the population, the rate at which it is reproducing itself, and how the material is consumed or dissipated.

Studies of productivity in lakes involve measuring the budget of energy and material for the biological community. We must know the source of material and energy for each of the species and we must know what consumers eat each species. The algae and higher plants are the primary producers which, by the process of photosynthesis, take inorganic carbon dioxide from solution in the water and build it into organic compounds. They can use inorganic sources of nitrogen and phosphorus, such as nitrate and phosphate. The consumer, animals, and other such organisms make use of this material by feeding, digestion, and assimilation. The idea of the "food chain" is a well-known generalization of the organization of biological communities. This paper is not the appropriate place to develop the idea extensively, but useful statements can be found in a variety of books (Odum, 1958; Ruttner, 1963).

If we want to understand the mechanism of control of productivity and abundance of the biological community in a lake, we must study the conditions of growth of the primary producers; that is, the algae in the open water, and the rooted plants and large attached algae inshore. They will obviously be influenced by the intensity of light and by temperature, both of which vary seasonally and with depth. They will also be influenced by the concentration of the nutrients in the water and the rate at which the nutrients are supplied. The abundance of the primary producers will be affected, not only by the rate at which they are produced, but also the rate at which they are consumed. If they are eaten as fast as they are produced, no increase will be seen; a high rate of consumption could mask a high rate of production. However, in the long run, it can be expected that the lakes with greatest abundance for prolonged periods of time will be the most productive because of the constant loss and consumption of organisms.

Considerable progress has been made toward understanding the factors that control productivity in lakes. The productivity of a lake at a given moment is set by the simultaneous operation of a number of controlling factors, including those listed above. The effectiveness with which a lake uses its nutrient income will be affected by such things as the shape of the lake, climate, and many other features, summarized by Sawyer (1954). Much of this understanding has been achieved by detailed studies of many lakes of widely different character in which correlations were established between productivity and environmental conditions. In a general way, lakes that develop higher concentrations of nutrients tend to produce large populations and are called eutrophic. Some writers tend to use the word almost as a synonym for "highly productive," but the two concepts should be distinguished. Eutrophication means enhancement of the supply of nutrients, and is generally followed by increased productivity (see Mackenthun and Ingraham, 1964; Mackenthun, 1965).

Comparative, descriptive field studies can yield only limited information, and physiological studies of algae under laboratory conditions are necessary to specify the details of the processes involved and to identify the mechanisms responsible for the correlations observed in nature. These two kinds of studies are the extremes of a range of approaches to the productivity problem. To connect the descriptive field studies with the simplified laboratory studies of isolated processes, we need field experiments.

Some progress has been made by deliberate fertilization of lakes; that is, a known amount of nutrient material is added to the lake and the response of the system is studied. Since the climate and shape of the lake remain the same, one can evaluate the specific effect of nutrients. Of necessity, most of this work has been done with small lakes, and knowledge is therefore biased. The Lake Washington situation gives us a chance to see how a large lake responds to large changes in nutrient income, both increases and decreases.

Pollution

The phrase "pollution of lakes" has meant to many people the discharge of raw sewage into lakes. Such discharge is obviously bad for lakes that are used as a source of drinking water, for swimming, or for any other purpose that brings people into contact with the water. However, even when the sewage is purified by treatment plants, there can be bad secondary effects because the effluent contains relatively large concentrations of several nutrient elements. The effluent from a large city can contain enough to fertilize even a large lake sufficiently to cause troublesome excess growths of plants and especially algae.

There has been a long history of this kind of trouble with lakes in various parts of the world, and on the basis of this experience, it is possible, under some conditions, to make reasonably secure predictions about the general effects to be expected in particular cases. Early in their regional history, these lakes were noteworthy for their clear, pure water. Naturally, as the regions were settled, the human populations became concentrated about the lakes; the lakes were good sources of drinking water, transportation, food, and recreation. At the same time, they were convenient receptacles for wastes, and the invention of sewage systems multiplied the delivery of wastes to lakes. As time passed, the characteristics of the lakes changed. The water became murky during much of the year, unsightly, odorous scums formed, and evil-smelling gases bubbled up from the depths, which were no longer inhabited by fish.

What all this amounts to is that the lakes became much more biologically productive than they were originally. The unpleasant features that developed are merely by-products of high productivity. The water was murky because large quantities of algae developed. Some kinds of algae float up to the surface in calm weather, blow downwind, and are piled up in decomposing masses on the shore. Unusually productive lakes are more likely to produce an abundance of colonial, floating types of algae than are less rich lakes. The particular species of algae that grow best in enriched lakes are more likely to produce unpleasant side effects than others. The density of rooted vegetation may be greater in productive lakes than in unproductive ones (Wilson, 1935, 1941), but in advanced cases of enrichment, the larger plants are shaded out by the algae and may virtually disappear (Pearsall and Hewitt, 1933; Olsen, 1964). All lakes contain some algae, but for a lake to produce nuisance quantities over large areas for long periods of time each year requires unusually large supplies of nutrients.

Lake Monona at Madison, Wisconsin, provides an example of the kind of conditions that may develop because of heavy enrichment:

> The prevailing winds at Madison are from the southwest. These tend to drive detached masses of putrefying algae onto the shores and beaches of the lake especially around the northeast end of the mouth of the Yahara River at points beyond Starkweather Creek. Masses of decaying algae thus strengthened, if stirred with a stick, look like human excrement and smell exactly like odors from a foul and neglected pig sty [Alvord and Burdick Report, quoted by Flannery, 1949].

The fertilizing effect of sewage has been known and recognized for a long time. For example, George C. Whipple, an eminent sanitary engineer, writing in 1918, commented as follows:

> Like other plants the algae in water grow best when fertilized. Nitrogen, potash, phosphates, and similar substances stimulate their growth. Polluted waters are, therefore, more likely to develop objectional growths of algae than the same water unpolluted. The elimination of pollution from a catchment area is desirable not only for sanitary reasons but also for lessening the growths of algae.

Whipple seems to have been ahead of his time, and it was many years before the fertilizing potential of sewage-plant effluent became widely recognized by sanitary engineers.

The emphasis in the literature about algal nuisances is on the microscopic or small floating (planktonic) algae because these are the organisms that make the water appear "dirty" and are the ones most obvious in forming scums and odors. Nevertheless, other types of algae are encouraged to grow by enrichment. Rocks, plants, docks, piers, and boats offer areas of attachment for considerable variety of algae which live attached to solid surfaces. A piece of wood exposed in Lake Washington during the spring accumulates a coating of "slimy" brown material which may be superficially displeasing. With microscopic examination this "slime" turns out to be a beautiful jungle composed of attractively colored and formed unicellular algae attached to the wood by clear gelatinous stalks. It is only through the mass of these organisms that their presence is felt as an unpleasant slimy aggregate.

Other types of attached algae form filaments perhaps the diameter of a hair and of a length to be measured in fractions of an inch or a few inches at the most. An aggregate of these may form a considerable beardlike growth on surfaces, and in very rich lakes develop such a bulk as to be very prominent.

One of the bulky attached algae most frequently noticed is *Cladophora*, and in Lake Zürich this organism has formed dense junglelike masses and much effort has been spent in some parts of the lake by men working in boats to rake them out (Thomas, 1950, 1951). In Lake Michigan, a *Cladophora* problem appears to be developing near the larger cities that put sewage into the lake, according to newspaper reports. The attached material may break loose and form dense floating mats. Swimmers find it distinctly unpleasant to become entangled in such mats. Characteristics of algae relevant to water pollution problems are described by Palmer (1959) and Hutchinson (1967).

Changes Observed in Lake Washington

Until recently, Lake Washington had been receiving increasing amounts of treated sewage, and by 1955 its condition had changed in such a way as to show clearly that its productivity had increased and its condition was deteriorating toward the production of algal nuisance conditions (Fig. 23; see Edmondson, Anderson, and Peterson, 1956).

Early in the history of Seattle, the lake was used for disposal of raw sewage, but delivery of raw sewage was minimized by the early 1930's. However, increasing amounts of treated ("purified") sewage entered the lake as Seattle expanded and as adjacent towns grew and built individual sewage-treatment plants, especially after the opening of the first floating bridge in 1940. By 1952 ten treatment plants emptied to the lake. In that year

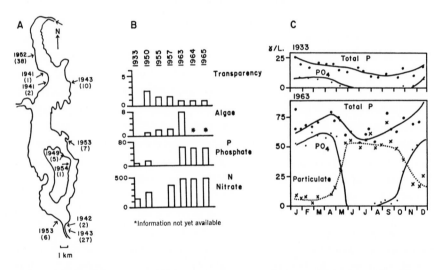

Figure 23. A. Lake Washington. Arrows show locations of sewage treatment plants, years of establishment, and percentage of sewage phosphorus contributed by each in 1957; data from H. M. Phillips, Seattle Engineering Department. B. Changes in condition of Lake Washington. Histograms show following features: minimum transparency as measured by the depth to which Secchi disc can be seen; mean abundance of algae during summer in surface as parts per million by volume; maximum concentration of phosphate phosphorus in surface water during winter; maximum concentration of nitrate nitrogen in surface water during winter. C. Seasonal changes in concentration of phosphorus during two years. Lines show major trends of total phosphorus and the phosphorus in dissolved inorganic phosphate. Note sharp decrease in phosphate during spring when algae are growing and absorbing phosphate from water. Data for 1933, Scheffer and Robinson (1939); for 1950, Comita and Anderson (1959).

the large Lake City plant was established that later became responsible for about 45 per cent of the volume of sewage effluent. The amount of phosphorus and nitrogen entering the lake in sewage in 1957 was about twice the average in the period 1931–40, and sewage accounted for about half the phosphorus income of the lake. (Treated sewage is rich not only in phosphorus and nitrogen but in other scarce elements as well. If one measures an increase in one component of sewage, increase in others is probably indicated.) In addition, significant quantities of nutrients were carried in by streams passing through areas served by septic tanks (Brown and Caldwell, 1958).

Lake Washington had been studied in detail during 1933 and 1950. Since the fall of 1956 the lake has been under essentially continuous investigation.* Measurements have been made of the abundance and activity of organisms, including the rate of primary production by planktonic algae. Measurements have also been made of chemical conditions that affect the growth of algae or that give information about biological activity in the lake. Of the many publications on Lake Washington, the following record the major studies or contain summaries and bibliographies: Anderson, 1961; Comita and Anderson, 1959; Edmondson, 1961, 1963, 1966, 1968; Edmondson, Anderson, and Peterson, 1956; Edmondson, Comita, and Anderson, 1962; Peterson, 1955; Scheffer and Robinson, 1939; Shapiro, 1960.

On the basis of all this work it can be stated that very distinct changes took place in the quantity and kinds of living things in Lake Washington and in the amount of various materials dissolved in the water (Fig. 23).

The first striking change noticed in the biology of the lake was the appearance in the summer of 1955 of a fairly dense population of the alga *Oscillatoria rubescens.* This organism forms hairlike filaments up to about ⅛ inch long. It has appeared in several enriched lakes early in the development of changes which later gave rise to nuisance conditions, a point that will be discussed in a later section of this paper. The alga has reappeared in Lake Washington from time to time. In 1962 a related species, *O. agardhii,* was so abundant as to attract widespread attention: one of the Seattle papers carried a large headline "Lake Washington Brown—That's Algae, Not Mud" (*Post-Intelligencer,* July 3, 1962, p. 1). Other species of algae have increased also, some forming clumps about the size of a pinhead.

* The research concerning Lake Washington reported below was supported by the National Institutes of Health (Grant R6 4623, 1956–58) and the National Science Foundation (Grants G–6167, G–24949, and GB–4851X, 1958–68), and the State of Washington Fund for Research in Biology and Medicine, Initiative 171.

The total quantity of algae present in the upper layers of the lake during the summer has increased very greatly since 1950, being about fifteen times as abundant on the average in 1962 as in 1950. The increase in the quantity of algae in the water has caused the water to take on a cloudy appearance during much of the summer. A method of determining the transparency of the water visually is to lower a white disc 8 inches in diameter (Secchi disc), into the water until it just disappears from sight. If this operation is carried out in a standard manner that has been established, reproducible results are obtained. In 1950, even when the lake was in its cloudiest condition, such a disc could be seen a full 10 feet into the water, while in 1957, the corresponding distance was only 4 feet, and 3 feet in 1963, 1964, and 1965. In very heavily enriched lakes, the distance may be reduced to a fraction of a foot.

The increase in the quantity of floating algae has not been the only observable biological change, but it is one of the most striking that affects the public. Almost as noticeable is the fact that attached algae growing on docks and stones have also increased.

The increase in living material in the lake is symptomatic of an increase in the nutritional materials which are used. As shown by Figure 23, the concentration of phosphorus measured in the surface waters of the lake has increased considerably since 1933 and 1950. Dissolved inorganic nitrogen has also increased greatly. It should be realized that the concentration of nutrient material in the lake water at any one time represents the combined result of the processes which are bringing nutrients into the water and the processes which are removing them. The concentration of dissolved phosphate and nitrate tends to be highest during the winter when consumption is at a minimum. During the spring, with increased light and temperature, dissolved nutrients are removed by the increasing population of algae. The concentration during the summer does not necessarily tell anything about the supply of nutrients actually available to the algae since the material may be removed from the water as fast as it comes in. The quantities of nutrients bound up in living organisms are increased, so the total phosphorus and nitrogen content of the water has increased over the years. Even a measurement of total phosphorus content by itself is not sufficient for a full evaluation of the situation since some of the algal material is consumed by small animals, and the undigested food is dropped down to the bottom of the lake where it is no longer measured.

The growth of algae can be affected by the concentration at which nutrients are supplied, as discussed in a later section. The maximum concentrations yet observed in the surface water of Lake Washington of phosphorus in phosphate and nitrogen in nitrate are 62 and 475 parts per billion, respectively. These are distinctly greater than the concentrations found to make a significant, summer-long increase in the abundance of algae when added as inorganic fertilizer to a small unproductive lake, 25 and 125 ppb respectively (Nelson and Edmondson, 1955). The corresponding values for Lake Washington in 1933 were only 8 and 170 (Scheffer and Robinson, 1939).

Another chemical change that has taken place is a marked reduction in the quantity of dissolved oxygen in the deeper waters of the lake toward the end of summer (Shapiro, 1960; Edmondson, 1961). During the summer, the upper water is warm and, being less dense, floats on top of the cold water, thus sealing off the deeper waters from contact with the air. Bacteria and animals in the deeper water consume dissolved oxygen so that the concentration decreases during the summer. It is not replenished by oxygen released in the process of photosynthesis by algae because there is not enough light in the deep water. Since dead material is constantly being dropped from the upper part to the bottom of the lake, the amount of food material available for the deep-water animals and the bacteria in the mud will depend in part upon the productivity in the upper water. Thus, a lake that produced or received nothing would consume no oxygen in the deep water; the more material that is produced, the more oxygen that is used and, hence, the less that is left by the end of the summer. Striking changes have taken place in Lake Washington in this regard and toward the end of the summer of 1957, for the first time in the known history of the lake, dissolved oxygen disappeared from the very deepest water lying against the bottom sediments. This is a very significant feature because when the water lying against the bottom has very little oxygen in it, certain chemical changes take place which cause an increased release of nutrients from the sediment. The oxygen concentration has not again reached the low values of 1957 for reasons that are not yet clearly understood.

An important change in Lake Washington that has been observed in other enriched lakes is a change in the kind of algae as well as the quantity. At present the lake is dominated by species that form groups or colonies easily visible to the eye. In 1950, the predominant species occurred either as single cells or as relatively small groups of cells. It appears that the massive, colonial species tend to occur in dense populations only in richer lakes. This can be understood on the basis that when cells are grouped, and especially if they are encased in gelatinous coats, they are not as freely exposed to nutrients in the water as are solitary cells. Thus, nutrients would have to be present in higher concentrations in order to support the same rate of intake as in solitary cells. On the other hand, the massive groups seem to have a survival advantage in that they appear to be less susceptible to loss by being grazed by the small animals in the lake. This hypothesis has not yet been fully tested, but it is reasonably consistent with a great deal of data on algae in lakes.

A feature of several of the colonial species of algae that have been abundant in the summer in recent years is an ability to float so that in calm weather they rise up from some depth, concentrate near the surface, and form a scum. This feature obviously enhances the nuisance capacity of any given quantity of algae.

Solution of the Lake Washington Problem

During the middle 1950's, the public in the Lake Washington area became aware not only that Lake Washington was showing signs of deterioration, but that general sewerage conditions in the area were in an unsatisfactory condition. Passage of the Metro legislation and the organization of Metro (Municipality of Metropolitan Seattle) resulted (Miller, 1960). The Metro sewerage project resulted in almost total diversion of effluent from the lake early in 1967. The projected cost was about $120,000,000; approximately $85,000,000 can be attributed to diverting sewage from Lake Washington and building the treatment plants required. It would not be fair to attribute that entire cost merely to the "cleaning up" of the lake. With the projected growth in population, new sewage-treatment plants would have been required and some of the old ones would have had to be enlarged in order to keep up with the requirements of the expanding population, partly as a consequence of the opening of the Evergreen Point floating bridge in 1963. The construction and operation of many small treatment plants would have cost the community a great deal more money. The development of a centralized, simplified system for treating sewage on a wholesale rather than retail basis has economic advantages over a system of many small, dispersed treatment plants. It has been stated that the entire Metro sewerage system can be justified on the basis of the financial savings that will occur in the long run through the mass treatment of sewage, relative to the cost that would have been required with the previous piecemeal system (Harold E. Miller, personal communication).

Although the deterioration of the lake has been enough that people have commented on its appearance and have complained about the "tide flat" odor, these conditions do not compare with the kinds of problems experienced in Lake Monona and Lake Zürich, and we have not seen a real nuisance condition in the lake yet. It is remarkable that the Lake Washington community has headed off trouble before it got really bad and before the lake had been so enriched that recovery would be a very lengthy process.

From the limnological viewpoint, the diversion of the effluent will be a useful, very large-scale experiment. While it was clear that the lake would revert to a much less productive condition fairly promptly, the details and actual rate of the changes will be most informative. During 1965, by which time about half the effluent had been diverted, the lake already seemed to be showing the effects of the reduced nutrient income (Oglesby and Edmondson, 1966), and during 1967 the improvement was distinct although subtle (Edmondson, 1968).

The question has been frequently asked as to what effect the diversion of sewage to Puget Sound will have. Puget Sound is very much larger than Lake Washington and has a much more rapid replacement of water. A study of water movement in Puget Sound was made before the outfalls were designed. On the basis of this, it is expected that the effluent will be very greatly diluted in deep water (Brown and Caldwell, 1958). Nutrient scarcity appears not to be a major limitation on productivity in Puget Sound, and conditions are not favorable for development of the kind of alga problem that would have developed in the lake.

Of course, alga problems are not the only difficulties engendered by the disposal of large volumes of sewage. Sewage may contain toxic materials and it may require much oxygen for biological decomposition of organic material present in it. These problems are not within the scope of this chapter. Whatever difficulties may arise, it seems likely that they will be less severe and easier to handle with the new facilities than with the old.

Evidence for the Fertilizing Effect of Sewage

To put the preceding discussion of Lake Washington in its context, and to make the most of it for evaluating other situations in the future, it will be useful to review the experience with enrichment of lakes by sewage and other drainage. The following sections will outline the various kinds of evidence which have led to the present views of lake deterioration, and will describe the variety of investigative methods which must be applied to a problem of this kind.

Sequence of Events

It has been a frequent experience that urban development has been followed by symptoms of increased lake productivity, especially when the development has included the disposal of sewage in lakes. Many such cases were reviewed by Hasler (1947). These facts alone are not proof, but they are suggestive and lead the way to investigations designed to establish the specific causes of particular cases of lake deterioration and the general principles of the control of productivity. In some localized cases, drainage from heavily fertilized fields may have an effect, especially on small lakes (Ohle, 1954, 1955), and lakes of naturally high productivity do not need much additional enrichment to produce nuisance conditions. Ordinary drainage from nonfertilized lands is much more like lake water in nutrient content than is sewage effluent, and even drainage from fertilized fields is less rich than sewage effluent (Sylvester, 1961; Engelbrecht and Morgan, 1961; Mackenthun, 1965).

A good many of the lakes in central Europe which give algal trouble now are relatively rich in nutrients. Some are lakes which formerly did not give trouble before they were enriched, and are near unenriched lakes which still do not give trouble (Thomas, 1949, 1953).

Nutrient Budget of Enriched Lakes

Another line of evidence comes from studies of the quantity of nutrients delivered by different sources. Sawyer and his associates made very detailed studies of the chain of lakes at Madison, Wisconsin (Sawyer, 1947). This, at the time (1941–43), was a unique investigation in which, by frequent measurements of concentration of nutrients in the inlets and outlets and by measuring the flow of water, it was possible to draw up a nutrient budget for the lakes. One of the reasons for making this very expensive and time-consuming study was that there had been some controversy as to whether domestic sewage or drainage from fertilized fields was responsible. The work showed that most of the nutrients in the lake came from sewage effluent, although the situation was complicated by the character of the industrial wastes involved. Agricultural drainage brought in less, and was less concentrated. A similar budget was subsequently made for Lake Zürich, Switzerland (Thomas, 1957). Sewage and sewage effluent contributed 55 per cent of the dissolved phosphorus entering the lake, and 24 per cent of the nitrogen. In Lake Washington in 1957, sewage contributed nearly half the phosphorus, and a considerably smaller fraction of nitrogen (Brown and Caldwell, 1958; data from H. M. Phillips, Seattle Department of Engineering).

These studies are important, but it is still necessary to find out more about the specific amount of fertilization required to cause nuisance conditions. For one thing, it is inadequate merely to specify the total amount of nutrient delivered to a lake and the proportion originating in sewage. The amount of algae produced by a given volume of water is related to the amount of nutrient in that water, and this means that the concentration must be considered.

Some of the published nutrient budgets give only the total amount of materials delivered annually from different sources, as pounds per acre, without giving information about the concentrations. Delivery of a large quantity in very dilute form may have less effect than a smaller quantity in very concentrated form (see Edmondson, 1961, and a subsequent section in this paper). Entry of a given volume of water of low concentration into a

TABLE 12

RANGES OF MONTHLY MEANS OF CONCENTRATION OF PHOSPHATE PHOSPHORUS
IN WATERS ENTERING LAKE WASHINGTON, 1957 *

The Cedar River is the major inlet of the lake, contributing 55% of the water. The Sammamish River is second, bringing 36%. Coal Creek flows through relatively sparsely inhabited land. Thornton Creek flows through heavily settled land served by septic tanks.

	Minimum (mg./liter)	Maximum (mg./liter)
Cedar River above Landsburg	0.002	0.004
Sammamish River	0.003	0.038
Coal Creek	0.009	0.033
Thornton Creek	0.044	0.103
Lake City Sewage Treatment Plant	1.66	5.66
Renton Sewage Treatment Plant	3.66	9.16
Ship Canal (outlet of lake)	trace	0.005

* Source: Hollis M. Phillips, Seattle Engineering Department.

lake merely displaces a like volume of water out the outlet, while entry of a concentrated source raises the general concentration (Sawyer, 1947).

Thus, the determination of the general nutrient budget of a given lake is only part of the work; the interpretation is another matter. Some people expressed concern that removal of effluent from Lake Washington would reduce the phosphorus income by only about half and the nitrogen income even less. The implication seemed to be that all phosphorus and nitrogen would have to be eliminated before any benefit would accrue, but this is an unwarranted assumption. To interpret the effect of the reduction one needs to consider that the source to be diverted has over one hundred times the concentration of phosphorus in the natural waters entering the lake (Table 12). It should be noted also that Lake Washington had shown for many years its ability to absorb fairly large enrichment without much deterioration.

Nothing in the above comments should be taken to indicate that only nitrogen and phosphorus need to be considered in evaluating lake situations. For example, Ohle (1954, 1955) has pointed out that the concentration of sulfate in a lake may make a difference in the consequences of enrichment because the more sulfate that is present, the larger the concentration of hydrogen sulfide that can be developed if the lake becomes anaerobic in the deep water. A lake which develops hydrogen sulfide will produce more complaints because of the smell of this gas and other products of anaerobic decomposition.

Studies of Adjacent Lakes of Similar Character
When Differently Enriched

A famous case is that of the large lake at Zürich, Switzerland. It has been thoroughly studied for many years, and much is known about the changes that have taken place. The present condition of the lake is especially well known through the publications of E. A. Thomas (1957; Thomas and Marki, 1949), but much limnological work has been done by many investigators over many decades (Minder, 1938, 1943). This case is of particular interest in relation to Lake Washington because not only is the lake of comparable size to Lake Washington, but the changes in Lake Washington have been very similar to those in Zürich sixty years earlier.

The lake at Zürich is composed of two basins separated by a very narrow, shallow connection: the Zürichsee (Lake Zürich) proper and the Obersee (Upper Lake). Water flows from the upper basin to the lower. During the nineteenth century, small towns and villages grew up on the shores of the lower lake but not the upper. The domestic waters from these communities, although not from the city of Zürich, entered the lake. The wastes from the city of Zürich itself are emptied into the outlet of the lower lake, and have not contributed to the problem. Over sixty years ago, the lower basin showed the first generally noticeable signs of enrichment from domestic drainage. In 1898, a large population of *Oscillatoria rubescens* developed. This alga was already known from other enriched lakes of Switzerland where it formed very dense populations, so dense that the water became a rusty brown and in Rotsee (Red Lake) was referred to as "Blood of the Burgundians" (*Burgunderblut*). This phrase in itself gives an impression of the quantity of algal material produced.

During the years that followed, the *Oscillatoria rubescens* population became very dense in Lake Zürich from time to time, and made the lake take on an unpleasant dirty appearance which was bothersome to many people. There was much public complaint about the appearance of the lake at certain times of the year, especially in the late summer and early fall.

As a consequence of the increased production in the upper layers of the lake, the quantity of oxygen in the deep, cool water decreased and was insufficient to support fish during much of the year, and by 1918 the coregonid fish population had disappeared from Lake Zürich, but the shallow-water coarse fish increased.

During all this time, the upper lake, which received very little domestic drainage, remained clear and pure and maintained a population of trout. However, after a period of time, the suburban developments reached out along the shores of the upper basin, and during the early 1940's the upper lake began to develop populations of *Oscillatoria rubescens,* although not as dense as in the lower lake.

This situation is about as close as one can come to having a controlled experiment with large lakes; here we have two connected similar bodies of water, one of which is enriched, while the other, which is not, serves as control. The unenriched lake maintained its original condition for many years while the lower lake was changing under enrichment. The subsequent increase of algae in the upper lake showed that it too was capable of responding to enrichment.

Thomas points out that the inlet of the upper lake brings in large quantities of nutrient-poor water, and that the dilution is very important in its effect on the productivity of the lake. In the two very dry summers of 1947 and 1949 when the inflow was greatly reduced, the enrichment was able to manifest itself more in the upper lake than in normal years when the dilution is greater, in that the oxygen decreased to lower concentrations in the deep water.

Agriculture has been developed in the drainage area of the inlet of the upper lake. The question arose as to whether this, in itself, would have an important enriching effect on the lake. A careful study was made of the nutrients in the runoff from the cultivated lands, and it was found that it was inconsequential as a factor in the nutrition of the lake (Thomas, 1954).

The public reaction to the dense alga production in the lake has been strong and, apparently, swimming has been inhibited. As Thomas says (1957:30), "A swim in the lake, however, should refresh not only the body, but also the spirit." The proposition has even been made that swimming pools should be built and filled with filtered water. There have been problems about the drinking-water supply of villages on the lake also. Thomas points out that if the water is not good enough to swim in, it probably is not good enough to drink either and, in fact, it requires much filtering and treatment at some times of the year to make the water palatable. Thomas (1957:32) quotes the Swiss President as saying in 1942, "Today there is no more pressing problem for the lake communities than this, 'Save the lake.'"

There appear to have been discussions among the communities on the lower lake for many years about how to handle the unpleasant situation that is expected to get still worse as the population continues to increase. In 1945, a study was made to see whether it would be technically and financially feasible to divert all the sewage by making a trunk sewer down both sides of the lake. It was found to be technically possible, but the cost was judged to be too high, and as yet, diversion has not been planned.

I have emphasized the appearance of *Oscillatoria rubescens* in the lake at Zürich. This is because this particular species of alga has developed large populations in a number of the enriched lakes in Switzerland and in other parts of the world. While the full physiological significance of the appearance of this alga in a lake is not fully known, it has characteristically appeared abruptly in large quantities quite early in the development of situations that, later on, produced algal nuisances (Staub, 1961). Its presence seems to be an important indication of significant enrichment with nutrients and to show the potentiality of future trouble. This species appeared in large numbers in Lake Washington in 1955 and was the first definite indication that Lake Washington was seriously responding to enrichment. It needs to be pointed out that problems may be generated by several different species of algae, and that *Oscillatoria rubescens* is not the only one involved, or necessarily involved at all.

The Zürich case is outstanding, and is relevant to the present considerations because of its similarity to Lake Washington. It is by no means a unique case of the effect of sewage. For example, of a group of six lakes near Copenhagen, three with high productivity receive considerable quantities of sewage, the others with relatively low productivity do not (Nygaard, 1955; Steeman Nielsen, 1955). The outstanding alga-producing lakes in Switzerland appear to be relatively rich in nutrients, and the richness is related at least in part to sewage (Thomas, 1949, 1953).

Results of Diversion of Sewage Treatment Plant Effluent

The lakes at Madison, Wisconsin. Only a few thoroughly enriched lakes studied by limnologists have had the sewage diverted from them. The lakes at Madison are an outstanding example (Flannery, 1949; Sarles, 1961). The city of Madison, Wisconsin, is situated on an isthmus between Lake Mendota and Lake Monona (Fig. 24). Water flows in the Yahara River from Mendota to Monona, and thence to Waubesa and Kegonsa in order. The lakes in this region tend to be naturally productive, and there have been alga problems in all the lakes, but Mendota has been the least troublesome, while Monona has been in very bad condition (see quotation on page 142).

Early in this century, people began to be bothered increasingly by evil odors from Lake Monona and by very unpleasant-looking scums. In 1912, copper sulfate was first used to kill off the algae, and in 1925, a regular program of treatment with copper sulfate was established. In some years, over 100,000 pounds was required to control the algae. (Monona is small

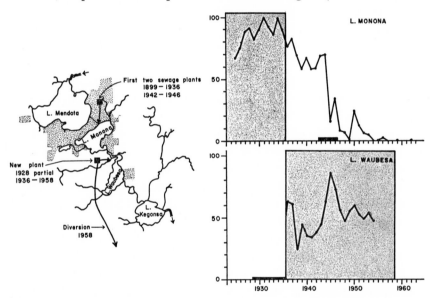

Figure 24. Outline of major features of history of algal nuisance at Madison, Wisconsin. *Left:* Map of region showing lakes and location of sewage outfalls. In general Lake Monona received large quantities of sewage through 1936, although partial diversion took place in 1928. After 1936 essentially all of Madison's sewage went through the Nine Springs Plant into Lake Waubesa, although some started in 1928. Monona received some sewage again during 1942–46. *Right:* Amount of copper sulfate (thousands of pounds) added each year to control algae in lakes Monona and Waubesa. Note that after complete diversion of sewage-plant effluent from Monona in 1936, requirement for treatment began to decline, with a small resurgence in 1943 and 1944 with return of some sewage from Truax Field. Simultaneously, as the sewage was now being sent into Lake Waubesa, Waubesa began to require treatment. Late in 1958 sewage was completely diverted from the lakes; no copper sulfate has been added since 1962. Periods of major sewage inflow are shown by shading, of minor inflow by bars on the baseline.

enough to make this practicable. Lake Washington is much too big for copper sulfate treatment.) A consistent record of the amount of algae has not been kept over the decades, but there is a good record of the amount of copper sulfate used. Since the dosage was adjusted to demand (K. M. Mackenthun, personal communication) the quantity of copper sulfate is probably a reasonably good measure of the intensity of the nuisance conditions, perhaps even better than a simple measure of the amount of algae.

Recent studies show that the quantity of algae may not have decreased as much as has the requirement for copper sulfate. In 1963, Lake Monona had almost as great a number of algal organisms as in the years before sewage diversion, but there has been a great qualitative change since the days of the large nuisances. At the present time the population is dominated by species of algae that do not rise to the surface of still water. Therefore, there is much less tendency to form scums in calm weather (G. Fred Lee, personal communication).

In 1928, partial diversion of the sewage was made, although much of the Madison sewage effluent still entered Lake Monona. In 1936, complete diversion from Monona was accomplished although there was still a certain amount of storm drainage and ground runoff. The lake still produced nuisance conditions, but required progressively less copper sulfate as time passed until 1942 when, rather suddenly, larger quantities were required during the war. This increase in requirement of copper sulfate coincided with the reactivation of the old treatment plant which had been abandoned in 1936. During the war years, it was used for the sewage from an air field staffed by about twenty thousand men. When this staff was reduced at the end of the war, the effluent was greatly reduced and there was a sharp drop in the amount of copper sulfate required to control algae in Lake Monona. Finally, in 1954 none was used, and since then only small amounts have been used occasionally, totaling 3,481 pounds in the years 1955–63 as compared to the 100,500 pounds used in 1934 alone. Other chemicals are applied to control weeds.

Trouble in the Madison lakes did not, however, end with the diversion of sewage from Lake Monona in 1936, because the effluent was simply moved downstream to Lake Waubesa. Lake Waubesa and the next lake downstream, Kegonsa, had been giving some alga trouble before 1936, but as soon as sewage effluent began to flow directly into Lake Waubesa, very distressing algal nuisances began to occur. The communities finally developed a plan by which the sewage plant effluent was diverted from three of the Madison lakes late in 1958.

The history of the sewage situation at Madison is marked by much argument and bickering about causes and blame among the various communities involved (Flannery, 1949). There were denials of the effectiveness of treated sewage in generating alga nuisances. Nevertheless, as the result of the experience with diversion it is quite clear that a major source of trouble in the Madison lakes has been the effect of sewage-plant effluent. It must be recognized that the effect of the sewage in this particular situation is amplified by the fact that the annual flow of effluent exceeded the volume of the lake (Edmondson, 1961).

Interpretation of the Wisconsin situation is a bit difficult to relate to Lake Washington because of local conditions. The water of the Madison region is richer in dissolved minerals than is the Lake Washington watershed, and the lakes naturally are more productive. Also, the Madison lakes are relatively shallow. Additional features are the greater agricultural development and the presence of a large meat-packing plant which produced very rich effluent. Lake Washington is a very different kind of lake, and less sensitive to fertilization.

Lake Monona had been very heavily fertilized for many years. The recovery period was roughly twenty years. It can be expected that the carryover will bear some relation to the intensity of enrichment. In this regard, Lake Washington is much better off since it has not been heavily enriched as long as Lake Monona and has never produced Monona-type nuisances.

Other experiences with diversion of sewage from lakes. A small lake near Copenhagen, Lyngby-Sø, has been studied in some detail (Olsen, 1955; Johnsen, Mathiesen, and Røen, 1962). The sewage was diverted in 1959, and year by year during the next four years, the productivity as measured by the rate of photosynthesis decreased steadily (Mathiesen, 1963). Unfortunately data on the abundance of algae appear not to be available. The submerged, rooted vegetation essentially disappeared from the lake after 1956, presumably from shading by algae, but is now becoming re-established (Olsen, 1964). In this case, recovery appears to be starting promptly.

In 1933, the sewage was diverted from Red Lake (Rotsee) at Lucerne in Switzerland at considerable cost; nevertheless, the lake has continued to produce nuisance quantities of alga ever since (Minder, 1948). This led to considerable consternation and confusion. The fact that this lake did not recover after diversion of sewage has led some people to suspect the general proposition of the effectiveness of sewage in enriching lakes and diversion as a remedy (Dr. Otto Jaag, personal communication). Nevertheless, the situation must be examined on its merits, and if this is done, it turns out that the continued alga nuisances in Red Lake are easily understood. It is a small, narrow, shallow lake, more a pond. Lake Washington has a volume about 670 times as large and an area 184 times as large as that of Red Lake. Lake Monona, which is regarded as a fairly small lake, has about 27 times the volume of Red Lake. The lake receives drainage from fertilized and cultivated land. It is possible that it receives enough enrichment from the fields to keep it blooming. Unfortunately, the lake has not been studied scientifically since 1945, so that it is not known if a gradual recovery is being made, as in Lake Monona.

In relating these studies to the Lake Washington situation, it must be recognized that there is nothing in the Lake Washington watershed like the relative amount of cultivation in the watershed of the Rotsee, nor are such developments likely to come. If much heavy agriculture were to develop anywhere in the Lake Washington watershed, there naturally would have to be reasonable land use practices followed to prevent wasteful erosion and a loss of fertilizer from fields.

Deliberate Fertilization of Lakes

Somewhat more controlled are situations in which a small lake has been fertilized deliberately with quantities of nutrients to increase the productivity just as fields and lawns are fertilized. Although much of the work on lake fertilization is devoted to fish management (Mortimer, 1954), several limnological studies have been aimed at the general productivity problem. For example, enough inorganic fertilizer was added to Bare Lake, Alaska, to give twenty-five parts per billion of phosphorus in the form of phosphate, and five times that quantity of nitrogen in the form of nitrate (Nelson and Edmondson, 1955). Fertilization was soon followed by a very great increase in the growth of algae, and the quantity became large enough to make the lake so cloudy in appearance that airplane pilots noticed the difference. The minimum Secchi disc transparency was reduced from 7 meters (23 feet) to 1 meter (3 feet). In general, as far as experience goes, most lakes appear responsive to fertilization most of the time, indicating a prevalent limitation of production by scarcity of nutrients.

An elaboration of this kind of work involves the use of large tubes of polyethylene or other clear material suspended in lakes (Thomas, 1961; Goldman, 1962). The water column may be isolated from or exposed to the bottom sediments. Addition of nutrients to the tube or other manipulations permit isolation and study of separate processes.

Enrichment of Samples of Lake Water: Bioassay

The fertilization of an entire lake or even a portion of it, even with relatively pure fertilizers in carefully measured quantities, is a fairly uncontrolled process since a great many different biological processes in the lake may be affected by the increase in nutrient concentration. To simplify the experimental situation further two kinds of bioassay can be made. In one, samples of lake water with the natural population are enriched with nutrients and the response of the population in growth or photosynthesis measured (Thomas, 1953). In a further simplification, one can inoculate filtered samples of lake water with pure cultures of a well-studied alga of known characteristics. The rate of growth of the alga and the maximum population developed under standardized conditions of light and temperature give an indication of the relative fertility of the lake water. Additional samples of the same water enriched variously with phosphorus, nitrogen, or trace elements, or a combination of these are similarly studied. If addition of an element is followed by increased growth of the algae relative to the unenriched control vessel, the interpretation is that growth is held in check by insufficiency of that element (Potash, 1954; Lund, 1959; Hughes and Lund, 1962).

Such studies have been useful in identifying the limiting nutrients and in showing how they may change with time; see the discussion of the relative importance of different nutrients, below.

Physiological Studies of Algae
Growing in Pure Nutrient Solutions

Finally, many highly controlled laboratory studies of the requirements and abilities of algae have been made with pure cultures of algae growing in nutrient solution of known concentration. The physiological literature is primarily directed toward an analysis of the cellular and chemical mechanisms of organisms. Much of this has a direct bearing on the problems under discussion, but the definitive information for the present discussion comes from experimental work organized around the specific ecological problems (Fogg, 1965). It is not the intent of the laboratory work to duplicate a lake in the laboratory, but rather to identify and analyze the component processes. This is only part of the problem, since the organization and integration of the processes in natural communities need to be known.

It is necessary to clarify two ways in which the concentration of nutrients affects the amount of algae. In a typical experiment, a flask containing a nutritive medium with specified concentrations of nitrate, phosphate, sulfate, and so forth, is inoculated with a small quantity of algae. The flask is placed in a culture chamber with controlled light and temperature, and daily counts made of the abundance of cells until the maximum number is reached and the population stops growing. When this experiment is performed with a series of flasks in which the concentration of one nutritive element varies while the others are kept constant, the maximum population varies in some proportion to the concentration of the varying nutrient. But all this means is that the flask contained a definite amount of this nutrient at the start, and when it is all converted to algae, growth stops. The larger the initial amount, the more algae can be produced. Additional growth can be generated by adding more of the missing nutrient as long as other necessary elements are present in relative excess. Beyond some concentration, another element will limit production, and addition of the first will not increase the yield of algae, although the amount of the first element in the cells may continue to increase (Gerloff, Fitzgerald, and Skoog, 1954, 1957; Ketchum and Redfield, 1949).

Thus in a lake, a given volume of water can produce a given amount of algae from the stock of nutrients present, and to produce more, it will have to receive additional nutrients. This may be accomplished by mixing with other water richer in nutrients, but such mixing may also dilute the algae present. The end result will depend on the actual quantities involved, and the rate at which the algae grow. It should be pointed out again that an important part of the alga nuisance problem is the secondary concentration of algae by flotation, once they have been produced.

The concentration of nutrients can also have a direct effect on the rate at which algae grow. There may be a range of concentration in which the rate of absorption and therefore the rate of cell division and population growth is controlled by the availability of nutrients to the algae. Experiments by Rodhe (1948) were carried out to show the growth of populations of the alga *Scendesmus quadricauda* in culture solutions with different concentrations of phosphate. The solutions were changed daily and the experiments were carried out in such a way as to minimize all the effects except the utilization of phosphate. There was a direct proportionality between the maximum abundance of algae achieved in the flask and the initial concentration of phosphate between 0.02 and 0.10 mg./liter with inconsequential growth below 0.02. One of the common nuisance algae (*Microcystis aeruginosa*) had a direct proportionality between the maximum abundance of algae in culture and the initial concentration of nutrients in the range investigated, 0.02–0.14 mg./liter of phosphate phosphorus and 4–15 mg./liter of nitrate nitrogen.

Thus, any addition of nutrients within these ranges can be expected to increase algal production (Gerloff, Fitzgerald, and Skoog, 1954, 1957). The exact quantities of algae produced and the threshold values for growth are strongly influenced by the specific culture conditions. For this reason and others, at present it is not possible to make an exact calculation of the consequences of a particular nutrient addition to a lake.

Relative Importance of Different Nutrients

The question of the relative importance of nitrogen and phosphorus has been widely discussed. This is only part of a more general problem of the relative importance in natural waters of all the nutritive elements and other materials required by algae such as sulfur, carbon, iron, vitamins, and others.

The idea of limiting factors or "bottle-necks" is a familiar one (see Odum, 1958). There are complications when this idea is applied to natural communities, and one must not take too simple a view of the situation. For one thing, lakes are inhabited by a variety of species, each with somewhat different requirements and capabilities. For example, *Dinobryon divergens* has not only a very small phosphate requirement, but appears to be damaged by concentrations which are far below the optimal concentrations for most other algae (Rodhe, 1948). Thus, although there are some ambiguities in the published records of the occurrence of the species, *Dinobryon* generally forms its largest populations at times after some other alga has grown and withdrawn most of the phosphate from the water. It seems possible that this organism would be encouraged by massive fertilization with nitrogen.

Further, the chemical composition of algae may vary within wide limits when they are grown under different nutritive conditions; in one case the phosphorus content varied between about 0.6 per cent and 3 per cent of the dry weight of the algae. Such algae can absorb nutrients at times of abundance and continue to multiply for some time after nutrients are exhausted from the water (Ketchum, 1939a; Ketchum and Redfield, 1949; Gerloff, Fitzgerald, and Skoog, 1954, 1957).

Interaction between environmental factors also complicates the application of a simple bottleneck idea. It has been shown for at least one species of alga (*Phaeodactylum tricornutum*) that the ability to absorb phosphate is affected by the concentration of nitrate (Ketchum, 1939b). Thus variation in either phosphate or nitrate within certain ranges may have an effect on the growth of the alga. The optimal temperature may be changed by nutrient concentration (McCombie, 1953, 1960).

Another alga (*Asterionella formosa*) has been shown to be able to absorb phosphate from very dilute solutions in the presence of an organic substance, while it requires very much higher concentrations in the absence of this substance (Rodhe, 1948; Mackereth, 1953). This phosphate-sparing factor is very important in affecting the growth of this common, widespread, and abundant alga. Phosphate absorption is also affected by inorganic components (Joseph Shapiro, personal communication).

Accessory nutritional factors or vitamins make a profound difference to the conditions of growth of the various species of algae. Most algae present in lakes are primary producers in that they can use carbon dioxide as a source of carbon rather than requiring organically combined carbon, and can use inorganic nitrogen and phosphorus. But a good many species of fresh-water algae have a requirement for one or more organic substances in traces, vitamins, and they are unable to grow or grow poorly in the absence of the vitamins (Provasoli, 1958; Provasoli and Pinter, 1960). Vitamin B^{12}, for example, is required by many species. This molecule is synthesized by bacteria, and presumably production of Vitamin B^{12} by bacteria may be stimulated in turn by conditions favoring the bacteria. Further, sewage is relatively rich in Vitamin B^{12}. Thus, enrichment of a lake may have secondary effects on alga production in addition to direct supply of nutrition.

As a result of this flexibility, it is fair to say that the rate of production of algae in a lake is set at each moment by a large number of factors operating simultaneously, and that a change in any one of them can change algal production, either increasing or decreasing it. This fact is very important for prediction of the effect on the lake of given changes in nutrient supply and is worth more discussion. It is useful to speak of these as controlling factors since the rate of activity is proportional to the concentration (Fry, 1948).

In spite of the flexibility and versatility of the algal population in lakes in exploiting varied nutritional sources, it is obvious that the production of living material cannot outrun the supply of nutrients, and if a critically needed nutrient is totally absent, production cannot continue, however much of everything else is present. Thus, one can expect to find situations in which the rate of supply of one particular element dominates the control of production. Phosphorus and nitrogen appear to be most often dominating. To some extent the relative importance of elements varies in different lake districts in relation to the primary supply of nutrients for geological or geographical reasons. Thus, the experience in several lakes has been that phosphorus has been more often limiting, but it appears that in some, such as Lake Tahoe, phosphorus is present in excess relative to nitrogen (Goldman, 1963b; Goldman and Carter, 1964).

In a given year the limiting nutrients may change as the season progresses as judged by bioassay analysis. Thus, in one lake that has been studied by this method, phosphate was chiefly limiting during the spring, but later in the year nitrate was limiting (Potash, 1956). On some occasions carbonate and sulfate had an effect in addition to that of phosphate. Also, at a given moment addition of any one of a number of substances can increase growth.

In Lake Washington at various times nitrogen and phosphorus have been limiting, so that addition of either one had a small but distinct effect while addition of both together gave a still stronger effect (Joseph Shapiro, personal communication). It is, of course, realized that when one element in critical supply is enriched, another element can become limiting. This kind of effect has been observed in other waters both with natural populations (Hutchinson, 1941) and with single species in bioassays (Shapiro and Ribeiro, 1965; Edmondson, unpublished research on Hall Lake). These points must be considered when thinking about the effectiveness of sewage-plant effluent which is rich in a number of elements in addition to nitrogen and phosphorus. One often emphasizes the phosphorus content of sewage effluent and describes changes in sewage in terms of change in the phosphorus budget largely because it is easier to measure than nitrogen, but it must be realized that there are proportional changes in nitrogen, carbon dioxide, iron, and other important elements.

Maximum Allowable Concentration

Various investigators have been looking for some sort of rule of thumb by which one could rate the nuisance capacity of a lake merely by the simple concentration of nutrients or rate of addition of nutrients. The prospects of success are small. In temperate regions during the winter, the algal crop stops growing for lack of light, some die, the material decomposes, and the processes returning nutrients to the water in general are in excess of the consumption. In many lakes the nutrient concentration increases to a maximum sometime during the winter or early spring (e.g., Fig. 23). As the days lengthen in the spring and algal growth increases, the nutrient concentration in the water decreases because consumption outruns replacement. The situation is a dynamic one and it is not very useful to look for definite concentrations as indicating potential nuisance. The concentration that is built up during the winter merely represents the difference between income and consumption. Not all lakes have strong winter maxima of nutrient concentration. This could result either because high consumption matches high regeneration or because regeneration is low. Obviously these two situations are quite different. A lake with a high rate of income is likely to develop both a high concentration of nutrients and high productivity.

The situation can be described by an analogy. If one starts water running into a bathtub without closing the drain, the level of water will build up in the bathtub until the pressure is enough to force the water out the drain as fast as it comes in. If one now closes the drain and shuts the water off, the water will stay at the same level, but in the first case there is a rapid "productivity" or turnover of the water, and in the second case the situation is static with no production and no consumption.

The rule-of-thumb approach may be useful in some situations but cannot be generalized indefinitely from one to another. For example, as a descriptive generalization, in a group of lakes in southern Wisconsin, those which regularly produced algal nuisances also developed a maximum of more than 0.010 mg./liter phosphate phosphorus (Sawyer, 1947). This does not mean that any lake anywhere which exhibits this concentration is going to produce a nuisance. For instance, Lake Washington in the winter of 1950 exceeded this value for several months, developing a maximum of 0.016, but the lake was not regarded as producing algal nuisances then. In the winter of 1957, the maximum concentration was only 0.005 at a time when the lake was noticeably deteriorating. For reasons not understood, the algal population remained relatively dense during that winter and retained the phosphorus; the total phosphorus present was 0.034 mg./liter. Further, it was not demonstrated in the Wisconsin situation that some substance closely correlated with phosphorus was not actually controlling production.

As mentioned previously, inorganic fertilization of Bare Lake with 0.025 mg./liter of phosphorus and 0.125 of nitrogen greatly increased the algal population rapidly (Nelson and Edmondson, 1955). Presumably if this concentration developed by natural processes, at the beginning of the growing season a similar growth would take place, but this does not mean that all lakes would respond in the same way. Because of the interaction of environmental factors and the influence of size, shape, depth, exposure to wind, and rate of replenishment of water on the ability of a lake to produce a crop of organisms with a given supply of nutrients, different lakes will have different sensitivity to enrichment. This does not mean that the problem is hopeless and incapable of being generalized, only that one should not expect to be able to recommend a single universally applicable, maximum permissible rate of enrichment. It may become possible to allow for the factors mentioned. For instance, moderately hard-water lakes are probably more sensitive to sewage enrichment than soft-water lakes, all other things being equal.

The theory of the control of productivity in lakes is fairly clear, but numerical values of certain processes and relationships are needed to permit quantitative predictions of the effect of any given change. It is expected that the present work on Lake Washington will contribute to this development.

Natural Changes in Lakes

During the public discussions before the formation of Metro it was frequently asked whether Lake Washington was not simply going through natural changes leading to increased productivity. Therefore, it is worth considering what is known about natural aging in lakes. As a lake ages, it goes through a succession of biological conditions and events.

Lakes are relatively unstable and impermanent features of the landscape on a geological time scale since they tend to fill in. Most of the familiar lakes in North Temperate regions were formed by glacial action during the Pleistocene roughly twelve thousand years ago. The sediment that has been building up consists largely of inorganic silt eroded from the land around the lake and organic matter, the remains of organisms produced in the lake and on the surrounding land. In districts such as northern Wisconsin where many lakes were originally formed, a good many of the small ones have filled in completely and now consist of land occupied by terrestrial vegetation. Others are nearing extinction by filling, while others, larger and deeper to begin with or situated so as to have little inwash of silt, are still present as large, deep lakes. As a lake fills in, more of the bottom becomes progressively shallow enough to be exposed to enough light to support rooted plants, and eventually plants will grow clear across the bottom. There may be a jungle of underwater vegetation when the lake becomes shallow all the way across. Also the exposure of sediments to light facilitates uptake of nutrients from the bottom by algae, and large mats of filamentous forms may grow. Thus, there is a tendency for small old lakes to support more organisms than large, deep, steep-side ones, other things being equal.

In this connection, it is worth pointing out that casual observation of lakes may be misleading. When driving around uninhabited country, one may see lakes in which there are mats of floating algae. People sometimes believe therefore that sewage or sewage-plant effluent cannot be the cause of alga problems since alga problems exist in uninhabited areas. Many of the lakes just described are actually rather shallow ponds in the last stages of succession.

A lake such as Lake Washington, however, is far from being a naturally productive lake because of age. It has many centuries to go before it fills in by natural processes. It is nowhere near ready naturally to produce the abundance of algae that it is now producing; these conditions are due to the exaggerated input of nutrient substances, without which the lake would remain fairly clear all year long, as it did in 1950.

Recovery of Lakes from Enrichment

To make a prediction about the recovery of a lake after diversion of concentrated sources of enrichment requires evaluation of processes supplying nutrients to the population. There has been so little experience yet with diversion that a very exact quantitative prediction is not yet possible, but it should be possible to fix some sort of limit. Again material exists for a fairly satisfactory theoretical background, but quantitative relationships must be established.

A key to the situation is the relation between bottom sediments and water, and an important fact is that much of the dissolved nutrient material entering a lake is incorporated into the bottom sediments by way of the settling of dead organisms. Some of the material is decomposed by bacteria, and the elements regenerated to the water. Thus the sediments serve as a reservoir of nutrients, and the relative part this plays in supplying the algae with their needs will determine what happens when the input of dissolved nutrients from outside the lake is sharply curtailed. The sediments are a limited reservoir because much of the dissolved nutrient material that enters a lake is permanently buried in the sediments. For instance in a group of three lakes in Switzerland, from 60 per cent to nearly 100 per cent of the phosphate that entered was retained in the sediments (Thomas, 1955). The Madison Lakes retain 30 to 60 per cent of the nitrogen (Sawyer, 1947); Lake Washington retained about 60 per cent of all the phosphorus that entered in 1951 and about 20 per cent of the nitrogen.

As judged by the uptake and release of radioactive phosphorus, only the top few millimeters, say ten, are ordinarily engaged in active exchange with the water, and possibly most of the absorptive activity is confined to the top millimeter (Zicker, Berger, and Hasler, 1956; Hayes, 1955). Phosphorus compounds are relatively insoluble, and some of the more soluble elements such as nitrogen may be available from deeper in the sediments. But, because of the slowness of diffusion in sediments, only a relatively thin layer of the material can be regarded as freely available for release of nutrients back to the water. In lakes with dense populations of bottom-dwelling insects, mixing and transport from deeper depths in the sediments may be made by animals, but this activity would seem to be hardly important below about 15 cm. depth (about 6 inches) in ordinary lake sediments. Lake Monona appears to be a fairly special case, in that copper appears to have penetrated measurably to a depth of about 4 feet (Nichols, Henkel, and McNall, 1946), but these sediments are probably much looser and more easily disturbed than ordinary lake sediments.

Thus, in general, when external concentrated enrichment of a basically unproductive lake like Lake Washington stops, the sediments deposited are less rich in nutrients than before, and eventually the richer sediments will have yielded up what they can and will be covered up with less rich sediments. While repeated recycling of elements between water and sediments may be important in setting the total productivity of a lake, to build up a dense population of algae at any one time requires more than rapid recycling; the input to the algae must dominate over the return back to the water by processes of deposition and decomposition. Rapid inflow of sewage effluent is an effective way of increasing the input to the algae.

Another process to be considered is the rate at which the water of the lake is replenished by the inflow of water poor in nutrients. In Lake Washington the replacement time is about three years. Nutrients that are regenerated from the bottom will either be redeposited or go out the outlet.

The question has been raised as to whether any lake enriched to the point of nuisance production can recover from enrichment, and judgment has been colored by experience with such lakes as Red Lake. Certainly a lake that has nearly filled in and has become productive of dense populations of plants through natural increase of productivity will be difficult to manage, although with small lakes there may be some hope that dredging and manipulating the water supply can alleviate nuisances (Green Lake, Seattle; Sylvester and Anderson, 1964; Oglesby and Edmondson, 1966).

Another phenomenon that has influenced thinking on these matters is the fact that once a lake has become productive enough that the oxygen is exhausted from the deep water during the summer, the regeneration of nutrients is greatly accelerated so that there is an automatic self-fertilization (Mortimer, 1941–42). There has been some thought that once a lake begins this process, it will be self-perpetuating. However, there is no evidence that this is true of basically unproductive lakes; the cases in which it is true seem to be lakes which have developed a high productivity naturally and are merely encouraged in this by artificial additional enrichment. It seems obvious that if a basically unproductive lake like Lake Washington is enriched to this point, once enrichment is stopped, production will decrease and eventually through dilution and exhaustion of the nutrients from the bottom the lake will, of necessity, return to a less productive condition.

In the particular case of Lake Washington one could easily predict that the diversion of effluent would be followed fairly promptly, perhaps irregularly, by a return of the lake to its original condition as it existed in 1950 or 1933. With the present state of knowledge, however, it would be difficult to state in detail how fast the return would be or what effect partial diversion would have.

Removal of Nutrients from Sewage

It has frequently been proposed that the enrichment problem should be solved by removing nutrients from sewage (e.g., Rohlich, 1961, and other papers in the same volume). The technology of sewage treatment is not my field and I am not prepared to discuss these matters, but it is important to relate the engineering possibilities to the facts of limnology.

A variety of systems has been proposed for precipitating or otherwise removing nutrients, many tried in the laboratory and some set up on a pilot plant basis (Føyn, 1964). Despite a great deal of attention, it appears that it is not yet practicable for a city to buy a treatment plant that will adequately remove nutrients in such a way that the effluent can certainly be disposed of in lakes without unpleasant consequences. It is an interesting fact that the Madison, Wisconsin, situation has been met by diverting sewage around the lakes, although the University of Wisconsin has long been a center for research in the field of nutrient removal.

It seems very likely that under pressure of necessity, improved and practical methods of nutrient removal will be developed. At each stage of development of new methods it will be necessary to evaluate the residual effluent. It is common to rate the removal in some such way as "80 per cent of the phosphorus is removed." Now the algae will not be affected by knowledge that 80 per cent of the nutrients has been removed. They will be affected by the concentration developed in the water in which they live, and it may be that 20 per cent of the original source is still concentrated enough in a given situation to make nuisances. Furthermore, most of the systems for chemical precipitation that have been proposed are much more effective at getting rid of phosphorus than nitrogen, so that the effluents from some processes are still quite rich in nitrogen, and the effects of massive enrichment with nitrogen need to be ascertained. Lakes in which nitrogen is a major limiting factor would be expected to respond to enrichment with a nitrogen-rich effluent, and in many lakes the growth of organisms like *Dinobryon* might be encouraged.

The case has been made very strongly by many people that it is the obligation of a community to take whatever action is required to avoid contamination of another community's water supply or other natural resource. Further it can be argued that it is not proper to waste the phosphorus and nitrogen contained in sewage and that we should pay the necessary price for conserving the elements that are becoming scarcer and more difficult to obtain.

For the present, with available techniques, it seems that diversion of effluent is the only sure way of controlling the enrichment problem. It may be hoped that before long practicable processes will be perfected which will permit conservation of sewage resources.

Developing Alga Problems in Other Areas

Algal problems have developed in several parts of the world in the past and are continuing to develop in places where human activity results in the input of effluents rich in nutrients (National Academy of Sciences, National Research Council, 1968). Most of the best-known examples of artificial enrichment are fairly small lakes such as those at Madison, but even fairly large lakes such as those of Zurich and Seattle have been involved. There is a growing body of evidence that even very large lakes cannot accept large volumes of rich effluent for an indefinite time without deterioration.

One of the largest lakes in Europe, Lake Constance, has for centuries been noted for its clarity and beauty. It appears at last to be showing distinct deterioration (Elster, 1961). As with the other lakes which have shown artificial eutrophication, Lake Constance exhibits several different kinds of changes. The abundance of planktonic organisms has increased between the 1920's and the 1950's; several of the species of algae increased by factors of 6–45, and the planktonic crustaceans increased by a factor of 10. There has been a distinct decrease in the amount of oxygen in the deep water of the lake, although it is not yet close to becoming depleted of oxygen.

The spread of *Oscillatoria rubescens* in Europe evidently is not finished. It appeared in Lake Neuchatel suddenly in 1960 (Wuthrich, 1965), and it has begun to appear in the prealpine lakes of Switzerland and northern Italy. It was first observed in Lake Lugano in 1945 (Tonolli, personal communication). Its recent appearance in Lake Maggiore in October, 1967, is of extraordinary interest (Bonomi, personal communication). This lake is the site of one of the major limnological institutions of the world, the Istituto Italiano di Idrobiologia at Pallanza, so that more is known about many aspects of the earlier condition of this lake than of any of the others invaded by *Oscillatoria rubescens,* including Lake Washington. Thus, another opportunity exists for finding out in detail what happens during the transition to nuisance conditions.

Even the Great Lakes of North America are not exempt from changes, and all but Lake Superior have already shown distinct deterioration (Beeton, 1965). Lake Erie, the smallest and shallowest, is most susceptible to enrichment. The population of algae has increased and changed in kind (Davis, 1964). In 1953, for the first time apparently, its deeper water became depleted of oxygen and there was a massive kill of bottom-living mayfly nymphs (Britt, 1955a). The population of these insects made a fitful recovery, but further depletion of oxygen has affected them (Britt, 1955b, 1963), and there have been major changes in the bottom fauna (Beeton, 1961). Even Lake Michigan, whose volume is about 2,000 times that of Lake Washington, has had localized alga nuisances near the cities which use the lake for disposal of sewage, and there has been increasing abundance of algae and difficulty in the filtration plants that prepare lake water for drinking in the cities (Damann, 1960).

A possible major change in the nutrient budget of Lake Michigan awaits decision of the Supreme Court of the United States. Chicago runs its treated sewage into the Chicago River, diluting it and flushing it with a large volume of water from Lake Michigan. A proposal had been made that not only should Chicago decrease its take of lake water, but that it should return effluent to Lake Michigan. Limnologists will await the decision with interest, for if this change is made, it will be the largest lake fertilization experiment yet carried out.

Growing public awareness of the enriching effect of sewage in contrast to the pollution aspect is evidently being taken into account increasingly in planning sewage disposal operations. For example, it is foreseen that the population surrounding Lake Tahoe is going to increase and will produce an increasingly large amount of sewage. A detailed study of the area has been carried out, including a limnological study with measurements of productivity and bioassay experiments. (Goldman, 1963a, 1963b, 1964; Goldman and Carter, 1965).

To deal effectively with the kind of pollution problem discussed in this paper requires application of limnological knowledge that is of current interest to scientists who are not directly involved in pollution-control work. Without entering into the debate about basic versus applied research, it seems reasonable to suggest that the future work on lakes and streams continue to be encouraged to range widely and not necessarily to be tied to pollution and management problems as we see them now. In the particular case of Lake Washington, when the practical problem arose, basic knowledge could be applied immediately. The understanding required to solve the problem already existed because of studies of lakes made purely for their general scientific interest. The work on Lake Washington in 1933 and 1950 was not done in anticipation that the knowledge would be needed in 1955 to control pollution.

To understand and properly evaluate the effects of various management practices on lakes requires a detailed knowledge of the principles on which aquatic communities are organized and function. It is to be hoped that increasing advantage will be taken of existing limnological knowledge in the management of aquatic resources and that converse advantage will be taken of opportunities to extend limnological knowledge.

REFERENCES

Listed below are the papers cited in the text. This is not a comprehensive bibliography on enrichment.

Anderson, G. C.
    1961 Recent changes in the trophic nature of Lake Washington. Pp. 27–33 in Algae and metropolitan wastes. Technical Report W 61–3, Robert A. Taft Sanitary Engineering Center, Cincinnati, Ohio.

Beeton, A. M.
    1961 Environmental changes in Lake Erie. Transactions of the American Fisheries Society, 90:153–59.
    1965 Eutrophication of the St. Lawrence Great Lakes. Limnology and Oceanography, 10:240–54.

Britt, N. W.
    1955a Stratification in western Lake Erie in summer of 1953. Effects on the Hexagenia (Ephemeroptera) population. Ecology, 36:239–44.
    1955b Hexagenia (Ephemeroptera) population recovery in western Lake Erie following the 1953 catastrophe. Ecology, 36:520–22.

1963 Some changes in the bottom fauna of the island area of western Lake Erie in the decade 1953–1963 with special reference to the aquatic insects (abstract). P. 268 in Proceedings of the Sixth Conference on Great Lakes Research. Great Lakes Research Division of the Institute of Science and Technology.

Brown and Caldwell Civil and Chemical Engineers

1958 Metropolitan Seattle sewerage and drainage survey: A report for the city of Seattle, King County, and the state of Washington.

Clark, E.

1967 How Seattle is beating water pollution. Harper's Magazine, 234:91–95.

Comita, G. W., and G. C. Anderson

1959 The seasonal development of a population of *Diaptomus ashlandi* Marsh, and related phytoplankton cycles in Lake Washington. Limnology and Oceanography, 4:37–52.

Damann, K. E.

1960 Plankton studies of Lake Michigan, II: Thirty-three years of continuous plankton and coliform bacteria data collected from Lake Michigan at Chicago, Illinois. Transactions of the American Microscopical Society, 79:397–404.

Davis, C. C.

1964 Evidence for eutrophication of Lake Erie from phytoplankton records. Limnology and Oceanography, 9:275–83.

Edmondson, W. T.

1961 Changes in Lake Washington following an increase in the nutrient income. Proceedings of the International Association of Theoretical and Applied Limnology, 14:167–75.

1963 Pacific Coast and Great Basin. Chap. xiii in Limnology in North America, ed. D. G. Frey. University of Wisconsin Press, Madison.

1966 Changes in the oxygen deficit of Lake Washington. Proceedings of the International Association of Theoretical and Applied Limnology, 16:153–58.

1968 Eutrophication in North America. In NAS, NRC, International symposium on eutrophication. Washington, D.C. (in press).

Edmondson, W. T., G. C. Anderson, and D. R. Peterson

1956 Artificial eutrophication of Lake Washington. Limnology and Oceanography, 1:47–53.

Edmondson, W. T., G. W. Comita, and G. C. Anderson

1962 Reproductive rate of copepods in nature and its relation to phytoplankton population. Ecology, 43:625–34.

Elster, H. J.

1961 Ist der Bodensee in Gefahr? Wasserwirtschaft, 51(10):1–3.

Engelbrecht, R. S., and J. J. Morgan
  1961 Land drainage as a source of phosphorus in Illinois surface waters. Pp. 74–79 in Algae and metropolitan wastes. Technical Report W 61–3, Robert A. Taft Sanitary Engineering Center, Cincinnati, Ohio.
Flannery, J. J.
  1949 The Madison Lake problem. M.S. thesis, University of Wisconsin.
Fogg, G. E.
  1965 Algal cultures and phytoplankton ecology. University of Wisconsin Press, Madison.
Føyn, E.
  1964 Removal of sewage nutrients by electrolytic treatment. Proceedings of the International Association of Theoretical and Applied Limnology, 15:569–79.
Fry, F. E. J.
  1948 Effects of the environment on animal activity. University of Toronto Studies in Biology, 55:1–62.
Gerloff, G. C., G. P. Fitzgerald, and F. Skoog
  1950 The mineral nutrition of *Coccochloris peniocystis*. American Journal of Botany, 37:835–40.
  1952 The mineral nutrition of *Microcystis aeruginosa*. American Journal of Botany, 39:26–31.
  1954 Cell contents of nitrogen and phosphorus as a measure of their availability for growth of *Microcystis aeruginosa*. Ecology, 35:348–54.
  1957 Nitrogen as a limiting factor for the growth of *Microcystis aeruginosa* in southern Wisconsin lakes. Ecology, 38:556–61.
Goldman, C. R.
  1960a Molybdenum as a factor limiting primary productivity in Castle Lake, California. Science, 132:1016–17.
  1960b Primary productivity and limiting factors in three lakes of the Alaska Peninsula. Ecological Monographs, 30:207–30.
  1962 A method of studying nutrient limiting factors *in situ* in water columns isolated by polyethylene film. Limnology and Oceanography, 7:99–101.
  1963a The measurement of primary productivity and limiting factors in freshwater with carbon-14. Pp. 103–13 in Proceedings of the conference on primary productivity measurement marine and freshwater, ed. M. S. Doty. U.S. Atomic Energy Commission, TID–7633.
  1963b Primary productivity measurements in Lake Tahoe. Appendix I, pp. 154–63 in Comprehensive study on protection of Lake Tahoe Basin. Engineering-Sciences, Inc. for the Lake Tahoe Area Council.
  1967 Integration of field and laboratory experiments in productivity studies. Pp. 346–52 in Estuaries, ed. G. H. Lauff. Publication No. 83, American Association for the Advancement of Science.

Goldman, C. R., and R. C. Carter
  1965 An investigation by rapid carbon-14 bioassay of factors affecting the cultural eutrophication of Lake Tahoe, California-Nevada. Journal of the Water Pollution Control Federation, July, pp. 1044–59.

Hasler, A. D.
  1947 Eutrophication of lakes by domestic drainage. Ecology, 28:383–95.

Hayes, F. R.
  1955 The effect of bacteria on the exchange of radiophosphorus at the mud-water interface. Proceedings of the International Association of Theoretical and Applied Limnology, 12:111–16.

Hughes, J. C., and J. W. G. Lund
  1962 The rate of growth of *Asterionella formosa* Hass. in relation to its ecology. Archiv für Mikrobiologie, 42:117–29.

Hutchinson, G. E.
  1941 Mechanism of intermediary metabolism in stratified lakes. Ecological Monographs, 11:21–60.
  1967 A Treatise on Limnology, Vol. II in Introduction to lake biology and the Limnoplankton. John Wiley & Sons, New York.

Johnsen, P., H. Mathiesen, and U. Røen
  1962 Sørø-søerne, Lyngby-Sø og Bagsvaerd sø. Dansk Ingeniørforening Spildevandskomiteen, Skrift 14, pp. 1–135.

Ketchum, B. H.
  1939a The development and restoration of deficiencies in phosphorus and nitrogen composition of unicellular plants. Journal of Cellular and Comparative Physiology, 13:378–81.
  1939b The absorption of phosphates and nitrate by illuminated cultures of *Nitzschia closterium*. American Journal of Botany, 26:399–407.

Ketchum, B. H., and A. C. Redfield
  1949 Some physical and chemical characteristics of algae grown in mass culture: Chemical composition of algae grown in various media. Journal of Cellular and Comparative Physiology, 33:281–99.

Lund, J. W. G.
  1959 Biological tests on the fertility of an English reservoir water (Stocks Reservoir, Bowland Forest). Journal of the Institute of Water Engineers, 13:527–49.

McCombie, A. M.
  1953 Factors influencing the growth of phytoplankton. Journal of the Fisheries Research Board of Canada, 10:253–82.
  1960 Actions and interactions of temperature, light and nutrient concentration on the growth of the green alga, *Chlamydomonas reinhardti* Dangeard. Journal of the Fisheries Board of Canada, 17:871–94.

Mackenthun, K. M.
   1965   Nitrogen and phosphorus in water. U.S. Government Printing Office.
Mackenthun, K. M., and W. M. Ingram
   1964   Limnological aspects of recreational lakes. U.S. Public Health Service Publication No. 1167.
Mackereth, F. J.
   1953   Phosphorus utilization by *Asterionella formosa* Hass. Journal of Experimental Botany, 4:296–313.
Mathiesen, J.
   1963   Om planteplanktonets produktion af organish stof i nogle naeringsrige søer på Sjoelland. Saetryk af "Ferskvandsfiskeribladet" 61(1):7–9; (2)20–25.
Miller, H. E.
   1960   Municipality of Metropolitan Seattle. First Annual Report.
Minder, L.
   1938   Der Zürichsee als Eutrophierungsphänomen. Geologie der Meere und Binnengwässer, 2:284–99.
   1943   Der Zürichsee im Lichte der Seetypenlehre. Neujahrsblatt herausgegeben von der Naturforschenden Gesellschaft in Zürich.
   1948   Der Rotsee. Schweizerische Zeitschrift für Hydrologie, 11:245–53.
Mortimer, C. H.
   1941–42   The exchange of dissolved substances between mud and water in lakes. Journal of Ecology, 29:280–329; 30:147–201.
   1954   Fertilizer in fishponds. Colonial Office Fishery Publications No. 5, London.
National Academy of Sciences, National Research Council
   1968   International symposium on eutrophication. Washington, D.C. (in press)
Nelson, P. R., and W. T. Edmondson
   1955   Limnological effects of fertilizing Bare Lake, Alaska. U.S. Fish and Wildlife Service, Fishery Bulletin 56(102):413–36.
Nichols, M. S., T. Henkel, and D. McNall
   1946   Copper in lake muds from lakes of the Madison area. Transactions of the Wisconsin Academy of Sciences, Arts, and Letters, 38:333–50.
Nygaard, G.
   1955   On the productivity of five Danish Waters. Proceedings of the International Association of Theoretical and Applied Limnology, 12:123–33.
Odum, E. P.
   1958   Fundamentals of ecology (2nd ed.). W. B. Saunders Co., Philadelphia, Pa.

Oglesby, R. T., and W. T. Edmondson

1966 Control of eutrophication. Journal of the Water Pollution Control Federation, 38:1452-60.

Ohle, W.

1954 Sulfat als "Katalysator" des limnischen Stoffkreislaufes. Jahrbuch vom Wasser, 21:13-32.

1955 Die Ursachen der rasanter Seeneutrophierung. Proceedings of the International Association of Theoretical and Applied Limnology, 12:377-82.

Olsen, S.

1955 Lake Lyngby Sø. Folia Limnologica Scandinavica, 7:1-152.

1964 Vegetationsaendringer i Lyngby Sø. Bidrag til analyse af kulturpåvirkinger på vand- og sumpplantvegetationen. Saertryk af Botanisk Tidsskrift, 59:273-300.

Palmer, C. M.

1959 Algae in water supplies. Superintendent of Documents, Washington, D.C.

Pearsall, W. H., and T. Hewitt

1933 Light penetration and changes in vegetation limits in Windermere. Journal of Experimental Biology, 10:306-12.

Peterson, D. R.

1955 An investigation of pollutional effects in Lake Washington. Washington Pollution Control Commission, Technical Bulletin 18.

Potash, M. A.

1956 A biological test for determining the potential productivity of water. Ecology, 37:631-39.

Provasoli, L.

1958 Nutrition and ecology of protozoa and algae. Annual Review of Microbiology, 12:279-308.

Provasoli, L., and I. J. Pinter

1960 Artificial media for freshwater algae: Problems and suggestions. In The ecology of algae, ed. C. A. Tryon, Jr., and R. T. Hartman. Special Publication No. 2, Pymatuning Laboratory of Field Biology. University of Pittsburgh.

Rodhe, W.

1948 Environmental requirements of freshwater plankton algae. Symbolae Botanicae Upsaliensis, 10:1-149.

Rohlich, G. A.

1961 Chemical methods for the removal of nitrogen and phosphorus from sewage plant effluents. Pp. 130-35 in Algae and metropolitan wastes. Technical Report W 61-3, Robert A. Taft Sanitary Engineering Center, Cincinnati, Ohio.

Ruttner, F.
   1963 Fundamentals of limnology, trans. D. G. Frey and F. E. J. Fry. 3rd ed. University of Toronto Press, Toronto, Ont.
Sarles, W. B.
   1961 Madison's lakes: Must urbanization destroy their beauty and productivity? Pp. 10–18 in Algae and metropolitan wastes. Technical Report W 61–3, Robert A. Taft Sanitary Engineering Center, Cincinnati, Ohio.
Sawyer, C. N.
   1947 Fertilization by agricultural and urban drainage. Journal of the New England Waterworks Association, 61:109–27.
   1954 Factors involved in disposal of sewage effluents to lakes. Sewage and Industrial Wastes, 26:317–28.
Scheffer, V. B., and R. J. Robinson
   1939 A limnological study of Lake Washington. Ecological Monographs, 9:95–143.
Shapiro, J.
   1960 The cause of a metalimnetic minimum of dissolved oxygen. Limnology and Oceanography, 5:216–27.
Shapiro, J., and R. Ribiero
   1965 Algal growth and sewage effluent in the Potomac Estuary. Journal of the Water Pollution Control Federation, 37:1035–43.
Staub, R.
   1961 Ernahrungsphysiologisch-autokologische Untersuchungen an der planktischen Blaualge *Oscillatoria rubescens* DC. Schweitzerische Zeitschrift für Hydrologie, 23:82–198a.
Steeman Nielsen, E.
   1955 The production of organic matter by the phytoplankton in a Danish lake receiving extraordinarily great amounts of nutrient salts. Hydrobiology, 7:68–74.
Sylvester, R. O.
   1961 Nutrient content of drainage water from forested, urban and agricultural areas. Pp. 80–87 in Algae and metropolitan wastes. Technical Report W 61–3, Robert A. Taft Sanitary Engineering Center, Cincinnati, Ohio.
Sylvester, R. O., and G. C. Anderson
   1964 A lake's response to its environment. Journal of the Sanitary Engineering Division. Proceedings of the American Society of Civil Engineers, 3786, SA1:1–22.
Thomas, E. A.
   1949 Regional limnologische Studien an 25 Seen der Nordschweiz. Proceedings of the International Association of Theoretical and Applied Limnology, 10:489–95.

1950 Auffallige biologische Folgen von Sprungschichtneigungen im Zürichsee. Schweizerische Zeitschrift für Hydrologie, 12:1–24.

1951 Der Verschmutzung des Zürichsees und die Strömungs- und Durchflussverhältnisse bei Rapperswil. Schweizerische Verhandlungen von Gas- und Wasserfachmännern, Monatsbulletin 3 and 4:3–16.

1953 Zur Bekämpfung der See—Eutrophierung = Empirische und experimentelle Untersuchungen zur Kenntnis der Minimumstoffe in 46 Seen der Schweiz und angrenzender Gebiete. Schweizerischen Vereins von Gas- und Wasserfachmännern, Monatsbulletin 2 and 3:1–14.

1954 Der Einfluss der Meliorierung der Linthebene auf die Überdungung des Zürichsees. Schweizerischen Vereins von Gas- und Wasserfachmännern, Monatsbulletin 10 and 11:3–18.

1955 Stoffhaushalt und Sedimentation im oligotrophen Aegerisee und im eutrophen Pfäffiker- und Greifensee. Memorie dell' Istituto Italiano di Idrobiologia, Supplement 8:357–465.

1957 Der Zürichsee, sein Wasser und sein Boden. Jahrbuch vom Zürichsee, 17:173–208.

1961 Vergleiche uber die Planktonproduktion in Flaschen und im Plankton-Test-Lot nach Thomas. Proceedings of the International Association of Theoretical and Applied Limnology, 14:140–46.

Thomas, E. A., and E. Märki
1949 Der heutige Zustand der Zürichsee. Proceedings of the International Association of Theoretical and Applied Limnology, 10:476–88.

Whipple, G. C.
1918 Technical and sanitary problems. In Freshwater biology, ed. H. B. Ward and G. C. Whipple. 1st ed. John Wiley & Sons, New York.

Wilson, L. R.
1935 Lake development and plant succession in Vilas County, Wisconsin. Ecological Monographs, 5:207–47.

1941 The larger aquatic vegetation of Trout Lake, Vilas County, Wisconsin. Transactions of the Wisconsin Academy of Sciences, Arts, and Letters, 33:135–46.

Wuthrich, M.
1965 Le phytoplankton du lac de Neuchatel. Schweitzerische Zeitschrift für Hydrologie, 27:1–75.

Zicker, E. L., K. C. Berger, and A. D. Hasler
1956 Phosphorus release from bog lake muds. Limnology and Oceanography, 1:296–303.

XII

RECEIVING-WATER MONITORING: KEY TO SEATTLE METRO'S POLLUTION-ABATEMENT PROGRAM

Charles V. Gibbs

EARLY in 1959, the Municipality of Metropolitan Seattle (Metro) undertook a major program of pollution abatement and prevention in the Seattle area. This program, which will involve an expenditure of $135,000,000 by 1972, was by 1967 about 90 per cent under contract.

To guarantee that its primary responsibility, protection of the environmental waters of the greater Seattle area from pollution, is accomplished at the least cost to the rate payers, Metro has initiated what is probably the most varied program of water-quality monitoring undertaken by a waste-disposal agency. Working under the philosophy that a discharger has the responsibility for monitoring its receiving waters, Metro has established a Water Quality Control Division and has assigned it the task of planning and implementing the necessary programs.

Early Recognition of the Value of Monitoring

At the outset of Metro's program, water-quality monitoring assumed critical importance. One of the two major sewer systems in the Seattle area terminates in a large activated-sludge treatment plant at Renton with effluent disposal to the Green-Duwamish River. When the Metro plan was presented to the state regulatory agencies for approval in 1960, conservation and fisheries interests voiced opposition. They assumed that the effluent from the treatment plant would threaten the annual runs of salmonoid fishes, an especially important natural resource in the Northwest. Metro assured the

Charles V. Gibbs is executive director of the Municipality of Metropolitan Seattle.

state that all water uses would be adequately protected, if not in fact benefited, and backed these assurances with the commitment to divert the effluent directly to Puget Sound if conditions in the river necessitated a remedy. A continuing program of monitoring was proposed to detect impending degradation of water quality that might affect fisheries resources or other water uses.

In approving Metro's plan, the Pollution Control Commission required that the monitoring program encompass all waters to receive effluent discharges and that the program commence no less than two years prior to any new discharge. As will be shown later, the state's action vastly increased the scope of the monitoring program by adding salt water, lakes, and canals to the receiving waters to be studied. The commission also specified that the monitoring program be subject to review and approval by a five-member board. The program, as ultimately developed, is an outgrowth of close liaison between the Metro staff and the board, and has the board's approval.

The following objectives were continually in mind while the Metro monitoring program was being planned:

1. To determine, evaluate, and demonstrate the effectiveness of the Metro program for abating water pollution.

2. To provide a basis for design according to specific needs rather than arbitrary standards.

3. To permit planning and scheduling of future projects in accordance with demonstrated needs.

4. To provide a basis for controlling operations to produce required end results.

5. To fix the responsibility for adverse conditions caused by other waste dischargers.

6. To insure compliance with the requirements of the state Pollution Control Commission and the state and local health departments.

Monitoring Programs

In staffing the Water Quality Control Division, Metro recognized that chemical and physical data alone do not constitute a monitoring program. Accordingly, the division is composed of a Water Quality Section, an Ecological Section, and an Industrial Waste Section, each under the direction of professional personnel with experience in their particular field.

To process the large number of samples collected, a laboratory was established in the central office building. Many of the latest developments in analytical equipment are incorporated in this modern $30,000 facility.

Because of the geography of the metropolitan Seattle area, it was necessary to plan, in effect, four separate monitoring programs, each with its own distinct problems to investigate. An inspection of Figure 25 reveals that Metro is faced with monitoring almost every conceivable type of receiving water. The Green-Duwamish River program presents the problems of a fresh-water stream and its terminal estuary. Puget Sound is an arm of the Pacific Ocean; therefore, the monitoring program for these waters is typical of many other salt-water studies except that the efficiency of four separate outfalls must be determined. The study of the Lake Washington–Lake Sammamish drainage basin requires work on two large lakes and many small tributary streams. Finally, the Lake Washington Ship Canal system necessitates work on several small lakes connected by deep-water canals, all influenced by intrusion of salt water through the Hiram M. Chittenden Locks.

The Green-Duwamish Program

The Green-Duwamish River presented the most complex monitoring problem that Metro faced. The fact that this river system is affected by tides dictated that a manual sampling program would be prohibitively costly if tidal influences were to be properly evaluated; therefore, the program had to be as automatic as possible. A lengthy inspection of automatic midwestern and eastern monitoring installations was followed, in March, 1963, by a symposium on the "Status of Water Quality Monitoring Instrumentation," sponsored jointly by the University of Washington and Metro. The result of the extended study was the decision to install four units, of the type pioneered by the Ohio River Valley Sanitation Commission (ORSANCO), on the river. The equipment above and below the outfall of the treatment plant continuously records surface temperature, pH, dissolved oxygen, and conductivity. The two units in the river estuary record the same surface parameters; in addition, they record temperature, dissolved oxygen, and conductivity of samples obtained near the bottom. In addition to on-site recording, all data are telemetered to the central office, where a paper tape is punched preparatory to computer processing. The data are also printed in log-sheet form for daily observation of data to indicate existing problem areas or mechanical problems.

Bacteriological, ecological, and nutrient monitoring programs are being conducted on a manual sampling basis. The ecological program consists of a study of the movement, distribution, and magnitude of resident and anadromous fish populations in the river; plankton studies to determine seasonal

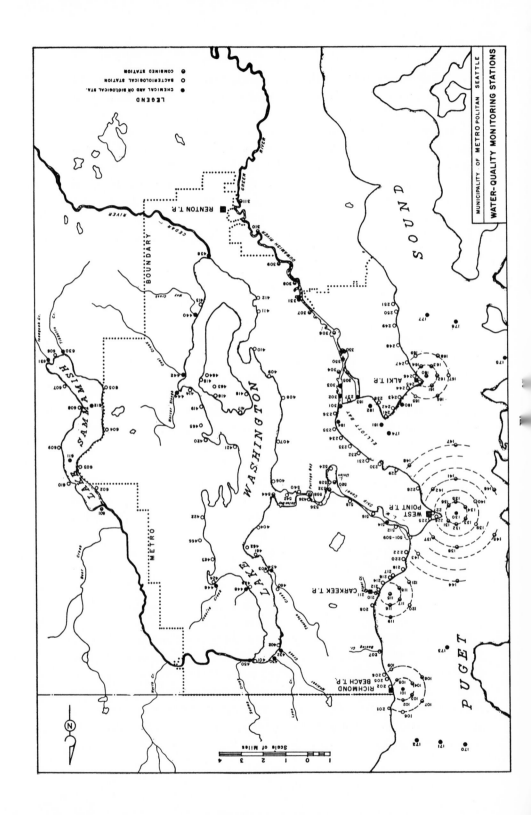

MUNICIPALITY OF METROPOLITAN SEATTLE

WATER-QUALITY MONITORING STATIONS

and long-term variations in relation to changes in available nutrients; and studies of attached growths and investigations of the density and diversity of benthic populations.

Why does the Green-Duwamish River, a comparatively minor stream from the standpoint of mean discharge, warrant one of the most intensive programs of water-quality monitoring ever undertaken as a continuing study? The answer, of course, is determined by the value of the beneficial uses to be protected, the most important of which is anadromous fish propagation.

On a tributary of the Green River is situated one of the state's most important salmon hatcheries. This facility supplies eggs and fry for much of the lower Puget Sound salmon fishery and also supports its own run of fish, a resource with an estimated minimum annual worth of $970,000. In addition, a large run of the steelhead (the Northwest's version of the Atlantic salmon) uses the river each winter as a migration route to upstream spawning beds. These fish support a sports fishery worth an additional $230,000 each year. The value ascribed to the salmon fishery is divided almost equally between commercial and sports catches. Whereas the figure assigned to the commercial catch represents only the wholesale value of the fish, the processed value is approximately three times as great. Thus, after considering the ultimate worth of the resource, we can say that the value of the Green-Duwamish fishery alone is well over $2,000,000 per year.

The fact that a stream with this potential as a fisheries resource flows through the heart of the industrial area of one of the nation's larger cities is in itself unique. To this situation add the Metro proposal for discharge of treated effluent in quantities that will equal the low flow of the river, and the need for an intensive study of water quality becomes apparent.

Metro's alternative to the problem of effluent disposal, discharge directly to Puget Sound, would, in itself, justify the monitoring program since such a project would cost $19,440,00, an estimate based on 1962 costs.

Studies of Puget Sound

Studies of Puget Sound waters, which began in July, 1964, are similar to those being conducted by the city of Los Angeles for the Hyperion outfall. Sampling stations located in concentric rings around the diffuser section of each outfall are spaced at intervals of approximately one-half mile. Surface and depth stations are sampled for dissolved oxygen, temperature, conductivity, and bacteriological analyses. During the sampling operation, observations for transparency and recognizable sewage solids are made. Bacteriological sampling of the Puget Sound beaches at thirty-five stations on a weekly schedule has been under way since January, 1963.

The ecological study of the sound encompasses all work necessary to determine density and productivity of planktonic populations as related to changes in nutrient concentrations and to ascertain the influence of any sludge deposits on the benthic community. If feasible, trawling in the offshore waters will be conducted to evaluate the influence of marine outfalls on bottom-fish populations.

Lake Washington and the Ship Canal

The monitoring program for Lake Washington has been designed, in consultation with Dr. W. T. Edmondson of the University of Washington, to augment his research study being conducted under a National Science Foundation grant.* Dr. Edmondson's work in the early 1950's called attention to the fact that Lake Washington was in danger of being lost as a prime recreational and aesthetic asset to the community. Large quantities of treated sewage were being discharged into the lake and, as a result, complete eutrophication was imminent. This fact, more than any other single factor, prompted the formation of Metro in 1958.

The Metro program consists of the determination of nutrient inflow to and outflow from the lake and also occasional cooperative studies to determine the nutrient reservoir. Eleven streams are sampled on a bimonthly schedule, with nitrogen and phosphorus analyses performed on each sample. Surveillance of Lake Sammamish involves a program similar to that of Dr. Edmondson's but on a smaller scale. Analyses for productivity, dissolved oxygen, temperature, and nutrient budget are carried out on a regular schedule. Bacteriological conditions of the two lakes are measured by sampling thirty-one stations including the major swimming beaches during the recreational season.

The Corps of Engineers monitors the Lake Washington Ship Canal system for conductivity in order to trace salt-water intrusion into the system and thereby schedule the operation of the Government Locks. The availability of this data to Metro makes duplication of this facet of the program unnecessary. The Metro program, therefore, consists of measuring dissolved oxygen and temperature at five locations on a biweekly schedule and sampling for bacteriological analysis at twelve stations on a weekly schedule.

* See Dr. Edmondson's description of his research, "Water-Quality Management and Lake Eutrophication: The Lake Washington Case," in this volume.

Cooperative Studies with the U.S. Geological Survey

As outlined in the brief description above, each program represents a large investment in manpower and capital which required that Metro seek outside assistance. The U.S. Geological Survey, Quality of Water Branch, now the Water Resources Division, agreed to cooperate with Metro on the Green-Duwamish and Puget Sound surveys on an equal cost-sharing basis. An extensive program of stream gauging in the Lake Washington basin has been undertaken with the Surface Water Branch, now Water Resources Division, of the federal agency.

The cooperative study of the Green-Duwamish River represented a total investment of over $168,000 in fiscal year 1964. A large portion of this total was invested in the automatic monitoring equipment. The remainder, nearly $100,000, represented the value of the equivalent services performed by the two agencies.

Since the original agreement, the cooperative program has been expanded to include various special studies on the Duwamish River system and initiation of the Puget Sound program in October, 1965. This has increased the cost of the total program to $300,000 which represents nearly a threefold increase in equivalent services since 1964.

Electronic Data-Processing

As indicated previously, the data collected from the automatic monitors are being computer processed. Such processing is a necessity based on the tremendous volume of data collected. Originally, the data were processed at the Northwest Research Computer Laboratory at the University of Washington. This included preliminary screening and conversion to magnetic tape for further processing and data correlation. The data are presently undergoing a further screening process which includes use of the BOMM program, a time series analysis computer program developed by Fisheries Research Institute, and multiple regression techniques to smooth out the data, i.e., removal of invalid data and filling in of missing segments of data over short periods of time. The final screened data are being stored on magnetic tape for generation of periodic reports and further data correlation. The periodic reports to be generated by the computer include a monthly summary of daily maximum, minimum, mean, and standard deviation values and a weekly mean for temperature, conductivity, pH, DO, and percentage of DO saturation. Further correlation will be carried out to relate existing conditions in the estuary to the many complex physical, chemical, and biological characteristics of the system and to study the effects of the present and future loading of the Renton Treatment Plant in order to assist in the present operation and design of future expansions of the treatment facility.

With approval of Metro's demonstration grant for computer operation of its remote facilities, preparation is being made to handle all future data processing of both automatic and manually collected data on Metro's own computer. This preparation includes training of key personnel in computer programing and developing various programs to handle data processing and data correlation.

Metro has found that the most economical means of handling the manually collected data is through punched cards. Accordingly card formats have been devised using a fixed field format based on the type of information generated. All laboratory work sheets have been revised so that they function as source material for the keypunch operator. Presently the data are being processed on an IBM 1130 computer for generation of periodic reports and for further data correlation. The reports include a quarterly summary for the Monitoring Review Board and a monthly report to management and the operations department.

In conclusion, Metro's monitoring program, although costly, is expected to be a wise investment in terms of the over-all benefits. It is an operating representation of the philosophy that any significant use of the public waters for waste disposal carries with it an obligation to monitor these receiving waters so as to assure their being used in the best interests of the public.

XIII

PULP-MILL WASTE-WATER DISCHARGES INTO PUGET SOUND: AN INDUSTRY VIEWPOINT

Donald J. Benson

THE basic Pollution Control Act for the State of Washington was passed by the Legislature in 1945. This law was not changed until 1967 when a number of housekeeping amendments were proposed to bring definitions into line with national trends. A major companion act to the basic 1945 law was enacted in 1955 which developed the "permit" system of licensing industrial discharges. The first permits to be issued to the Washington sulfite pulp mills contained, among other operating and reporting requirements, a clause requesting that recovery techniques for spent sulfite liquor be developed.

A primary reason for the interest in the amounts of spent liquor discharged was the controversial area of SSL (spent sulfite liquor) toxicity for oysters. Because of the great cost of recovery, the pulp industry was reluctant to proceed without more definitive information regarding the effect of their discharge. To resolve this problem, in 1959 the Pollution Control Commission sought the services of two widely acclaimed scientists in the fields of sanitary engineering and oyster culture, Gordon Gunter and Jack E. McKee, to examine conditions in Puget Sound. The document resulting from their study, known as the Gunter-McKee Report, took over a year to prepare. It pointed out areas requiring more scientific study and research, but recommended, as a result of knowledge about the effects of spent liquor on oysters, interim standards that were generally within the conditions in the sound.

At a public hearing early in 1960, the Pollution Control Commission failed

Donald J. Benson is executive secretary of the Northwest Pulp and Paper Association, Seattle, Washington.

to adopt the report; instead it asked the larger pulp mills to recover their spent liquors under a precept of the basic law relating to the use of all "available and reasonable" methods for the control of water pollution. The mills, which were essentially under orders through their permits, asked for a hearing in the matter, contending that the requests were not "reasonable" under the terms of the law. The legal aspects of the issue were explored until January of 1962, when the state of Washington asked for technical aid from the U.S. Public Health Service.

A conference held under Public Law 660 in January, 1962, resulted in a comprehensive joint state-federal study of Puget Sound. As a result of this action, the complicated legal procedures were dropped, permanent five-year permits were issued to the sulfite mills, and it was agreed that the resolution of the problem would have to be in the technical rather than the legal arena.

In April, 1967, the results of the survey were issued by the new Federal Water Pollution Control Administration. The study (which evolved into primarily a federal effort) showed that sludge deposits in the vicinity of the mills could generate gases toxic to fish life and that low concentrations of spent sulfite liquor could cause abnormalities in laboratory-spawned oyster larval forms under specific conditions known as the oyster larval bioassay. A similar laboratory test showed a sensitive response by egg forms of the English sole to SSL.

On the basis of these findings the FWPCA requested recovery of spent liquor solids from all but the two smallest sulfite mills on Puget Sound and removal of settleable solid by clarification from all mills. At one location where the need for the removal of settleable solids was first evident, the necessary facilities were installed immediately. During the federal study several of the mills also intensified their own field study programs which reconfirmed their position that no serious pollution problems are evident and that the abundance of fish life and related forms in the receiving waters were ample evidence of their position.

They further contend that laboratory tests used as a basis for some of the federal requests are no substitute for field information, particularly when the species and form used is not found naturally in the waters because of low temperatures such as is the case for the oyster larvae.

These technical issues will be resolved when either the conference is reconvened or federal water-quality standards hearings are held relative to this matter. At such meetings the evidence from both sides of the issue will be heard and a decision could be enforced by the courts, if necessary.

A Philosophy of Water-Quality Control

A philosophical question as well as a technical one appears to be at the heart of the problem manifested in Puget Sound. If both management and agencies (or public) can come to an understanding in this area, problems are much more likely to be handled on a rational and technical basis, and not through the time-consuming legal or irrational emotional route.

Definitions

The term "water-*quality* control" is preferred to "water-*pollution* control." The second is a relatively negative term that implies failure—or making the best of a poor situation. The sanitary engineer should be pleased to use a term that hints at some skill and achievement in manipulating our environment successfully. This in essence is what a professional engineer is trained to do, i.e., adapt the environment to man. Conversely, the medical profession is dedicated to adapting man to his environment.

Downstream Beneficial Use Theory

A basic concept of water-quality control is the theory of downstream beneficial use. This, simply stated, means that the residents upstream will control discharges so that beneficial uses downstream are not impaired.

Categories of beneficial use have been listed many places, and the following are a composite to give us terms of reference for water use: (1) domestic water supply; (2) industrial water supply; (3) irrigation; (4) stock and wildlife watering; (5) propagation of fish, shellfish, and aquatic life; (6) recreational use; (7) power production; (8) navigation; (9) waste assimilation; (10) aesthetic use.

Following now is a list of terms used to denote the various types of contaminants or pollutants that can reduce water quality below levels necessary for the beneficial uses (it must be kept in mind that in any given situation a time, place, and concentration element are necessary before a beneficial use is actually affected): (1) harmful or indicatively harmful bacteria; (2) toxic materials (both acute and chronic, including radioactivity and pesticides); (3) temperature; (4) oxygen depression; (5) undesirable growths; (6) excessive bottom deposits; (7) color and turbidity; (8) floating material.

Most people are probably familiar with the problems of low oxygen caused by excessive organic decomposition and its effect on fish life. This is not always caused by the discharge of man-made materials. Upwelling in the offshore or deep portions of the sound can cause dangerously low oxygen levels. A fish kill in Hood Canal in 1963 was attributed to this cause. The annual oxygen deficit during the summer in the upper Klamath River is caused primarily by the decay of natural algae from the shallow Klamath Lake.

An example of undesirable growths is the complicated slime problem in the Columbia River. Very low amounts of organic enrichment materials, not enough to lower the dissolved oxygen, occasionally trigger the formation of *Sphaerotilus* which can clog the nets of the commercial fishermen downstream.

The effects of toxic materials can be either dramatic or very subtle. Both manifestations are often difficult to document in the laboratory or define in the field. Bacteriological pollution is almost exclusively caused by the discharge of inadequately treated domestic wastes.

Enforcement of the Beneficial Use Theory

Enforcement—or to phrase it perhaps more pleasantly, "application"—of the beneficial use theory usually results in a two-pronged approach. First, a program of continuous assessment and evaluation of water quality and beneficial uses must be practiced; second, waste-discharge requirements which are dependent upon such stream determinations must be developed. As a practical matter this procedure becomes quite complicated with our rapidly developing economy. Changes are occurring much too rapidly to allow this cause-and-effect approach to be tightly aligned. A level of treatment must be anticipated that will satisfy the downstream beneficiaries for a number of years, not just immediate needs.

Another innovation paralleling the beneficial use theory is the application of the "known and reasonable" methods of control. With a strict application of the beneficial use theory, we can visualize that a single discharge into a large body of water with few or no users downstream would allow perhaps a very loose or even wanton discharge situation. In these circumstances a carefully arbitrated set of "minimum" control measures may be applied with the constraints of "known and reasonable" to maintain good housekeeping and careful discharge operation.

Parenthetically, the use of legal enforcement to require known and reasonable measures is often less than satisfactory. As a matter of fact, the most efficient "enforcement" in any of these areas is a mild blend of informed public opinion (not uneducated public fervor), salesmanship on the part of the control agency, and good faith on the part of management. This is not to say that legal enforcement proceedings are unnecessary, but for the most efficient use of technical personnel the salesmanship approach is far superior. This not only relieves the necessity for a "policeman" at each outfall, but spares the long and arduous court proceedings that require so much unproductive time from groups of technical people involved, those from both agency and management.

Complications in the Beneficial Use Theory

The theory of upstream control to protect downstream uses is a satisfactory way to approach water-quality control in a static situation, but what happens in our dynamic community typified here in the Pacific Northwest? Assume, for instance, that Mill A locates on a stream and through moderate treatment and good inplant control is able to satisfy the water-quality requirements for the downstream uses.

Now comes Industry B, prepared to do as well or perhaps, because of newer equipment, a little better than Industry A in reducing their discharge. However, the combination of the two effluents would exceed the stream's assimilative capacity, and so the water quality would be degraded below that desirable for other users.

The problem must be solved, but how and by whom? One choice would suddenly cause Industry A to increase treatment capacity to the degree imposed upon Industry B, thus to some extent penalizing the established industry through action begun by another, perhaps a direct competitor. A second choice would require Industry B to assume a much higher degree of treatment than the established Industry A, thus in a way penalizing Industry B for merely being second in time. The third choice, usually an unacceptable one, is to allow a degradation of the downstream water below the established standard, perhaps penalizing the downstream users.

An equitable solution is difficult to derive. Application of the "clean as possible" theory would face this dilemma eventually, even if a satisfactory agreement as to the term could be wrought. The application of effluent requirements, discharge tied to production levels, the use of prescribed treatment methods—in fact, all approaches to control—must face this typical problem at some point in time.

The Selection of Industrial Locations

Before tackling a proposed solution to this problem, let us digress for a background on how one industry, pulp and paper, locates a manufacturing site. The major goal in business enterprise is to make a needed competitive product that will yield a return great enough to service the investment capital. To plan for this, an estimate of the costs of doing business is necessary. In the pulp and paper industry, major considerations include pulpwood prices; nearness of market; satisfactory water supply; waste-disposal requirements; tax rates; and power, fuel, chemical, and labor costs. Supplies of wood and water, together with disposal requirements, are cost items related closely to natural resources that probably have the greatest variation from site to site, especially in a given region.

As is easily recognized, if the advantage gained by savings in freight rates to markets or in low prices for wood were great enough, it would be reasonable to pay more for water supply and waste disposal.

Several pulp and paper mills in the South employ biological-degradation systems to treat wastes from the kraft process before discharging them to very small streams. Others may hold wastes for periods of time and release during favorable water flows. A mill at Springfield, Oregon, not only has reduced loadings to the McKenzie River by rather strenuous inplant controls and water reuse, but by secondary treatment and irrigation of land with a portion of the remaining mill discharge during the summer for perhaps the lowest waste-discharge rate per ton in the nation. A mill at Shelton, Washington, prior to shutdown in 1957, recovered an unprecedented 97 per cent of the spent sulfite liquor and burned it without recovery of heat or chemicals.

These mills recognized the exceptional water-quality needs of the receiving water when they planned to build or expand. If the estimated costs were still favorable for their situation, they proceeded with construction. But the fact that they could justify these extraordinary procedures in their particular physical and market situation should not reflect upon lesser measures taken by mills in other locations, notably on large receiving waters, which chose their location at least in part because of the great assimilative capacity of the recipient waters, perhaps paying a higher premium on wood or freight.

A Rational Approach to the Waste-Treatment Problem

Water-quality management depends for its success on broadly based planning. As a first step, some gazing into the crystal ball is necessary. In most areas, water planning is functioning through the several levels of government. With these plans, forecasting is necessary to determine the future water requirements of the basin involved. To establish these figures, some estimate of population and industrial growth is necessary. Would it not be possible to refine the industrial growth pattern to a degree that would give reasonably reliable answers to the potential of a basin for supporting particular kinds of industry?

Zoning

Maximum beneficial use of water resources can be achieved to a degree by the use of zoning procedures—for both land and water. For instance, it is not desirable to withdraw water for domestic use immediately below even the most modern of sewage-treatment plants. The zoning plan then would aim to reserve sites above the predicted location of treated waste discharges for water withdrawal. The same approach would hold true for the location of water-related recreation sites, or the relative location of industry and other high-quality water users and uses.

It is agreed that, if necessary, appropriate precautions must be taken that will permit both needed uses, even if one should occur at an awkward position with regard to the other. To achieve maximum water use, however, we should plan to avoid as many of these problems as possible through the tool of land and water zoning.

Criteria and Standards

In the development of plans for zoning, scientific information regarding how various water uses interfere with one another is essential. In the study of waste discharges this information is usually referred to as water-quality criteria. Much work has been done and more is being done to develop such information; however, the criteria developed cannot be applied willy-nilly to all waters in all locations.

The application of selected criteria to fit a given situation is a highly technical engineering matter that policy-makers should recognize when making decisions. Questions of the general use of the state's water, the establishment of zones, and the hiring and firing of the technical people are in the purview of the administration. On the other hand, the job of setting up standards picked from the tool chest of developed criteria is a job for the professional engineer much as is the determination of how much steel should be placed in the footings of City Hall.

Fortunately the Federal Water Quality Act of 1965 generally recognized these principles. The requirement that the states establish water-quality standards for interstate streams by June, 1967, was coupled with a requirement for public hearings for various sections and segments of the waters involved. At these hearings lay citizens and other water users were afforded the opportunity to express their desires for water use. Those possessing technical competence could comment upon the adequacy of the particular criteria proposed. The federal law further requires that the standards proposed be practical and feasible. From this supply of data in addition to their own information, the professional engineers of the state pollution-control agencies would develop final standards. These would then be further scrutinized by their federal counterparts for promulgation.

The parameters expressed with numerical values tend to be those backed by adequate information. For other parameters where adequate knowledge is lacking, limiting values are specified by a no-adverse-effect clause and backed by field and laboratory bioassay techniques.

Summary

With a workable model that includes plans to achieve the potential of a basin, zoning to avoid conflicting uses, and the wise application of criteria to determine the standards required, the dilemma of meeting the classic problems illustrated in Industry A and B can be met and solved.

In the circumstances just outlined, Industry A would have been in a better position to know that Industry B would someday exist. The time of its coming would probably be dependent upon market conditions and availability of investment capital. Industry A, building and operating with this knowledge, would be able to plan both technically and financially to reduce their discharge at the appropriate time. Then, with both industries providing comparably adequate treatment, they would plan for the time when further expansion in the basin would take place.

Admittedly many problems are attached to this proposal. At best, planning and forecasting are risky business. Expansion is taking place rapidly, and problems of lead time in the requirements for treatment facilities have to be recognized. It is also possible that the limit of a basin's water assimilation would be reached faster than the technical development of waste-treatment ability. At this point the control agency must be firm in not granting further permits until technology catches up with the need.

The forcing of one manufacturer or city to go to higher levels of discharge control because of the action of another municipality or industry is not a pleasant task. But what is the alternative? At present essentially this same procedure is taking place, with great stress and strain, both on the quality of water and upon industry and the control agency. Agency people are frustrated because they have difficulty selling the need for control measures beyond those immediately recognizable in the receiving stream. Management, in order to properly plan and install facilities ahead of absolute need, requires much advance information not presently available.

The basin plan would not eliminate all of the problems, but at least the perspective of the over-all situation—past, present, and future—would be available for all to examine. The management of our water would be enhanced immeasurably through understanding and appreciation of the complexities involved and of the increased predictability of future requirements.

XIV

THE CHANGING ROLE
OF THE COURTS IN
WATER-QUALITY MANAGEMENT

Ralph W. Johnson

FIFTY years ago few people were concerned about water quality. Ample water—good, clean water—was available for just about any use; few worried about how to make it cleaner. The phrase "water-quality management" still lay dormant in the mind of some wordy academic. Throughout most of the nation we were more concerned, it seemed, with how to get rid of water, clean or otherwise, than how to conserve it.

Now all that has changed. The combination of rapid industrial expansion and population explosion has put clean water in short supply. Greater demands have brought greater conflict; and with them enters the law, our institutionalized device for resolving conflicts.

In the short span of about twenty-five years the law has tried to create a system of priorities and standards of quality for water use. In many ways the effort might still be called "rudimentary" and "halting," primarily because of the novelty of the problems and the emergence of new social values. In the past fifteen years, however, the increasing demand on water has brought a sharpened tempo of conflict and a stepped-up growth in the law. We now have a substantial body of law on the subject. In this paper I shall try to summarize that development.

Common-Law Control of Water Quality

Historically, water quality in this country has been controlled by the "riparian rights" system. This system has been applied by the courts in all

Ralph W. Johnson is professor of law at the University of Washington.

states of the Union except the tier located in what was once called the "Great American Desert," including Montana, Idaho, Wyoming, Nevada, Utah, Colorado, Arizona, and New Mexico. These latter states, along with Alaska, have rejected the riparian rights system completely in favor of the appropriation system of water rights. The two systems are quite different. The riparian system * says that each landowner adjacent to a stream or lake has a right of reasonable use of the water vis-à-vis other riparians. This right is always relative, and may be diminished or expanded as the circumstances change and other uses of the water develop. At no time does it become fixed or certain. The appropriation system † on the other hand, says that the first in time is the first in right; it applies to nonriparians as well as riparians. The first person, riparian or otherwise, who "appropriates" the water, i.e., puts it to beneficial use, acquires a legal right to continue that use. This right remains the same throughout time, even though other uses or demands for the water develop later. The appropriation system has historically been used to control quantitive allocations of water for irrigation and mining and has had little to do with the control of water quality, although it probably can be adapted for the control of quality as needed.

The riparian system has concerned itself both with quantity and quality, although more with the latter. It is a court-centered, common-law system, and remains largely so today, whereas the appropriation system evolved from a court-centered system to a statutory and administrative law system about the beginning of the twentieth century.

Early riparian rights cases, decided during the latter part of the nineteenth century, sometimes adopted what is called the "natural flow" theory, under which a lower owner on a river was sometimes permitted to enjoin an upper owner who changed either the quality or quantity of the flow of the river, whether or not the change actually caused the complaining lower riparian any damage. However as more and more people and industries used the waters of the rivers and streams, the impracticability of this system became apparent. By the turn of the century nearly all courts had changed to the "reasonable use" theory.‡ Presently all states using the riparian rights system adhere to it. A lower owner can enjoin an upper owner only if the upper's

---

* For a description of the riparian system, see *Restatement of the Law of Torts,* Vol. II, Sec. 849, pp. 239–43.

† For a description of the appropriation system, see Wiel (1911) and Hutchins (1942); for an analysis of Washington's water law, see Johnson (1960:580).

‡ See, for example, the discussion in Sandusky Portland Cement Co. v. Dixon Pure Ice Co., 221 F. 200 (1915), involving a cement company whose use of a stream warmed the water slightly and made it impossible for the ice company to cut ice.

use is "unreasonable" as to him. Needless to say, this leaves much uncertainty as to the legal rights of the parties. For example, a use that was reasonable in 1940 may be in doubt by 1950, and may be clearly unreasonable by 1960. This has been the pattern of many industrial uses of rivers where the public has increased the use of the lower sections for recreation during recent years.

One other legal theory deserves special mention, to wit, nuisance. In practice it is often so similar to the riparian rights theory as to be indistinguishable. It is based on the rule that a person cannot interfere "unreasonably" with another's use of his land. Nuisance has, of course, been applied to many situations not involving water, such as rendering plants or houses of prostitution in residential districts, noisy or smoky factories in residential areas, and blasting operations near businesses or dwellings. As to water use, the nuisance theory has sometimes been used to prevent an upper water-user from unreasonably polluting a river to the damage of a lower riparian. Again, however, the rule is based on the "unreasonableness" of the polluter and thus each case depends on its own facts.

Limitations of These Legal Remedies

A number of limitations, seriously impairing the usefulness of these legal remedies connected with the control of water quality, have brought about their gradual decline and replacement by administrative control.

Uncertainty

An investor desiring to use a stream for the location of an industry should be able to depend on the quantity and quality of water that the industry needs. If he cannot do so his investment risk may be too great, causing him to locate elsewhere, or possibly to stay out of the business entirely. The investor's need for certainty is frequently not met by the "reasonable use" theory of riparian rights. What was "reasonable" at one point in time may be unreasonable a few years later. For example, suppose Industry A locates on Blue River in 1940. Virtually no one uses the water downstream at the time. Between 1940 and 1960 three other industries—B, C, and D—establish themselves upriver, contributing slightly to the further pollution of the water. Then, between 1960 and 1964, several resorts open up near the mouth of the river, below the industries. Industry A's use of the water may cause insignificant harm to the resorts by itself, but combined with the pollution caused by B, C, and D, it may cause substantial damage. If the resorts seek a court injunction, they may or may not prevail, but the threat is real enough that it may discourage industrial development, even where such use might be the best one for the particular river.

This element of uncertainty in the riparian system was the root cause of a major study of the riparian system in the eastern states in the early 1950's, and the drafting of a Model Water Use Act. The Model Act attempts to introduce an element of certainty into the system through a licensing program.* Industries apply for and receive a license to use the water in a certain way. Thereafter they can be assured of a continued right to use the water without interference for a specific number of years.

The Public Interest Not Protected

Barring legislation permitting the state to sue on behalf of the public, the riparian rights system offers little protection to the public. Historically, it has been used by one individual against another. The public, or a large group of persons, have found the remedy too unwieldy to be practicable. Thus if the public has an interest in a particular river for recreational purposes, but the portion of the river usable for recreation is located in a wild area where there are no resorts to complain, the public interest may go unprotected. The potential benefit, or loss, to any individual member of the public is too small to justify his bearing the time and expense of litigation.

Loss of Riparian Right through Prescription or Laches

Statutes of limitations exist in every state to limit the time in which a person can bring a lawsuit. The limitation period for actions involving water use varies from about three to ten years; thus, if for ten years Upper Owner makes use of a river that is unreasonable to Lower Owner the statute of limitations may forever bar legal action by Lower. Although *public* nuisances may not be barred by such statutes they can bar actions based on private nuisances, and riparian rights.

Similarly the defense of "laches" (inexcusably sitting on one's rights) may be interposed to bar an action by a lower owner against someone above him who has used a river for waste discharge over a long period of time, has come to rely upon its use for this purpose, and has received no earlier complaint from the lower owner.

* For an analysis of this uncertainty element in the riparian rights system and the approach of the Model Act in remedying it, see University of Michigan Law School (1958:15–18).

Consistent Policies Not Evolved by the Courts

The criteria adopted by the courts for controlling water quality, "reasonable use," are too vague to permit long-range planning by industries, individuals, or the public. Nor are the courts themselves constituted in a way to make long-range policy about water quality. They tend to deal in *ad hoc,* piecemeal problems. Different cases come before different judges, at different times, and with different lawyers. The proceedings are adversary. The primary interest of the parties is usually to win that particular case; they are, for the most part, only incidentally concerned with the establishment of significant "principles." The interest of the other users, both present and future, or of the public, is not their primary responsibility or concern.

Hit-or-Miss Enforcement

Lawsuits are started by people whose rights have been injured. However, a person whose rights have been stepped on is not compelled to bring a lawsuit, and there are many reasons why he may not wish to: the injury to his rights may be small; he may be in poor health; the defendant may be a large company difficult to beat in court; or the plaintiff might simply dislike lawsuits. Often when the public suffers substantial loss or injury because of the defendant's conduct, no legal action is brought to rectify the situation. The harm to each individual is too small to justify the expense and time. The result is hit-or-miss enforcement and a tendency toward laxity in water-quality standards.

Cost of Court Action

A lower owner may be faced with overwhelming costs if he desires to proceed through the courts to enjoin pollution. Any lawsuit is expensive, but those involving injunctions for water pollution are even more so. Scientists and engineers must be consulted; and specific damage to the plaintiff must be proven. There may be five, ten, fifty, or one hundred individuals and companies contributing to the pollution upstream, and the specific contribution of each must be proven. On many streams such lawsuits have become so complex and expensive that they are simply not started.

The Courtroom-Centered System

A legal trial is an *ad hoc* treatment of an important, but small, part of a very large and continuing problem. The courts are expert at recapturing and analyzing past events, such as a robbery, an automobile collision, or a breach of contract, but are limited in handling continuing problems that run from the past into the future, as does water-quality control. Court decisions do not themselves constitute, nor do they particularly encourage, the kind of long-range planning that is essential to effective water management. Nor do these decisions bring about the creation of uniform standards that can be relied on by industry or the community for future planning. Lastly, legally trained judges are not necessarily the best-qualified persons to determine long-range policy about water usage. Their lack of technical, scientific, and economic training sometimes inhibits their full understanding of the problems involved.

One consequence of the failure of the court-centered system demands special notice. Because the courts could not act effectively there has been, in reality, no way for those wanting cleaner waters to make their voices heard. The complaints made to the courts both by industry and the public were ineffectual, but there has been no other place to go. Only the water users at the headwaters of a stream, with no one above them, could be certain of the quality of the water flowing past their property. Others desiring cleaner waters had no effective sanctions. This means that the real decision-makers were those who wished to pollute the waters. An individual, industry, or city that found financial advantage in dumping waste products into a nearby stream had only to obey its conscience in deciding whether to do so, and although in Shakespeare's time it may have been true that "conscience does make cowards of us all," it certainly has not been true of the water polluters of the mid-twentieth century.

This is not to suggest that in every case we should stop using rivers for carrying away waste. For some rivers this may be the most desirable use. But such decisions should be consciously and knowledgeably made, with a full understanding of the alternatives and a freedom of choice among them. Such choices have not been available under the common-law, courtroom-centered system of water-quality control.

Movement toward a More Rational and Efficient Approach

As the public became aware of the inadequacies of the common-law, court-centered system, various alternatives were tried. Some states tried flatly to legislate away pollution. Statutes were enacted and regulations issued that made unlawful the discharge of *any* polluting materials into rivers and lakes. However, blanket prohibitions such as this proved unworkable. Virtually any use of water changes its quality. If a blanket prohibition were strictly enforced, many industries would shut down and cities would be at a loss to handle their waste sewage. The objective of water-quality control may be a good one but it must be approached with an understanding of its potential economic costs. Time must be given cities and industries to consider whether and to what extent they can use other methods of waste discharge.

The Present Trend

During the past few years the trend has been strongly toward the administrative agency for water-quality control. Thirty-six states and Puerto Rico now have comprehensive pollution-control agencies. Thirty-eight states have agencies empowered to issue orders to individuals and organizations using the waters within the states, although only twenty-nine of these have actually issued any orders. Twenty-five states have brought legal actions at one time or another to enforce orders or enjoin pollution.

In spite of this impressive array of legal proceedings, the inclination of nearly all administrative agencies has been to persuade, educate, and cooperate instead of enforce by law. Over the past ten years nearly everyone concerned with pollution control has received considerable education about the problems it poses. "Purists" now recognize that cleaning up a watershed may take many years, and that the economy of the region may suffer unduly if too much haste is demanded; on the other hand, industries and cities realize they must get on with planning toward a gradual cleanup.

Do these developments mean that the courts no longer play a part in pollution control? No, clearly not. Their role is changed, but is nonetheless important.

First, the common-law remedies are still available. They supplement the administrative remedies. For example, in eastern Washington an irrigation district has for years used slightly treated sewage in its irrigation water for fertilizing purposes. Lower owners have complained, but to no avail. The lower owners now have their choice: they can bring a private lawsuit to enjoin such pollution on grounds of nuisance or riparian rights, or they can ask the Pollution Control Commission to take administrative action. In the case in question the commission has been unsuccessful in obtaining compliance through persuasion and has now asked the Attorney General to bring legal action to enjoin further pollution.

Second, both state and federal administrative agencies use the courts from time to time to enforce their orders. In these cases the courts are not creating new law, or policy, as they did in the early common-law actions; rather they are carrying out announced policies of the legislature and the administrative agencies.

Third, the courts still interpret the meaning of statutes creating administrative agencies, determining the nature of the agency and the limitations on its powers.

Fourth, the courts still pass on the constitutionality of statutes and regulations. All statutes and regulations must conform to the provisions of the state and federal constitutions. If they contravene such provisions, they may be stricken down. They must, for example, meet the "equal-protection" and "due-process" concepts as expressed in those constitutions and as interpreted by the courts.

Fifth, the courts continue to review administrative action to insure that the agencies act fairly and reasonably, not arbitrarily and capriciously. On the other hand, such agencies do not have to adopt what the court believes is the *best* solution to the problem at hand. They only need to adopt "a" reasonable solution to meet the standards of reasonableness.

Sixth, a fair hearing is generally required upon the issuance of pollution-abatement orders. When an administrative agency issues orders, it must generally do so in such a way as to permit all interested parties to have their say. The hearings must be conducted fairly, and all sides be given reasonable opportunity to present their arguments.

Conclusion

Over the years the role of the courts has changed significantly in the control of water quality. The center of decision-making has moved away from the courts to the administrative agencies. Nonetheless, the courts still play a significant part in the total process through their review of legislation and administrative action.

REFERENCES

Hutchins, Wells
  1942 Selected problems in the law of water rights in the west. U.S. Department of Agriculture, Miscellaneous Publication No. 418.
Johnson, Ralph W.
  1960 Riparian and public rights to lakes and streams. Washington Law Review, 35:580.
University of Michigan Law School
  1958 Water resources and the law.
Wiel, Samuel C.
  1911 Water rights in the western states. 3rd ed.

XV

A SURVEY OF
WASHINGTON WATER LAW

William Van Ness

Introduction

WATER law, like other areas of law, is influenced by what men do in actual practice. Consequently, it is often undergoing change and adjusting to the needs and demands of people in particular times and in particular places. Historically, these changes may be seen in the types of uses to which water has been put. In the nineteenth century and early in this century water was used almost exclusively for agricultural and domestic purposes. Gradually, however, the nature of predominant uses has changed and today water is of increasing importance for municipal uses, for hydroelectric power, for industrial development, and for recreation. With these changes in types of predominant uses there has developed a need for increasingly sophisticated legal methods for the control and allocation of water resources. In Washington and most other western states, detailed statutory water codes were enacted around the turn of the century in an effort to provide a legal framework and the skilled administrative staffs necessary to insure a just resolution of the complex problems and conflicts which have accompanied changed patterns of water use.

Today, midway in the decade of the sixties, water law and water institutions are again being reviewed, re-evaluated, and in many states changed, so

The present paper was written under the sponsorship of the State of Washington Water Research Center. The author is indebted to Professor Ralph W. Johnson of the School of Law, University of Washington, for his advice and counsel in the preparation of this survey.

William Van Ness is Special Counsel to the United States Senate, Committee on Interior and Insular Affairs, and a member of the Washington State Bar Association.

that they may continue to be responsive to the changing needs of people. These changes may be seen in connection with efforts to control the shameful manner in which our streams and rivers have been polluted in many areas of the state and nation. They may also be seen in connection with efforts to provide comprehensive regional planning which will weigh all alternatives in reaching decisions as to how best to develop water resources. In addition to the review of law and institutions designed for dealing with water resources, studies are also being carried on to assess present water supplies and future needs of Washington and the Northwest.

One of the most important aspects of change that has marked the twentieth-century history of water law and water resource development has been an increasing level of federal participation in the resolution of water resource problems. The role of the federal government has manifested itself in many ways. Most graphic and concrete have been reclamation, hydroelectric, flood control, and navigation improvement projects. The state of Washington has been a fortunate beneficiary in all of these areas. Washington has over 1,200,000 acres of irrigated, reclaimed land; the lowest electrical power rates in the nation; great rivers which are being harnessed and controlled for wider public benefit; and excellent sea and river ports.

In part, this shift in responsibility and effective participation from state and local government to the federal government is explained by the simple fact that often the particular project or problem at hand has been of national scope and impact and, therefore, required a national solution. This has been particularly true in the planning and financing of large-scale projects. A second important factor, however, has been the reluctance and, in some cases, the inability of state and local government to undertake responsibility for resolving water resource problems.

Today, this trend is being arrested and states are rising to the challenge of meeting water resource problems and doing what is necessary. A new era of equal partnership—which some refer to as "creative Federalism"—finds states assuming positions of leadership. This trend is seen in the state of Washington's participation in the recently created North Pacific River Basins Planning Commission; in the federal grant-in-aid Water Resources Research Acts; in state-initiated water resource studies; and in the work of the Washington State Legislative Interim Committee on Water Resources.

This paper has been written under the sponsorship of the State of Washington Water Research Center for use in future water resources planning to provide a general survey of the basic principles of water law which are applicable in this state. It is purposely as nontechnical as the subject permits, and it is hoped that it will provide the reader with: (1) a generalized overview of the rights, duties, powers, and interests of the various private and public groups that are concerned with state water law; and (2) an outline of the state and federal institutional machinery which is charged with the responsibility of administering water law and water resources.

To date, there have been no similar surveys of this nature in the state of Washington. For those readers who desire to pursue particular problems in more depth, a number of articles and treatises which provide excellent starting points are referred to in the text and listed in the References at the end of the chapter. References to statutory and case law are very limited.

Prefatory to a discussion of substantive principles of state water law, it is necessary to define and briefly outline some of the terminology and concepts used in classifying and talking about water rights.

Water appears in three general forms, all of which are interrelated: (1) in the oceans, lakes, and streams; (2) in the soil and in underground storage places; and (3) in the atmosphere. Water from the ocean evaporates, forms clouds, and falls as rain or snow on the earth's land masses. It then percolates into the soil or runs off and follows streams, reaching rivers, and eventually flowing into the ocean where the cycle begins again. Scientists regard this recurring, interrelated cycle as a unity and refer to it as the "hydrologic cycle."

The law, however, does not treat water as a cycle or a unity. Partly for historical reasons and partly because it was initially a practical way to deal with water problems, the law classifies water depending on *where* it appears in the hydrologic cycle. A different legal rule will, for example, apply to water in lakes than would apply to a spring, a stream, or underground water. As a result, it is important to be aware that the source of the water in dispute or the point in the hydrologic cycle at which the water in controversy appears will often determine the correct legal doctrine to apply. In Washington, for example, there are special statutes relating specifically to lakes, streams, or underground waters.* Different rules, dependent upon the source of the water, are also found in the opinions of the Washington Supreme Court. The advent of weather control and modification will require new laws.

The major classification of water with which this survey is concerned is the law of "watercourses" or "natural streams." Generally speaking, a natural

---

* The Surface Water Code of 1917 applies to lakes and streams (*Washington Review Code* 90.03), but a special statutory code is necessary for public ground waters (*Ibid.* 90.44). Similarly, these are special statutes relating to lakes (*Ibid.* 90.24) and artesian wells (*Ibid.* 90.36).

stream may be defined as a stream of water flowing in a definite channel which has a bed and sides or a bank. The flow of water need not be constant, but must be more than occasional surface drainage occasioned by extraordinary causes. Other sources of water which have in some respects led to the application of special rules are "seepage and spring water" (sometimes referred to by the courts as "diffused surface water"), "foreign waters" (waters developed or made usable through artificial means), "lakes and ponds," and "ground (underground) water," which is further subdivided into "percolating waters" and "underground streams." The special rules and considerations applicable to these sources will be briefly developed in subsequent portions of this paper.

In addition to applying different rules of law, dependent upon the source of the water, in the resolution of water controversies, the law also makes another major distinction related to the physical shape, size, and commercial utility of a body of water. This is the distinction between "navigable" and "nonnavigable" bodies of water. This distinction is very important for a number of reasons. First, if a body of water is determined to be navigable, the ownership or title to the bed of the body of water in question resides in the state, rather than in the abutting landowners. If the body of water is nonnavigable, the title resides in the adjoining landowners. Second, determinations of navigability have significance in defining the extent and nature of the rights an abutting (riparian) landowner may exercise over the body of water in question. Third, determinations of navigability are significant in defining the extent of federal power under the commerce and the admiralty clauses of the United States Constitution. The significance of the concept of navigability will be discussed later, but for now it should be noted that navigability is defined in different ways for each of the purposes mentioned above.

Before proceeding, it is also appropriate to discuss units of measurement used in water law. In Washington the legally recognized unit of measurement for flowing water is the cubic foot per second (cfs). For absolute volume or quantity, the legally recognized unit is the "acre-foot." One cubic foot of water comprises 7.48 gallons. A 1 cfs flow amounts to 448.8 gallons per minute, 646,272 gallons per day. The acre-foot is the amount of water required to cover 1 acre of land (43,560 square feet or 1/640 of a square mile) to a depth of 1 foot. A flow of 1 cfs for a 24-hour period is equivalent to 1.98 acre-feet of water.

A third unit of water measurement that was often used in Washington and other states in the early days of water law was the "miner's inch." The miner's inch varies in meaning from place to place and is now generally considered to be an imprecise form of measurement. In Colorado, by statute, 38.4 miner's inches equals 1 cfs; in other states 1 cfs is equal to 40 or 50 miner's inches. The miner's inch is not officially recognized as a unit of measurement in Washington today, although it was used in many early court opinions.

General History of Water Law

The law of water rights is extremely complex and varied in the different states. This is because each state may adopt its own system of water law so long as federal constitutional interests in the resource are not affected. Also, part of this complexity results from the failure of early courts to comprehend fully the unity of the hydrologic cycle with the result that many disparate rules and doctrines were engendered. More important, however, are two other factors. The first of these is the fugitive and fleeing nature of the resource. As water flows through different farms, cities, counties, and states, many different people, industries, and governmental users claim certain rights to its use. Some uses are consumptive and may restrict or deny water to lower users. Others seek to use water as an economical means by which to discharge pollutants, which may mean that lower users are restricted or denied in their use of water. Still others seek to use water as a means of navigation, recreation, or simply an aesthetic source of spiritual solitude and well-being. Quite obviously, these disparate uses are often in conflict with one another.

The early courts and legislatures provided institutional means for the settlement of conflicts between competing users by adapting many of the rules of ownership which governed real property to cover water rights. As might be expected, application of the legal rules of real property to water did not always work well. This resulted in the creation of many exceptions and special rules in the adaptations of the law of real property to water, to handle adequately the unique and unforeseen problems that arose in water conflicts.

The second major source of confusion is that there have been two major contrasting doctrines of water law. In the eastern states the "riparian doctrine" has traditionally been used. In the western states, the "appropriation doctrine" is solely used in some states, while in others both doctrines are used in varying degrees. Further complications are presented in that some eastern states have by statute recently enacted modified forms of the appropriation doctrine.

A water right is generally treated the same as real property. It is usually considered to be a "usufructuary right" which simply means that it is a right to make *use* of the water, but not a right of ownership or physical possession of the water so long as the water is flowing in a natural watercourse. An appropriative water right is said to be appurtenant to the land on which it is used. This means that if the land is sold and no mention of the water right is made in the deed of conveyance, the water right passes with the land to the new owner. As will be discussed later, the appropriative water right may also, under certain conditions, be transferred apart from the land. The riparian water right, on the other hand, always passes with a transfer of the land because it is considered by the law to be "part and parcel" of the land itself.

The Washington court has treated water rights as an "incorporeal heredit-ament." This means that for purposes of inheritance the right is treated as realty even though it is an intangible right to *use* water rather than a fixed and definite quantity of water. Water may take the character of personal property, the ownership of which vests in the appropriator, once it has been diverted from a natural water course and reduced to some form of actual possession such as placing it in a ditch or pipeline. A fixed quantity of water reduced to possession is to be distinguished from a water right which is a "legal right to appropriate water in the future." A legal action to determine ownership or quiet title to a water right may be maintained just as an action to quiet title to reality. In addition, there are special statutory procedures for the determination of the ownership of water rights. These are discussed later. A water right, like the rights of ownership in realty, may be lost through condemnation, abandonment, estoppel, and by the continued adverse use and possession of others.

The land which is now the state of Washington was originally acquired by the federal government through an 1846 treaty with England.* Subject to rights which had accrued and vested prior to acquisition by the United States, this land became part of the public domain and was subject to the regulatory and dispositional powers of Congress. Though much of the land originally subject to Congressional powers has since passed into private ownership by way of private grants, grants to the states as school lands, townsites, and the homestead acts, all lands which presently remain under federal ownership continue to be subject to federal control.

Early federal legislation on the water law applicable to federally owned land and water courses in the Washington territory and in other western

* For a detailed discussion of the early history of Washington water rights and the impact of federal, territorial, and state laws, see Morris (1956) and Horowitz (1932).

states did not bind the states to any predetermined system of water law, but did recognize the doctrine of prior appropriation. The early federal legislation adopted the law within the states' boundaries. In the western states this meant that the system of water law was the appropriation doctrine or, in some states such as Washington, the California Doctrine of a dual system of water law.

Washington adopted the dual system of water law and recognized both appropriation and riparian water rights. Trying to fit these two different systems of water law together in a manner which does not bristle with conflicts and incongruities has been one of the major problems in the history of Washington water law.

The riparian system of water law first came into use in the 1820's in America and was subsequently adopted in England. In America it has been used primarily in those states where there are relatively abundant supplies of water. The principal feature of the riparian system of water rights is that legal rights in water arise from the ownership of land which adjoins or abuts upon a natural body of water. The right to use the water exists solely because of the relationship of the land to the water. Thus, the land itself must be riparian (adjoining a natural body of water) before there is or may be a water right.

There are two principal allocation theories under the riparian concept: the "natural flow" and the "reasonable use" theories. Under the natural flow theory, each riparian was entitled to the full natural flow of the river; to have, in other words, the stream continue to flow past their land in precisely the same manner as it always had in the past. Washington and most other states have rejected the strict natural flow theory as unduly restrictive on the uses which could be made of available water. In its place they have adopted a "reasonable use" theory.

The reasonable use theory provides that each riparian owner may make a reasonable use of the available water, taking into consideration the uses and needs of all other riparians on the same water course. The concept of reasonable use will be discussed later in the section on the riparian system.

Because of the uncertainty, place-of-use restrictions, and nontransferability of riparian rights, many western states have rejected the doctrine as being inapplicable to an agricultural economy in an arid setting. The states which have rejected the riparian doctrine and adopted the appropriation system as the sole basis of the right to use water are Arizona, Colorado, Idaho, Montana, New Mexico, Utah, Wyoming, and Alaska. These states are said to follow the "Colorado Doctrine" because Colorado was the first state to reject the riparian doctrine and adopt the appropriation system. A second group of states, those on the Pacific Coast and the tier of states lying east of the Colorado Doctrine states adopted a dual system of water law which to some extent recognizes both the riparian and appropriation systems. This dual system is referred to as the "California Doctrine" and is followed in Washington. Other states which recognize it are California, Oregon, the Dakotas, Kansas, Nebraska, Oklahoma, and Texas. The remaining states in the East all follow the riparian doctrine. As has been mentioned, however, some of these eastern states have modified the riparian system by statute in a manner so as to create water rights which have many of the characteristics of appropriative rights.

The appropriation system of water law, in contrast to the riparian system, gives no preference to the use of water to adjacent landowners. Indeed, under the appropriation doctrine landownership is generally said to be irrelevant to the acquisition of water rights. An appropriative water right is acquired by applying the water to some beneficial use. The first person on a water course to use the water has a priority or a preference over all later users: "First in time means first in right." No attempt is made to share the available water as would be done under the riparian system. Rather, the party who initiated his water right first will have first priority and will be able to use the available water to the full extent of his right. If water is left over, the party having second priority may then fill his water right, and so on down the line, with the result that in times of shortage the latest person to beneficially use the water and perfect his appropriative right will be the first to be denied water.

In Washington there are substantial climatological differences between the eastern and western parts of the state. The average yearly rainfall in the eastern half is approximately eight inches per year; in the western half the rainfall averages approximately thirty inches per year. In addition, there is a difference in the types of activities in which water is used: in the eastern part of the state, water is used primarily for irrigation; in the western part water is used primarily for support of the municipal and industrial complex which has grown up there (Johnson, 1960:580; U.S. Geological Survey, 1966). In both areas, recreational use of water is becoming of increasing importance. Because of the relative scarcity of water in the eastern part of the state, most of the disputes and litigation over water rights have originated there. Water disputes which have arisen in the western part of the state have usually centered around lakes and the relative rights of their owners. These disputes have tended to involve recreational and aesthetic uses of water rather than consumptive uses.

As a result of the disparate differences in climate, rainfall, and types of water usage it is possible to contend that different rules of law should be applied in the resolution of water controversies in the eastern and western parts of the state. To date, however, neither the courts nor the legislature have made distinctions on this basis.

The appropriation and riparian systems represent theoretical models. In Washington and other jurisdictions each of these systems has been subjected to many minor and some major modifications. Some of these modifications are the result of legislative and judicial attempts to provide resolutions to specific problems which have occurred in their jurisdictions. Others are traceable to attempts to define and articulate a system of water law which best serves the economy and climatological needs of different states. Perhaps the most significant of these modifications has been the formulation of comprehensive water codes in states which have adopted the appropriation system.

Washington's basic statutory water code was adopted in 1917 * and basically serves three purposes: (1) it sets up a statutory system for the determination and recordation of pre-existent water rights; (2) it provides a permit system and procedures for the application for, and granting of, new water rights; and (3) it sets up an administrative agency with delegated authority to control water rights, to study water problems, and to assist the courts, the legislature, and parties having water rights in resolving particular problems. In addition, the administrative agency assists the legislature in formulating long-range policies.

Though the Water Code of 1917 purported to apply to "all water within the state" there is some indication in case law † that the statute applies only to surface waters and not to underground waters. The issue has never been clearly resolved and was at any event rendered largely academic in 1945 when the legislature enacted the present "Ground Water Code" ‡ which complements the 1917 Water Code (now commonly referred to as the "Surface Water Code"). The ground-water code and the unique problems associated with underground water will be discussed in a subsequent portion of this paper.

* *Washington Review Code* 90.03.
† Evans v. Seattle, 182 Wash. 450, 47 P. 2d 984 (1935).
‡ *Washington Review Code* 90.44.

The Appropriation System

In terms of relative significance, the doctrine of prior appropriation has been in the past and continues today to be the principal legal system used for the acquisition of water rights in Washington. Acquisition of water rights through the appropriation of water on the public domain in conformity with local customs, laws, and court decisions was early recognized by federal legislation which was applicable to the territory of Washington. The "local customs" for the acquisition of water rights practiced in Washington and recognized by the Federal Acts of 1866 and 1872, the Desert Land Act of 1877, and other federal legislation. The territorial legislature of Washington accorded recognition to the appropriative system in several early laws among which were authorizations for irrigation, mining, manufacturing, and other beneficial uses. Other legislation predating statehood inferentially recognized the appropriative doctrine by authorizing cities to provide water for the consumptive use of inhabitants and for fire protection. Though the Washington State Constitution declares that the use of water for irrigation, mining, and manufacturing shall be a public use, it expresses no preference for either the riparian or the appropriation system. The first legislation on water rights after Washington became a state in 1889 did, however, expressly recognize the doctrine of prior appropriation. In virtually every legislative session following 1890 some form of legislation which affected appropriative water rights was enacted.*

In general, the following observations may be made as to the nature of the appropriative water right. These should be contrasted to those describing the riparian right (described later) to appreciate fully the dramatic differences.

1. Landownership is irrelevant to the acquisition of the water right. The water right is obtained by appropriating the water and applying it to a beneficial use.

2. An appropriative water right may be lost by a continued failure to use the water for a beneficial purpose.

3. There are no place-of-use limitations on the appropriative water right. The water may be used near the source or it may be transported by ditch or

---

* The early history of Washington water law is discussed in part in Hutchins (1964); Johnson (1960); Morris (1956); Van Ness (1966); Horowitz (1932). The most comprehensive treatment of Washington water law available is found in Johnson (1961). Useful texts and treatises on western water law in general are Trelease, Blodmenthal and Geraud (1965); Sax (1965); Hutchins (1942).

pipe or other method of conveyance for use on lands far removed from the source. The water right or water appropriated under the right may be leased or transferred to someone else, either with or apart from the land. The only limitation is that the transfer must not injure or interfere with other rights.

4. In contrast to the "natural flow" and "reasonable use" theories of riparian water law which are used as a means of resolving conflicts between competing water users, the appropriative system resolves conflicts on a more objective basis: "Priority in time of use" is determinative as to who has the better right. The appropriative water right is a right to a "specific" quantity of water rather than a "reasonable" amount. The right may be further defined as a right to a specific amount of water, to be appropriated at specific times of the year, at a specific place on the stream, and by a certain method.

Methods of Obtaining Appropriative Water Rights

In general, Washington has utilized three different formulations of the appropriation doctrine during its water law history. The first of these was the "customary" method and predates statehood. The second was a "notice" method which was enacted in 1891 and remained effective until 1916. The last and present method is the "permit" system, which was enacted as part of the comprehensive Water Code of 1917.

As early as 1894, the Washington Supreme Court held "that the right to prior appropriation as recognized by . . . Congress existed as a part of the laws and customs of the locality." To effect an appropriation by custom the claimant had to establish an intent to appropriate water to a specified tract of land, followed by reasonable diligence in applying water to a beneficial use. If reasonable diligence in applying water is established, the priority of the water right relates back to and dates from the time of the initial diversion. The appropriation-by-custom method for establishment of a water right was operative from the date of the first settlements in Washington until the passage of the present water code in 1917.

There is some indication that the statutory notice system for the acquisition of water rights which was enacted in 1891 was perhaps intended to be the exclusive means of acquisition, but subsequent cases found the notice method to be merely permissive, and customary appropriations made between 1891 and 1917 were given effect without regard to whether the procedures of the notice statute were followed or not.

The notice method of acquisition of water rights was borrowed from legislation existing in other western states. By and large it did not prove to be a satisfactory method and was abrogated in Washington and most other western states by the enactment of comprehensive water codes based on a mandatory permit system. The 1891 statute provided that water rights for certain designated uses—irrigation, mining, manufacturing, and supplying municipalities with water—could be "acquired by appropriation and as between appropriators the first in time is first in right." An appropriator under the statute was required to post a notice at the contemplated point of diversion indicating his intent to appropriate, the amount of water sought, purpose of the appropriation, place of use, and means used to make the diversion.

The statute also provided that rights acquired could be the subject of a sale and that rights existing at the date the act became effective should not be prejudiced. Strict compliance with the terms of the act was required, but as has been noted the method was not exclusive, and if an appropriator made an actual appropriation in accord with the "customary" procedures discussed earlier, his water right would be valid. The chief advantages of the notice method were that it provided an evidentiary basis on which to date the priority of the water right and that it operated to relate the time of acquisition back to the date of posting the notices.

The permit system established by the 1917 water code * provided an exclusive means for the acquisition of all water rights after 1917. Though all "vested" water rights (rights in existence prior to 1917) were preserved, the code provided that all new rights must be initiated under the mandatory permit system and the procedures established by the code. The procedures for acquisition of water use permits will be discussed later. The chief advantage of the mandatory permit system is that it provides a method for state regulation, control, and recordation of water rights.

The Riparian System

It is not surprising that the earliest reported decisions of the Washington Supreme Court recognized the riparian doctrine, because by the time Washington became a state, it was firmly established as a part of American jurisprudence. The first Washington State Legislature also recognized the riparian system of water law by providing that all holders of possessory interests in land on the banks of natural streams were entitled to the use of the stream's water for irrigation purposes.

* *Washington Review Code* 90.03.

Though the precise form the riparian system takes varies in different states, in Washington the concept is defined in terms of the following characteristics:

1. The riparian water right arises from and is an incident of the ownership of the land which is riparian to a natural body of water. Under the riparian system, *all* land abutting upon a natural water course carries with its ownership a water right.

2. Historically, the riparian water right could not be lost by failure to use it. Recently, however, Washington and some other states have modified this general rule and under certain circumstances failure to use the water, which constitutes an exercise of the legal right, may result in its loss.

3. A riparian owner may use the water *only* on the riparian tract of land. This means he may not use the water unless the land physically abuts or adjoins the water course, nor may he sell the right or the water for use on other land.

4. The amount of water to which the holder of a riparian water right is entitled is determined on a reasonable use theory of allocation. What is reasonable will depend on past uses, the needs of other riparian owners, the amount of water available, the nature of the use contemplated, and other factors.

5. The riparian water right may not be sold or transferred apart from the land to which it is attached.

Reasonableness of use relates to both the amount of water used and the purpose for which it is used. What constitutes a reasonable use will vary with every stream, the number of users, the nature of the uses, the place, and the time. Between competing uses it has generally been held that domestic uses are preferred over other types of uses and, to some extent, established uses have been preferred over new uses. Some uses may be found to be unreasonable by their nature. Pollution or excessive waste would be examples here. Determinations as to what is reasonable at one point in time are, however, always subject to change with changed conditions.

One of the most desirable aspects of the riparian system is its flexibility. The concept of reasonableness provides a standard that can be shaped to meet future needs and unforeseen situations. However, because of the reasonableness standard, the exact content (in terms of amount, purpose, and time of use) of a riparian right can never be accurately defined. Any determination is always subject to a redetermination at a later date. In addition to this uncertainty as to the precise extent and nature of the riparian right, the concept has also been criticized because it limits the use of water to lands which adjoin the water course. A further undesirable limitation is that the riparian right cannot be sold or transferred apart from the land. If a riparian owner declines to make use of available water under his water right and no other riparian owner uses it, it may be wasted even though needed for use on nonriparian land which is near the water source.

The Supreme Court of the state of Washington has held that the riparian water right accrues with the passage of title to land from the government to a private owner. This is true whether the governmental owner was the United States or the state of Washington. The riparian right does not legally vest in the new owner, however, until the patent on the land is issued. When the patent to the land is issued, the water right relates back to the date of settlement or of filing.

The date at which title to riparian water rights vests is a matter of considerable importance because of conflicts which may arise between riparian and appropriative claimants. These conflicts are resolved on the basis of priority (the date at which the respective claims to the water accrued). Thus, appropriations made upon the public domain take precedence over riparian rights attached to land which later passes into private ownership. And, correspondingly, riparian water rights attached to land which has been patented in the name of private owners take precedence over any subsequent claims to appropriative water rights.

It should be remembered, however, that while the relative superiority of conflicting riparian and appropriative claims to the same body of water are resolved on the basis of earliest priority, there still remain dramatic legal differences within each system. For example, all appropriative water rights, in relation to other appropriative rights on the same body of water, have a ranking of priorities based on their date of initiation. Riparian rights, however, in relation to all other riparian rights on the same body of water, are governed by principles of sharing and reasonable use. Priority or date of initiation is of no significance between competing riparian rights.

The cardinal principle of the riparian system is that a person may make only reasonable use of his own water right, and must allow (or suffer as the case may be) reasonable use by other riparian users on the same body of water. Based on this principle, some of the riparian rights—both consumptive and nonconsumptive—which the Supreme Court of the state of Washington has recognized as reasonable are: access, swimming, bathing, fishing, boating, irrigation of riparian land, watering stock, generation of electrical power, manufacturing and industrial uses, storage, and satisfaction of domestic uses.

In addition, the court has recognized that the owner of a riparian right may prevent others from infringing upon or damaging his water right. Examples of this include enjoining the use of water for boating, swimming, or fishing by others in so far as these activites constitute a nuisance; ejecting trespassers from the bed of nonnavigable waters in which a riparian right is held; preventing nonriparians from appropriating water on private land; preventing nonriparians from boating or fishing on a stream where the riparian holder owns the bed (although this was a 1900 decision that might not be followed today); and preventing a city from supplying the domestic needs of its citizens through the use of a city-owned riparian right when to do so would be to the detriment of downstream riparian owners.

These are only a few of the many different rights that have been recognized. In the discussion that follows, some of these rights will be considered in more detail. A point that should be remembered in connection with these recognized rights is that while they were found to be reasonable uses in past cases, it does not necessarily follow that this would be true in future litigation. This is because the reasonableness of use must be judged on the basis of a specific controversy between conflicting claimants at a distinct place and point in time. Typically, the litigation would never have come about unless the competing uses were in some respects incompatible. The court's function is to determine which use is the most reasonable under the circumstances. It is characteristic of the judicial process that it is called upon to furnish "either-or" and "yes-or-no" answers to problems of this nature. Fortunately, however, in the area of riparian water law, courts are coming to recognize that an equitable solution often requires an adjustment of the rights, interests, and activities of both parties, rather than a choice between alternative uses.

One riparian right which is coming to be of increasing significance as the value of stream- and lake-front property for homesites is recognized, is the right to constant water levels. One landmark Washington case has held that an appropriator has no right to lower the level of a lake so as to expose a muddy bottom to the damage of the riparian owners.* In this case, the riparian owners had purchased their property for homesites and recreational purposes. The appropriator had a state permit and sought to appropriate an amount of water which would have resulted in lowering the lake level approximately a foot and exposing part of the muddy lake bottom. The court

* In re Martha Lake Water Co., 152 Wash. 53, 277 Pac. 382 (1929). See also Litka v. Anacortes, 167 Wash. 259, 9 P. 2d 309 (1950).

held that this could not be done unless the riparian owners were first compensated for the damage.

This holding does not change the rule of other cases, however, in which the state Supreme Court has held that a riparian owner who owns all the land around a lake cannot prevent an appropriator from taking *some* of the water from the lake *if* no harm or damage would result to the riparian property.*

In a more recent case involving a conflict between riparian and appropriative rights, another aspect of the hazily defined content of the riparian right was outlined. In this case, a water district sought to have an appropriative water right issued for domestic use. The body of water involved was a lake, and the riparian owners protested against issuance of the right because state health statutes and regulations forbid swimming, fishing, boating, or the discharge of any pollutants on a body of water used for drinking purposes. Thus, if the permit were issued, the riparian owner's use of the lake would be drastically curtailed. The court agreed with the riparian owners and refused to order that an appropriative permit be issued to the water district.†
In connection with this case it should be noted that as a municipal corporation, the water district could always exercise the right of eminent domain and condemn the riparian rights on the lake. This, however, would require the payment of just compensation for the rights taken.

Navigability and the Riparian System

Earlier in this paper it was noted that determinations of navigability were very important in water law. It was also noted that navigability is defined differently for different purposes. Some of these purposes are to determine: title to the bed of the body of water; rights of public use; and the extent of federal power under the commerce and admiralty clauses to the Constitution of the United States.

Title to the beds of all navigable lakes, streams, and other bodies of water vests in each state when it is admitted into the Union. This is based on the doctrine of "equality of states." Because the thirteen original states exercised control and ownership over the beds of their navigable waters, it was held that the same rights of ownership and control vested in the new states as they were formed.

The test to determine whether a body of water is navigable for purposes of

---

* Proctor v. Sim, 134 Wash. 606, 236 Pac. 114 (1925).
† In re Clinton Water District, 36 Wn. 2d 284, 218 P. 2d 309 (1950).

determining title is a test laid down by the Supreme Court of the United States. Simply stated, the test is that those bodies of water are navigable in law "which are navigable in fact. And they are navigable in fact when they are used, or are susceptible of being used, in their ordinary condition, as highways for commerce, over which trade and travel are or may be conducted." Other cases have gone on to say that it is not "every small creek in which a fishing skiff . . . can be made to float . . . which is navigable." *

The significance of the test and the determination that a body of water is or is not navigable, of course, is that this determines who holds title. If found navigable, the state owns the bed. If found nonnavigable, the riparian owner owns the bed. Some cases have stated that there are no riparian rights whatever on navigable waters. A careful examination of case law, however, indicates that there are riparian rights, but that they are less extensive; they do not, of course, include ownership of the bed of the water course.

The test to determine navigability is, as we have seen, relatively general, and it has been applied in a somewhat contradictory fashion in the history of Washington water law. Early cases tended to find lakes navigable even if they were very small. One case found a forty-acre lake that was ten to thirty feet deep navigable. Later cases, however, indicate that if a lake is small and is used principally as a pleasure resort and for recreational purposes, it will be found not navigable. The modern test requires that the lake be large enough for use as a highway for trade and commerce and also that it be located where it has been or can be used for these purposes.

These same general rules also apply in determining navigability of streams for purposes of title. A river that is used only sporadically for purposes of floating logs is not navigable. But, if used regularly to carry logs and other commercial products, the river will be found navigable for title.

Even if it is determined that a body of water is *not* navigable for purposes of determining whether the state or the riparian owner holds title (thus placing title in the riparian owner), this does not necessarily mean that the riparian owner can deny the public access to the use of the water. What it does mean is that title to the bed belongs to the riparian owners. If the body of water is a lake, and if there are a number of riparian owners around the lake, they will all own pie-shaped pieces of the bottom which join at the hypothetical center of the lake. But ownership of bed does not necessarily give the owners the right to prevent others from traveling over the lake's surface.

* Daniel Ball v. United States, 77 U.S. (10 Wall.) 557, 563 (1870).

The Washington Supreme Court has held that riparian owners on a nonnavigable lake own the rights to boat, fish, swim, and so forth, in common, and that any of the owners or their licensees (anyone to whom they give permission) is entitled to use the whole surface of the lake so long as they do not unreasonably interfere with the exercise of similar rights by other owners.* The court has reasoned that to allow each owner to fence in the surface of the lake and exclude others from traveling freely would greatly restrict the desirability of owning lake- and water-front property. In effect it would mean that each owner would be confined to his own wedge-shaped piece of the lake.

Riparian Rights and the 1917 Water Code

Before beginning a detailed discussion of the 1917 Water Code, it is appropriate here to relate the impact of the code on riparian rights. One of the major problems in the history of Washington state water law has been how to work out a satisfactory theoretical and operational accommodation between the appropriative and riparian systems.† We have already noted that where there is a direct conflict involving pre-1917 rights between the two systems, the rule of priority or "first in time, first in right" prevails.

Though a few minor amendments have been made since enactment, the critical section of the water code provides:

The power of the state to regulate and control the waters within the state shall be exercised as hereinafter in this chapter provided. *Subject to existing rights, all waters within the state belong to the public, and any right thereto, or to the use thereof, shall be hereafter acquired only by appropriation* for a beneficial use and in the manner provided and not otherwise; and, as between appropriators, the first in time shall be first in right. *Nothing contained in this chapter shall be construed to lessen, enlarge or modify the existing rights of any riparian owner,* or any existing right acquired by appropriation, or otherwise. . . .‡

A number of things should be noted about this section of the water code. First, it declares that the ownership of all water "subject to existing rights" resides in the public. Second, it provides that all future rights to water may be acquired *only* by appropriation, and then only in accord with the provisions of the water code. Third, it preserves without modification all "existing rights" (pre-1917 rights) of both riparian and appropriative owners.

* Snively v. Jaber, 48 Wn. 2d 815, 296 P. 2d 1015 (1956).
† For a discussion of riparian rights in Washington, see Johnson (1960).
‡ *Washington Review Code* 90.03.010. My italics.

The first point, the question of state ownership of all unused water, has in the past been the basis of a dispute between the federal government and the states. This conflict will be discussed later; for now, it suffices to say that on the reserved lands of the federal government, on interstate streams, and on navigable waters, the state has no power to regulate water use in a manner that conflicts with the purposes of the federal government.

The second point, that all future rights in water after 1917 may be "acquired only by appropriation," means that after 1917 there could accrue no new consumptive riparian water rights. Thus, any transfer of land from the public domain or from state-owned lands to private owners after 1917 does not transfer consumptive riparian water rights even if the land abuts or adjoins a natural water course. The effect of the code is to provide an "exclusive" means for the acquisition of all future consumptive water rights. The means used is the mandatory permit system in accord with the procedures of the water code.

The third point, that all "existing rights" are preserved without modification, is the most significant in relationship to the riparian system of water law in Washington.

The first issue this provision raises is: what were the existing riparian rights as of 1917? Traditionally, courts have said that riparian rights are inseparably appurtenant to, and part and parcel of, the land itself; and that using the water or failing to use it does not affect the right. Thus, it could be contended that enactment of the 1917 code had no effect whatsoever on riparian rights attached to land which was held in private ownership as of 1917, whether or not the rights had been exercised by actually using the water. The contention is that *all* riparian rights are preserved by the savings clause in the code.

Surprisingly, case law in this state has never directly answered this question. There is a line of cases which have, however, provided part of the answer and have served to provide the basis for an accommodation between the riparian and appropriative doctrines. These cases, beginning with *Brown* v. *Chase* * establish the principle that "waters of nonnavigable streams in excess of the amount which can be beneficially used, either directly or indirectly, within a reasonable time, on, or in connection with riparian lands, are *subject to appropriation* for use on nonriparian lands."

The effect of the cases which have followed this rule is to delimit and cut down the content of the "existing" riparian rights which the code purports to

* 125 Wash. 542, 217 Pac. 23 (1923). My italics.

preserve. Thus, if a holder of a water right failed to exercise the right within a reasonable time following the 1917 enactment of the code, it may be held that he has lost his water right. It should also be noted that the loss of the riparian right is apparently not the loss of a property right for which "just compensation" must be paid. The court has apparently reasoned that what has been lost has not been a traditional property right, but something more in the nature of an opportunity or expectation which failed to mature as a result of the holder's failure to exercise it.

Finally, it should be noted that under the water code and present case law, it is not clear what result would follow if a riparian owner should seek to make use of his pre-1917 water right in a situation where there was no conflict with appropriators. In *Brown* v. *Chase* and other cases, there has been a direct conflict. It is probable that the court would apply the "use within a reasonable time" rule and say that exercise of the riparian water right for consumptive uses is not valid, and that the claimant must comply with the provisions of the water code and apply for an appropriation permit. This is the position which the Division of Water Resources has taken in administering the water code. Also, it accords with the general philosophy of the water code, which is to reduce the uncertainty associated with riparian rights and to provide a comprehensive recording system for all state water rights.

In speaking of the court-made rule that riparian rights which are not used within a reasonable time after 1917 are lost, we were speaking primarily about consumptive uses. It is entirely likely under the present law that this same rule would not apply to other aspects of the riparian right such as swimming, fishing, boating, and constant lake level. There are indications in cases that many of the nonconsumptive features of the riparian right are still viable.

The Water Code of 1917

Washington was one of the last of the western states to enact a comprehensive water code. Basically, the enactment of the Water Code of 1917 did little to change the substantive rules of law which govern the extent and nature of water rights or how controversies between users were to be resolved. These tasks were left to the courts to handle on a case-to-case basis relying upon the wisdom of the past and rules of law derived from prior litigation. The significance and impact of the code was immense, however, in that it (1) set up an administrative agency, and (2) provided a procedural framework for the resolution of most prospective and many past conflicts over water.

The Division of Water Resources

The Water Code of 1917 established the Division of Water Resources, headed by the supervisor of Water Resources, under the Department of Conservation. The purpose for establishing an administrative agency was to assemble a body of experts in the fields of law, hydrology, engineering, climatology, and geology to deal with the complex problems of administering one of the state's most important natural resources. Lawyers and judges often were not conversant with the legal and scientific intricacies associated with water problems and, as a result, it not infrequently happened that, at the behest of over-zealous counsel, learned judges were placed in the ludicrous position of decreeing rights to ten times as much water as was in fact available in a particular stream basin. Obviously, this increased rather than resolved conflicts. What was needed was an administrative agency with an expert staff to advise the courts and water users on technical matters.

The Division of Water Resources, then, is charged under the law with the function of generally supervising all "public waters within the state and their appropriations, diversion, and use." The division has the power to regulate and control diversions of water in accord with the water code and the rights of the water users. There is also a duty to inspect the construction of all dams, canals, ditches, irrigation systems, and hydraulic power plants. When necessary to ensure safety, the division may require such changes in construction as are necessary.

One of the most important functions of the division is the compilation of an accurate inventory of Washington's water resources. This requires a great deal of field work and gathering of basic data on the flow of streams; the capacity of lakes and reservoirs; methods, extent, and location of present water uses; and other statistics. The division has the authority to promulgate rules to govern the administration of the water code, though the authority has never been fully exercised. It is also charged with the duty of representing the state and the public interest when court action or the action of private parties threatens those interests.*

The Division of Water Resources has authority to control all waters of the state, including those which have already been appropriated. In performing these delegated functions, it is vested with a good deal of discretion. Actions taken by the division, however, are administrative rather than judicial. When

* The powers and duties of the Division of Water Resources are set out in various places in the ground and surface water codes, *Washington Review Code* 90.03 and 90.44 and in *Washington Review Code* 43.21.120-30.

the division grants an appropriation permit, then, this does not constitute an adjudication of private rights. Actions taken by the division are always subject to review by the superior courts. Division personnel may assist in settling disputes between private parties, but they do not have the authority to make binding decisions in controversies between private parties. However, when the division gives an opinion on a contested matter, the Supreme Court of the state of Washington has indicated many times that it accords great weight to the determinations made by the division's expert staff members.

The water code authorizes the supervisor and his deputies to sit as referees for the purpose of taking testimony in statutory stream-bed adjudications. These proceedings are conducted under the supervision of the superior courts and represent a compromise between the judical and administrative branches in which the expertise of the division staff is incorporated into the court's function of resolving complex legal disputes. This function of the supervisor and his deputies will be discussed in more detail below.

The three primary functions of the Division of Water Resources are (1) the allocation of new water rights to applicants, (2) the determination and recordation of all rights which were in existence prior to 1917, and (3) the regulation and administration of all water rights. Each of these functions is discussed separately below.

Since the 1917 enactment of the water code, all new water rights may be acquired only in compliance with it. To acquire a water right an appropriator must apply for an appropriation permit with the state Division of Water Resources. Pending the division's determination as to whether the permit will be issued, a temporary permit may, under certain circumstances, be obtained. Before issuance of the permit the division must determine whether there is adequate water available for appropriation, the beneficial uses to which it may be put, and whether the proposed use interferes or conflicts with existing rights or the public interest. The prospective appropriator is required to publish a newspaper notice of the application in the county where the diversion will take place and the water will be used. If the permit is granted it will relate back to the date of application and will have a priority dating from that time. The permit then is recorded in the division's office in Olympia and the records provide a form of title registry which is similar to the records maintained in the various counties for the recordation of land titles. The acquisition of a permit is mandatory, and until this is done, a person claiming a water right gets no title and has no rights as against other water users.

The theory behind the mandatory permit system is to provide a basis for eliminating excessive claims to water and needless conflicts between competing users. It also provides comprehensive records and statistics on ownership, use, and location of water rights.*

It has been seen that prior to the enactment of the 1917 water code the courts had difficulty in making equitable resolutions of water disputes for several reasons: (1) lack of technical knowledge and information; (2) the problems of adjudicating riparian as against appropriative rights; and (3) judgments of the courts bound only people who were parties to court actions, while the collective effect of the water use of many others who were not parties to a particular court action might negate or render trivial the findings of the court.

What was needed was a mechanism which would bring *all* of the water users on a particular stream bed into court at the same time. Then the testimony of each could be taken, their rights sorted out in terms of priority and validity, and a formal certificate of right to use water could be issued. The judgment of the court would then be binding on all water users on a particular stream basin and anyone who sought to initiate new rights would have to do so through the mandatory permit system. The permit would fix the date of priority, the amount, and the place of use, and would thus obviate future controversies. Thus, when the water code was enacted, a substantial portion of it was directed towards providing such an adjudication procedure.

In summary form, the adjudication provisions of the water code provide that on the petition of a private party or on his own motion, the supervisor of the Division of Water Resources may, if he determines an adjudication would be in the public interest, initiate proceedings to adjudicate *all* claims on a water course. He does this by filing a statement of material facts, the names of all known parties claiming a right to the water, and a map of the area with the superior court in the county in which the contested water is located. The court then causes summons to issue to all known and unknown parties claiming a right to divert water.

Following service of summons, the claimants are joined as defendants and are required to file statements disclosing information relevant to their claims. The court then refers the matter to the supervisor or his deputy who serves as a referee in taking testimony. Following the testimony, the referee files copies of the transcript with the court together with his report which sets out his recommendations as to the relative priorities of the parties, the amount of

---

* Provisions relating to the permit system are found at *Washington Review Code* 90.03.250–340.

water to which they are entitled, any date restrictions, and a description of the land on which the water is to be used. Any prior decrees litigating the relative rights of parties involved in the adjudication are conclusive as against the parties originally involved, and are *prima facie* proof as against claimants who were not a party to the decree.

Pending final adjudication, regulation of water rights between the claimants is made on the basis of the referee's report. Provision is made for taking exception to the report and filing a bond pending the disposition of an appeal. Though the statute does not expressly say so, presumably a claimant would then be entitled to the water he had customarily been using, provided that this did not unreasonably interfere with the rights of others.

If a party fails to appear, judgment is entered according to the evidence and a nonappearing claimant is estopped to claim any rights except those given under the decree. Provision is made for any of the claimants to take exception to the referee's report at a hearing which is held in the superior court following the filing of the referee's report and transcript. If no exceptions are taken, a decree is entered according to the evidence and the report. Claimants then have a right of appeal to the Washington State Supreme Court. Following entry of the final decree a copy is filed with the Washington State Supervisor of Water Resources. The supervisor then issues diversion certificates to each of the claimants which define the nature of their right. These rights are then recorded.

Though these procedures provide an effective method for determining water rights, the procedures have not been extensively utilized. In the first twenty years following enactment of the water code, fifty-six statutory streambed adjudications were completed. In the last thirty years, however, only a few have been completed though there are a number now pending. One of the major reasons for the failure to adjudicate more of the streams in the state lies in the failure to provide the Division of Water Resources with the staff and budget necessary to the task.*

The regulation and administration of water rights is handled primarily through the rule-making powers of the Division of Water Resources. In areas of very intensive water use, which require the direct supervision of qualified and disinterested third parties, water masters or stream patrolmen may be appointed to administer the division of available water among the

* Provisions of the water code relating to the adjudication and determination of vested rights are found at *Washington Review Code* 90.03.110–240. An extensive discussion of the background of the adjudication system, its use in Washington, and the problems involved is found in Van Ness (1966).

claimants.* The water master inspects the diversion works used by appropriators and has authority to open, close, or adjust the amount of water appropriated so that it accords with the claimant's legal right. The water master also enforces the regulations of the division and has the authority to arrest any person who acts in violation of the provisions of the water code.

Water masters have been used in very few areas of the state. Use of their services has been limited to areas where there is extensive irrigation development that requires periodic regulation of channel and ditch flow and an equitable division of the available water resources.

The job of regulating and administering water rights is a relatively minor one once the legal rights of the parties have been determined. In areas where there are no water masters, a private court action may be initiated to enjoin and prevent any unlawful uses of water.

The Water Code and the Doctrine of Prior Appropriation

Though the water code declares that all waters in the state belong to the public and provides procedures for their acquisition, it does not indicate what water may or may not be appropriated. Obviously, water that has already been legally appropriated may not be appropriated by another. Further, the courts have ruled that water may not be appropriated if to do so would diminish or injure any existing rights.

In early cases the Washington court held that on a navigable body of water only the water between the high and low water marks was subject to appropriation. In later cases, however, it has been held that "there is no reason why the rights of appropriators should depend upon the navigability or non-navigability of the water appropriated." This would appear to be the general rule today and it is qualified only in that the appropriations must not impair the navigability of the water course.

Early cases also held that "waters flowing through state school lands were not subject to appropriation." This rule was later changed, however, when the court held that the state had granted its riparian water rights in state school lands to the public, thus waiving its rights and making water on school lands subject to appropriation.

One of the most important limitations on the availability of water for appropriation arises from the conflict between riparian and appropriative rights. If all the land bordering upon a particular water course were owned by parties claiming riparian rights, this would theoretically mean that there

* *Washington Review Code* 90.03.060 and 90.08.040.

would be no water available for subsequent appropriations. Only the riparian owners could use the water and they would divide it under a reasonable use theory. When faced with this conflict between the riparian and appropriative rights, the Washington State Supreme Court resolved it by holding that any water in excess of the amount which could be beneficially used, either presently or within a reasonable future time, by the riparian owners was subject to appropriation under the water code for use on nonriparian lands.* This rule limits the extent of a riparian right to the amount of water actually used, and is applicable to both streams and lakes. In making an appropriation, however, the appropriator has no right to trespass on the land of riparian owners. Appropriate arrangements for easements and rights of ways must be made.

Under the water code any individual, firm, association, corporation, irrigation district, or municipal corporation may appropriate water. Specific statutory provisions grant the federal government the right to appropriate water for a variety of purposes. It is possible that the often criticized Alien Land Laws prevent the acquisition of water rights by aliens, because water rights are real property. As yet, however, this question has not been presented in the courts.

Though the water code does not make ownership of land a prerequisite to the appropriation of water, the Supreme Court has rendered conflicting opinions on the question. One early case indicated that a "squatter" could not appropriate water on an Indian reservation prior to its being opened to settlement. It was held that an appropriator must own the land or be a settler having a possessory interest with evidence of intent to acquire title. Later cases, however, have indicated that it is not necessary that an appropriator be the owner of any lands before he could make an appropriation. All that is required is that the appropriator exercise reasonable diligence in putting the water to a beneficial use.

It was held in one case that an appropriation of water may be made for the purpose of selling it to others. Thus, the present rule would appear to be that landownership or exclusive use is not a prerequisite under the water code.

A person owning riparian land and claiming a riparian water right may also claim an appropriative water right. It has been held that these claims are not antagonistic and that the claimant does not have to select one theory of ownership over another.

---

* Brown v. Chase, 125 Wash. 542, 217 Pac. 23 (1923); see also the discussion of the case in Johnson (1960).

As has been noted, the Water Code of 1917 sets up a permit system for the acquisition of water rights. The water code and the decisions of the Supreme Court define the principles and procedures applicable to making a valid appropriation of water. In addition to the application for the permit and the other steps outlined earlier, a number of general rules and requirements which are derived from the common law are relevant. These rules were all that existed prior to enactment of the code, and at present they supplement and spell out the code's meaning and provide general principles for resolving conflicts between competing claimants when the issue between them is priority. These rules, which will be discussed in turn, cover questions of (1) diligence in completing an intended appropriation, (2) the doctrine of relation back, (3) beneficial use, (4) initiation by trespass, and (5) reservoir permits and the storage of water.

Once a party decides that he will make an appropriation of water and commences work to do so, as, for example, by digging a ditch or laying pipe, he must follow up this initial work with "reasonable diligence" and finish the appropriation without unnecessary delay. If an unreasonable amount of time should pass between the initiation of the first effort to make the appropriation and its actual completion, the claimant's water right will date from the time of completion and actual use of the water, rather than the date at which he commenced the necessary work to begin the appropriation. What constitutes a reasonable time will depend on the facts of each case.

Under the water code the supervisor has discretion to prescribe a reasonable time within which construction work necessary to an appropriation must be completed. If reasonable diligence is not made in appropriating the water and securing final issuance of the permit, the supervisor may cancel it.

Closely related to and complementing the concept of reasonable diligence is the doctrine of "relation back." As was noted in the earlier discussion of the appropriation system of water law, the appropriative water right dates from the time of the first beneficial use of water. This is very important because earlier water rights have priority over all later rights, and in times of water shortage, later rights must give way to earlier rights. As a result of the importance of priority in time there have been many water-law controversies between competing water users to determine which right was first initiated.

Courts have resolved problems of this nature by providing that if a party proceeded with reasonable diligence in effecting his appropriation, the priority date of the water right relates back to the date of first use. The result of applying the doctrine is that the acts of intervening claimants do not necessarily cut off or interfere with an original appropriator's plans, investment, and justifiable expectations. If, however, reasonable diligence in applying the water or prosecuting the work necessary to its application is lacking, the water right will not relate back to the date of the initial diversion. In this case, the initial appropriator's water right would probably be valid only to the extent that there has been an actual diversion and beneficial use of water.

Under the permit system water rights "acquired by appropriation . . . relate back to the date of filing of the original application" for the permit. The theory is that because the application for the permit is on file in the division's Olympia office, it serves to give his warning and notice to all subsequent users of the water right claimed. If an application is defective for any reason (e.g., improper land description) its priority will be protected if the defect is corrected within a reasonable time and if the rights of innocent third parties are not impaired.

Finally, it should be noted that many controversies involving the doctrine of "relation back" are not governed by the simplified procedures of the water code and will continue to arise in the future. These involve pre-1917, so-called vested water rights. Resolution of questions involving pre-1917 water rights often depends on factual determinations of what happened fifty to eighty years ago. This presents very serious evidentiary problems which are growing worse with the passage of time, and thus provides a persuasive argument for completing statutory stream-bed adjudications on a state-wide basis.

The beneficial use criterion for appropriative rights, both by statute and court decision, applies to the purpose of use and, frequently, to the period of use as well. Generally speaking, most uses which are not unduly wasteful, and which are of some benefit, will be found to be beneficial.

In some cases, use in a manner which pollutes the water course will be enjoined and forbidden. This represents an aspect of the more general rule that water may not be used in a manner that injures the rights of other water users. In Washington there are many statutes which either specifically or inferentially authorize the use of water for a great variety of purposes. In recent times the importance of recreational uses of water have been recognized as a beneficial use. Though recreational uses are not within the historical definition of a beneficial use, it is likely that the trend to enlarge the concept to include this and other uses will continue.

The concept of beneficial use and restriction on the purpose of use grew out of the idea that the goal of water law is to obtain the greatest possible benefit from the water supplies available for appropriation. Therefore, unjustifiable and unnecessary wastage of water is prohibited. In other western states, uses which have been held nonbeneficial include claims to water for no other purpose than speculation; using water to carry off debris in months when the water is needed for irrigation; and winter flooding of fields to produce an ice cap for moisture retention. The limitations on purpose of use and the definitions of beneficial use are operational rather than static, and they will vary from case to case and in different times and different places.

In issuing an appropriation permit, the supervisor may and often does limit the period during which water may be used. Many irrigational use permits, for example, are valid only between the months of March or April and September or October. The Supreme Court has held that in adjudications concerning water rights, the courts may determine the period of use of a water right as well as its priority and amount.

The Washington courts have recognized the general rule of other jurisdictions that an appropriative water right cannot be initiated by an unlawful trespass upon the private land of another. When a person has land which does not abut on a water course but desires to get a water right and to transport water to his property, he usually accomplishes this by purchasing an easement or right of way over the other person's property. When this is not possible, he may under some circumstances condemn a right of way or easement. He must, of course, compensate the party whose property is taken.

Applications for reservoir permits are subject to the same procedures as applications for any right to appropriate water.* Also any user of water from a reservoir must apply for and obtain a secondary permit which states that an agreement has been reached with the owner of the reservoir permit for the use of the water, and defines the nature of the interest the secondary permit-holder has in the water.

Any person or association intending to construct or modify a dam or controlling works capable of storing more than ten acre-feet of water is required to submit the plans to the supervisor for his approval as to its safety. Any construction which does not meet the supervisor's minimal safety standards may be abated as a public nuisance. Like all other appropriators, the holders of reservoir permits are required to maintain appropriate measurement devices which will assist the state in the practical allocation and regulation of water.

Restrictions on the Right to Appropriate Water

Diversion of water for use in another state or in Canada is expressly allowed by the water code unless the laws of the other state provide that

* *Washington Review Code* 90.03.370.

water may not be lawfully diverted from there for use in the state of Washington. If the law of the other state so provides, the supervisor may, at his discretion, decline to issue a permit.*

This type of statute is referred to as "reciprocity" legislation. In some other states, there are statutes which expressly forbid the transfer of water across state lines. California has "county of origin" legislation which forbids the use of water outside the county where diverted. Other states have "watershed of origin" legislation.

It should be noted, however, that protective legislation of this nature will not suffice to prevent Congress from diverting water from one state or region to another as has been recently advocated by some southwest states.† Indeed, an interstate compact between states could not prevent the export of a region's waters, if Congress passes legislation authorizing such a diversion. The basis of Congress's powers over interstate and national water resources will be examined in detail later in this paper.

If, on receipt of an application to appropriate water, a conflict is found, the supervisor is under a duty to reject the application. If the applicant can resolve the conflict by purchase or condemnation of the injured right, the supervisor may grant the permit. The supervisor may, at any event, issue a permit for less water than was applied for. In actual practice, a permit will usually be issued for the requested amount of water unless there is a direct conflict with existing rights. This is true even if there is little water available. The permit in these cases is analogous to a "hunting license." The permit does not guarantee that there is or will be water available, but if there is, the holder has the right to appropriate it after all rights having higher priorities are satisfied.

The Division of Water Resources may close certain waters and areas to general appropriation for periods of time to enable the United States to make field examinations, studies, and surveys in connection with utilizing the water for reclamation projects, dams, and other federal projects. Also, the Department of Game and Fisheries may appropriate a portion of the flow of a stream to ensure that the stream will always have sufficient water flowing in it to support wildlife and fish. The Fisheries Department may accomplish a similar result by closing a stream to all future appropriations.

The determinations and decisions of the supervisor in connection with the issuance of permits are by statute *prima facie* correct. Any party aggrieved

* *Washington Review Code* 90.03.300.
† For a good discussion of the proposed diversion plans and references to the legal literature on the subject, see Meyers (1966); Clark (1965).

with the supervisor's decisions may, however, appeal to the superior court to have the matter reviewed. Appeal will lie from the judgment of the superior court as in all other civil cases. The Supreme Court has stated on many occasions that it accords great respect to the expertise and knowledgeableness of the personnel of the Division of Water Resources. This does not mean, however, that their decisions will not be overruled on occasion, if an abuse of authority can be shown.

Though the essence of an appropriation is the right to use water and "the means by which it is done are incidental," there are a number of restrictions on the method used to divert and transport the water. The owners of ditches, canals, and reservoirs are required by statute to maintain controlling works and measuring devices at the point of diversions. Generally, any method of water conveyance will be acceptable providing that it is a reasonably efficient method considering the available technology, feasible alternatives, their cost, and local community customs. The general rule is that any method of diversion which is unnecessarily wasteful or injurious to third parties will not be allowed.

Private Agreements in the Use of Water

Subject to the approval of the district water master or the supervisor, private parties may agree to temporary or seasonal changes in use or point of diversion. These are commonly known as "rotation" agreements. Parties might, for example, agree that A should have all the water available from a stream on Mondays, B should have it all on Tuesdays, and so on. An individual water user holding different rights on separate lands may also rotate the use of the water to fit his individual needs. All rotations are conditional upon being made without injury to the rights of others. The Supreme Court has recognized the use of rotation agreements in a number of cases.

Transfer of Water Rights and Changes in Point of Diversion and Use

An appropriative water right may be transferred apart from the land upon which it was originally used providing that the change in point of diversion, place of use, or purpose of use may be made without injury or detriment to existing rights. Changes of this nature may not, however, be made until public notice has been given to all interested parties and the supervisor has issued a certificate allowing the change. Changes contemplated under this section of the water code are either permanent or changes which will last more than one irrigation season. Riparian rights, in contrast to appropriative rights, may not be transferred apart from the land to which they are attached. The rule with respect to riparian rights that the water may be used only on riparian lands, and may not be transferred apart from the land, is generally agreed among legal writers and economists to comprise an undesirable constraint on the use and development of water resources.

If it can be shown that a change in point of diversion would injure existing rights it will, of course, be denied. In one case, however, it was held that the statute authorizing the change of use did not clothe the supervisor with powers to interfere with the internal affairs of an irrigation district that contracted with landowners to supply water.

It should be noted here that irrigation districts are municipal corporations chartered by the state and that they operate under special statutory provisions. Generally, it may be said that their internal operations are governed by their charter and bylaws and are beyond the power of the supervisor to regulate. Some irrigation districts hold water rights in their own name. Others lease the rights of members, and still others contract with agencies of the federal government on a long-term basis for their water supplies.

Underground Water

Earlier it was noted that the law does not treat water resources as a hydrologic cycle or unity, but rather has devised different doctrines and rules dependent upon the source of the water. This tendency towards separate treatment has been marked in the law of "underground water" or "ground water." Further, it is likely that entirely new and different rules of law will necessarily evolve concerning "appropriations" of atmospheric water as technology continues to advance in cloud seeding and weather modification activities. This question is not treated in the present paper, however.

Today it is estimated that ground-water reservoirs supply more than 20 per cent of the nation's total water needs. Some experts believe that in the next thirty years ground water will become an even more important source. While wells have long been a source of water for domestic use, it is only in the past few decades that technological advances in drilling techniques and pump design have made ground water an economically feasible source of supply for irrigation. In the Southwest and other areas where surface water is scarce, the use of deep wells for irrigation and other high-volume consumptive uses is now commonplace.

Unfortunately, large-scale pumping of ground water involves many problems of administration which have not been clearly resolved in many states.

Ground-water reservoirs or "aquifers" commonly cover a large area. The ownership of the land may reside in many parties who utilize the water for different purposes. The activities of one party will have an effect on the uses which others may make of the water. In addition, the availability of surface-water resources and the uses to which they are put will have an impact on ground-water supplies. The reverse is also true to some extent.

In many states there are no laws regulating the use of ground water. Thus, in these areas anyone who desires to use water without a permit, or who has a permit but desires to use more than is permitted, can merely drill wells and pump underground water free of state regulation. Because this has become a problem in recent years, many states, including Washington, have enacted ground-water codes which parallel the surface-water codes. These codes have special provisions designed to deal with the unique problems associated with the conservation and management of underground water supplies. Before discussing Washington's ground-water code, a brief review of the common-law rules which governed the appropriation of underground water prior to the enactment of ground-water codes will serve to enhance an understanding of the problems involved.

The law has traditionally divided ground water into two categories—"percolating water" and "underground stream." In the case of underground streams, the same rules that are applied to surface water will be applied in resolving the rights of parties. The rationale behind this treatment is that "a stream is a stream" whether it is above or below ground.

If, however, the water at issue is determined to be "percolating water," different rules apply and a different result may be reached. In Washington and most other western states, there is a presumption that *all* underground water is percolating water.

The legal rules which apply to percolating water are a great deal different from those that apply to the appropriation of surface water or underground streams. A number of states have adopted a rule of "absolute ownership" with respect to underground water. The rule originated in England and is founded upon the idea that a landowner should have complete dominion over the water which lies under his land. Essentially, the rule is one of "capture," and allows the owner all the water he can take into his possession. The result of the rule is that a landowner is permitted to pump and drain water from beneath his neighbors' land free of state control or regulation. One state, Texas, has even held that a party may pump and waste the water maliciously to prevent a neighbor from using it. Under the absolute-owner rule the injured party is left with no cause of action or right to sue.

A second theory that is followed in Washington and some other states is a rule of reasonable use with respect to underground water. This rule is quite similar to the riparian concept of reasonable use. Like the riparian rule, however, the concept is very flexible and difficult to administer. For example, is it "reasonable" that X should use all the water he can pump to irrigate a valuable crop even if this means that Y must drill deeper wells to continue his own use? In spite of some problems, the reasonable use rule represented a considerable improvement over the English rule of absolute ownership.

A few states, as the result of court decisions, have applied the doctrine of prior appropriation to underground water as well as to surface water. In the past few decades, many states have adopted this rule by statute—usually in connection with the adoption of a comprehensive ground-water code.* When Washington adopted its Public Ground Water Code of 1945, it rejected the common-law rule of reasonable use and made the law of prior appropriation applicable to underground water.

The trend towards adoption of appropriative ground-water codes and rejection of the common-law rules of absolute ownership and reasonable use was in large measure dictated by the inadequacy of these systems to regulate and control the use of ground water. In some areas, such as Arizona and New Mexico, water users have not only depleted the ground-water supply and thus forced each other to drill deeper and deeper wells, but they have so lowered the ground-water level that there now exist serious problems of supply for municipal and domestic uses.

The Washington Ground Water Code of 1945

The Washington statutes † which provide for the regulation of "public ground waters" are in many respects similar to the Water Code of 1917, with the additional special provisions related to the unique problems associated with ground-water regulation. The statute provides that it supplements the 1917 water code (now commonly referred to as the surface-water code.)

Under the code, the doctrine of appropriation or "first in time, first in right" governs the acquisition of ground-water rights. The rule of priority also governs in the event of a conflict between an appropriator of surface water and an appropriator of ground water.

The use of ground water requires that a permit be applied for unless the purpose of the use is domestic or noncommercial and will not exceed five

* The statutes and their application in different states are reviewed in Hutchins (1955).

† *Washington Review Code* 90.44.

thousand gallons per day. This exception covers the great percentage of the wells now in existence in the state. The permits are handled in the same manner as under the surface-water code, except that the information required is in some respects different. An appropriator of ground water must give the depth of the well, its diameter and capacity, the distance to other wells in the area, and information concerning the subsoil characteristics. The statute also requires that the person or company which drills the well provide certain additional information.

The Supervisor of the Division of Water Resources divides areas in which there are many wells into ground-water areas, subareas, and zones. When necessary to prevent overdraft or lowering of the ground-water table, the supervisor has the authority to regulate the use of water in the area involved to assure that the "safe sustaining yield" is not exceeded, although this provision has not yet been used in this state. Permits will not be granted beyond the capacity of an area to replenish its supply and maintain a relatively constant ground-water level. While this is a statutory rule, it is similar to the general rule that the holder of a water right may not use water in a manner which will damage existing rights.

One of the very significant problems in administering ground water is the difficulty in obtaining information about the resource. Fortunately, in Washington the problem has not assumed critical importance as yet, because large-scale underground pumping in areas of water shortage has been confined to a few small areas of the state. In some states, Nevada for example, the problem has been faced and information is collected concerning ground water, its use, and availability in different parts of the state. The state engineer's office regulates the water and the allocation of new rights on the basis of a computer-programmed decision model.

Under the Washington Ground Water Code, a distinction is made between "natural ground water" and "artificially stored ground water." The former may be appropriated while the latter may not. While the distinction is not too important in Washington at present, it is in many other states where cities and irrigation districts purchase water and allow it to drain into the ground for storage.

Under the ground-water code "vested rights" (rights predating the code's enactment) are handled differently than they were under the surface-water code. The ground-water code provides that parties claiming a vested right to the use of ground water must file a declaration with the Division of Water Resources setting forth certain information concerning the claimed right. If the supervisor finds the claim valid after an investigation, the claimant is issued a permit. If the claimant fails to file a declaration, the water right presumably would not be valid. The code, however, surprisingly enough does not address itself to this possibility or indicate what the consequences are of failing to file a declaration.

The ground-water code, unlike the surface-water code, contains an abandonment provision. If the use of a ground-water right has been discontinued for a period of five years, the supervisor may presume that the right has been abandoned. The statute, however, does provide for notice and a hearing before a right may be found to have been abandoned.

Loss of Water Rights

Under some circumstances, water rights may be lost by abandonment, adverse possession, estoppel, laches, acquiescence, or condemnation. These will be discussed in turn.

Though it is established in Washington and other states that an appropriative water right may be lost by abandonment, the courts do not favor losses of this nature.* To prove abandonment of a water right, it must be affirmatively shown that there was an *actual relinquishment* of the use of the water right, and that the owner of the right relinquished his use with the *intent* to abandon the water right. "The intent to abandon and an actual relinquishment of use must concur" and be proven to exist simultaneously. Thus, if a party subjectively intended to abandon his water right, but continued to make use of water, there would be no abandonment. And conversely, if he failed to use the water for a period of time without intending to abandon the right, there would be no abandonment. The issue of abandonment is always a question of fact with the burden of proof on the party who alleges that it occurred. A failure to make use of water for ten years, without more evidence, is not sufficient to justify a finding of abandonment. Though not directly in point, it was held in one case that a failure to use a ditch for eleven years was an abandonment of the right to discharge waste waters into it. A distinction should be made between the abandonment or failure to use specific water, and the abandonment of the right to use or appropriate water. No ownership rights attach to the water itself until it is appropriated, so failure to use the water does not constitute an abandonment. Prolonged

---

* For citations to cases involving the loss of water rights by abandonment, adverse possession, estoppel, and condemnation, see Morris (1956).

nonuse of water may, however, be some indication of an intent to abandon the right to make use of water in the future.

In the law of real property it is possible to gain rights in the ownership of the real property of another person simply by prolonged and continuous use of his property. These concepts are known as "adverse possession" and "prescriptive rights." The public and social policy they reflect is that when one person uses the land of another for a prolonged period of time, the community comes to recognize that person as the owner. As a result, certain expectations are created: people may extend credit in reliance upon the appearance of ownership, or the party in possession may make significant improvements to the property. Rules of this nature are characterized as "rules of repose," and their purpose is to shift the title and place the ownership of land and its appurtenant rights in the person who for all outward appearances is and has been the owner.

The concept of prescriptive rights has been recognized as applicable to the law of water rights in Washington. Though most litigation has concerned riparian rights, it is recognized in other states that an appropriative right may also be lost by prescription. The extent and nature of the water right acquired is dependent on the nature and extent of the character of the use upon which it is founded. Once acquired, it results in a vesting of title in the claimant the same as if the right had been conveyed and transferred by a formal deed.

The Washington State Supreme Court has often said that "prescriptive rights are not favored by the law." This is because they result in the loss of forfeiture of the original owner's rights of ownership. As a result, it is very important that the claimant of rights by adverse use or prescription establish all the essential elements of a right of this nature. The claimant bears the "burden of proving the existence of a prescriptive right" and should he fail to prove the necessary elements, no right will be found to have vested in him. The essential elements which must be proven are (1) open, visible, and notorious use; (2) possession adverse and hostile to the original owner; (3) continuous, uninterrupted, and peaceful use; (4) exclusive use; (5) claim of right or color of title; (6) knowledge and acquiescence of the true owner; and, (7) continuous use for the statute of limitations period. It should be noted that the elements overlap, and most courts try to reach an equitable result on the facts of a given case. A discussion of these elements, respectively, follows.

The use of water must be open, visible, and notorious. The purpose of this requirement is to make sure that the original owner will be advised that someone else is claiming rights in derogation of his own. Thus, a prescriptive right could not be gained by stealth or under circumstances not known to the original owner or the community at large.

The party claiming superior rights of ownership by adverse use must show that he claims the property as owner, rather than as a lessee or in recognition of the superior rights of the true owner. Thus, use of a water right with the owner's permission, no matter for how long a period of time, will not lead to a prescriptive title because the requisite hostility or claim in derogation of the true owner's rights is lacking. The invasion of the record owner's rights must be sufficiently open so as to notify him his rights are being invaded and the invasion must be substantial enough to give the record owner a cause of action, such as trespass, for example, against the claimant.

A lower owner on a stream cannot gain a prescriptive right to the use of water against an upstream user. This is because the downstream use is not hostile to or in derogation of the upstream owner's rights. The upstream owner makes no claim to waters he allows to flow by, and an appropriation by a lower owner does not give him a cause of action for the invasion of any of his property rights.

Though continuous use is a requirement in the acquisition of a prescriptive right, this does not necessarily mean that the use must be uninterrupted. The court will look to the nature of the use, and the requirement of continuity may be satisfied if the adverse claimant uses the water whenever he needs it. If, however, the record owner should reassert his rights of ownership in a manner sufficient to give notice to the adverse claimant, the running of the statute of limitation may be interrupted.

The adverse claimant must make an "exclusive" claim to the water right. If he intends to share the water right with the owner or to use the right only in times when there is plenty of water available the requisite adversity will be found lacking.

The adverse user must claim the water right as his own and his use of the water must be hostile to the true owner.

If the adverse use occurred without the owner's knowledge and if he had no reason to know of the use, no adverse rights may be obtained. If, however, there has been a substantial invasion of the owner's water right, knowledge of the use will be presumed and a prescriptive right will be found to have accrued to the user.

The use must have existed for a period of ten years under the law of the state of Washington before an adverse right will be found. The statute of limitations begins to run only after there has been an actual invasion of the rights of the true owner.

Water rights may be lost by estoppel, laches, or acquiescence in the prolonged use of another. The most important of these is estoppel. Estoppel is a remedy the courts will sometimes apply to get an equitable result when no legal remedy is available to prevent an injustice. If, for example, a landowner having riparian rights changes the channel of a stream bed for a period of time and other parties use the water from the stream in its new location, the landowner may be estopped from returning the stream to its original channel. The new user must show that he "relied" on the permanency of the change. Also, the change must have been prolonged, though not necessarily the ten years required for the acquisition of a water right by prescriptive or adverse use.

As was noted previously, the water code has a statutory estoppel provision which prevents any party who fails to appear at a stream-bed adjudication from claiming a water right after the adjudication has been completed. For the provision to apply, however, the owner must have been notified of the proceedings and had an opportunity to appear.

The water code and the constitution of the state of Washington both provide that the use of water for certain purposes shall be deemed a "public use." The water code also provides that under certain circumstances private persons may exercise the power of eminent domain and condemn water rights and rights of way to transport water. The right of condemnation may also be used to enlarge an existent structure as, for example, to make a ditch larger and more efficient for the carriage of water.

Whenever the right of condemnation is exercised, just compensation must be paid to the original owner for any damage or deprivation which he may have suffered. When riparian rights are condemned, compensation may have to be paid for rights which go beyond consumptive uses of the water. Damages might, for example, be found if a lake level has been lowered, or even if the only loss incurred was the use of the water for recreational purposes.

Protection of Water Rights

In the early days of winning the West and settling the frontier, water rights often had only as much protection as their owners were able to provide in the form of self-help and threats of violence to would-be encroachers. Gradually, however, as formal social and legal institutions were established, water rights came to be recognized as valuable property rights and received the protection of the courts.

Early actions could be maintained for damages in the event a property right had been violated. To prevent future damage, a court order could be issued against third parties enjoining them from interfering with the water rights of another.

Following the adoption of comprehensive water codes in the western states, a number of legal remedies were made available to protect water rights. Today in the state of Washington there are at least four distinct remedies which may be pursued in the protection of water rights:

1. A civil action for either damages or injunctive relief.

2. A statutory stream-bed adjudication which brings all the disputing parties claiming water rights into court and determines their respective rights. The decrees which result from proceedings of this nature usually contain an order that all parties are permanently enjoined and restrained from violating the rights of the others.

3. A request to the Division of Water Resources that a water master or a stream patrolman be appointed to prevent the use of water by others "in excess of the amount to which the owner of the right is lawfully entitled." Administrative protection of this nature will usually require that the water rights in question have at some time in the past been adjudicated or that the parties all base their claims on state water permits. If legal questions as to the extent and nature of the water rights are involved, court action to determine the nature of the rights may be necessary.

4. A criminal action may be brought against any person who commits certain acts in violation of the state water code. These acts include the unauthorized use of water entitled to another; willful or negligent waste of water to the detriment of another; the willful injury to or destruction of water works; placing or maintaining obstructions in the right of way of another; and so forth. Conviction of any of these acts constitutes a misdemeanor.

Pollution and Water Law

In a preceding portion of this paper the participation and the expanding role of the federal government in dealing with various aspects of water resource problems and development was noted. Federal participation in the area of water pollution has in recent years received wide public attention, and is one of the most significant of the federal water resource programs undertaken. The extent and nature of the federal role in this area will be outlined

244 WILLIAM VAN NESS

following a discussion of the background of the problem and the efforts of Washington and other states to adequately resolve pollution problems.

The traditional methods of dealing with pollution problems within the context of the riparian and appropriative water-law doctrines have been inadequate. Within the traditional riparian doctrine, it is always possible to argue that pollution is not a "reasonable use" of the water. At times this argument has succeeded, but a strong counterargument has been that the reasonableness of the use must be weighed against the importance of the polluter's contribution to the economic well-being of a particular community. Thus, if the alternative to pollution is the shutdown of a community's primary industry the courts will quite likely find that the polluter's use *is* a reasonable use of the water resource.

Certain segments of industry have very effectively exploited a combination of threats against local authorities to move their operations and the competition among regions and municipalities for locations of new plants, to forestall or avoid abatement of their pollution. Usually installation of special equipment or adoption of different processes that either reduce or avoid pollution are feasible, but at considerable expense. It is a question of who is to bear the cost—the community by accepting pollution, or the industry by installing equipment to eliminate it. Municipalities have frequently been willing to accept pollution as the price of inducing industry to locate there rather than in another municipality. Some industrial spokesmen have advocated that the public bear the cost in any event by granting tax incentives or other forms of subsidy to industry for installation of equipment to eliminate or reduce pollution.

Devising a theoretical basis for handling pollution problems within the appropriation doctrine has been even more difficult than in the case of the riparian doctrine. Two related arguments have been used with limited success. First, it may be contended that use of water to discharge, disperse, and transport pollutants is not a beneficial use of the water. Second, it may be contended that pollution constitutes a waste of water and may, therefore, be enjoined. One of the difficult problems courts have had to deal with in this area is the contention—usually made by the polluter—that later or junior appropriators initiate their water rights "subject to" the water conditions created by the activities of senior or early appropriators. In effect, the contention is that the appropriative right deals only in terms of quantity and gives no assurance that the water will meet any minimal qualitative standards.

In addition to the limited remedies which exist within the common-law theories of appropriative and riparian water rights, Washington and most other states have developed a great body of specific statutory restrictions on the pollution of water. Typically, these include: (1) statutes which make it a public nuisance to pollute specified bodies of water (these may provide for a civil remedy in the form of injunctive relief and damages, or may involve criminal penalties); (2) statutes relating to fish and wildlife; (3) health-related statutes designed to protect the purity of water used for domestic uses.

With respect to these remedies, it should be noted that their coverage is incomplete, their administration resides in scattered agencies, the laws are remedial rather than preventive, and, finally, reliance is placed upon the courts and private citizens for their enforcement rather than on an administrative agency.

In an effort to provide a more adequate basis for resolving pollution problems, Washington and some other states have moved to enact modern and fairly comprehensive pollution-control laws.

The first official Washington State activity in the pollution-control field was the creation of a State Water Pollution Control Commission by proclamation of the governor in 1937. Previous to this, however, there had been studies of the problem by state agencies. In 1945, the state legislature acted to create the Washington State Water Pollution Control Commission. Amendments to the act in 1949 directed the agency to cooperate with federal programs. Amendments in 1955 directed the commission to issue permits for the discharge of waste materials.

Under the 1955 act, the commission, which is composed of the directors of the departments of conservation, fisheries, game, agriculture, and health, is empowered to determine water-quality standards. The discharge of pollutants in violation of the commission's standards is prohibited. The method of enforcement requires the commission to bring an action at law or equity in superior court. Plans for sewage or disposal systems must be submitted to the commission for approval before construction may begin. The act gives the commission a right to enter public and private property at reasonable times for purposes of inspecting conditions related to pollution.

In the event that the commission has reason to believe that a person, company, or corporation is violating or about to violate the pollution-control laws, it may require a report on the matter. The report may lead to hearings and court action. Willful violation of the pollution-control laws or orders of the commission constitutes a misdemeanor.

One of the most significant aspects of the pollution-control law is that any person who conducts a commercial or industrial operation of any type which results in the disposal of solid or waste materials into waters of the state is required to secure a state waste-disposal permit. The commission is required to issue the permit unless it finds that the discharge of the pollutants will unduly violate the public policy declared by the act.

The commission has authority to condition the issuance of permits on meeting certain standards and undertaking necessary action to reduce pollution and improve water quality. The act requires that the terms of the permits be periodically reviewed and adjusted.

Washington's pollution-control problems have primarily centered on the control of municipal sewage and the discharge of effluents by the pulp and paper industry. In general, the act and the commission have worked fairly well in trying to solve some very difficult problems. The commission has provided a good agency for working with and coordinating its programs with those of the federal government.

In addition to its other activities, the commission serves as a member of the Pacific Northwest Pollution Control Council. Other members in addition to Washington are Oregon, Idaho, Montana, and Alaska. The council also works and cooperates with the Canadian government and the federal government.

Prior to 1948, the role of the federal government in the field of water pollution was determined by three acts of the Congress: the Refuse Act of 1899, the Oil Pollution Act of 1924, and the Public Health Act of 1912.

The Refuse Act of 1899, which is still in effect, makes it unlawful, unless a permit has been obtained from the United States Army Corps of Engineers, to discharge refuse or pollutants into navigable waters. The act does, however, make an exception for refuse flowing from streets and sewers. A recent United States Supreme Court case breathed new life into the act by holding that it applies to all pollutants and covers discharges from manufacturing mills and establishments. The corps, however, has not aggressively enforced the act.

The Oil Pollution Act of 1924 prohibits oil discharges by vessels on navigable waters or on the coasts of the United states. Recent amendments to the act were made by the Clean Waters Restoration Act of 1966.

The Public Health Act of 1912 authorizes investigations of water pollution insofar as it relates to disease and human health.

In 1948 the Federal Water Pollution Control Act was enacted. It was originally intended to authorize only a five-year program. Subsequently, it was extended, and in 1956 it was replaced by the permanent Federal Water Pollution Control Act. The act of 1956, with subsequent amendments, constitutes the federal government's basic statutory authority for a comprehensive federal program for the prevention, control, and abatement of water pollution.

Originally, the Department of Health, Education and Welfare administered the act. 1965 amendments to the act created a new agency within that department called the Federal Water Pollution Control Administration. In 1966, pursuant to a reorganization plan, the Federal Water Pollution Control Administration was transferred to the Department of the Interior. The Federal Water Pollution Control Administration has primary authority for administering the act.

The 1956 act provided authority for continued federal-state cooperation in the development of comprehensive pollution-control programs; increased technical assistance to states; strengthened research and the compilation and dissemination of data on pollution. The act also encouraged state action through interstate compacts, uniform state laws, and grants to state and interstate agencies. One of the most important provisions of the act was broadened authority for federal enforcement measures to control pollution of interstate waters by providing simplified procedures for pollution abatement.

Amendments to the act in 1961 increased money for research and grants. The most significant provision, however, was to expand federal enforcement authority to include navigable as well as interstate waters. The Water Quality Act of 1965 further strengthened the Federal Water Pollution Control Act by providing for a program of grants and development contracts to find new or improved methods of controlling pollution caused by sanitary and storm sewers; increased authorizations for pollution abatement and control programs; and, most significant, the establishment of water-quality standards for all interstate waters.

The provisions relating to the establishment of water-quality standards contain a very complex set of procedures for the adoption of standards by the states, or, in the event the states fail to act, by the federal government. Thus, the problem of industrial water polluters playing one locality against another may be circumvented.

The complexity of these procedures reflects three things: first, the complexity of the problem itself; second, a very rigorous attempt to induce the states to assume the responsibility of promulgating and administering acceptable standards; and third, an effort to observe and maintain the traditional balance and constitutional separation of state and federal powers.

Washington and most other states are currently in the process of conducting public hearings which are part of the procedures designed to result in the adoption of water-quality standards and a plan for their enforcement. If the state adopts criteria and an enforcement plan which is determined by the Secretary of the Interior to be consistent with the purposes of the act, the state will set standards and plan control. If, however, a state fails to adopt an acceptable plan or standards, the secretary may, pursuant to certain procedures, promulgate standards applicable to interstate waters within the state.

The act also provides that if the quality of interstate waters should fail to meet standards approved by the secretary, or endanger the health and welfare of persons in a state other than where the pollution originates, the secretary may request the attorney general to bring an abatement suit.

The Clean Waters Restoration Act of 1966, which was passed by the Eighty-ninth Congress, makes a number of strengthening amendments to the Federal Water Pollution Control Act.

The 1966 amendments greatly expand the authorizations for research, grants to state and local governments, and demonstration projects. In addition, enforcement procedures have been expanded and strengthened and a new provision provides that the federal government will provide up to 50 per cent of the costs of interstate, state, or local planning agencies which develop comprehensive pollution-control plans for entire watershed areas.

The growth and expansion of the Federal Water Pollution Control Act has been paralleled in many other areas of federal legislation. Authorization acts for reclamation and flood-control acts now commonly contain provisions addressed to pollution problems. This is also true in other areas of federal legislation.

It is becoming increasingly clear that the grant-in-aid federal approach and the present programs of states to control pollution will need further emphasis and new approaches. It appears probable that the future will see increased reliance on economic incentives to control pollution. This may take the form of federal tax incentives or state imposed surcharges prorated to the extent and nature of the effluents discharged.

Interstate Water Problems, the Federal-State Relationship, and Water Law

Interstate water problems, whether they involve pollution control and abatement or devising some way by which to apportion the waters of a stream that flows between two states, are problems which occasionally arise in water law litigation.

Article III of the United States Constitution provides that the federal judicial power extends to "controversies between two or more states." The

Supreme Court has original jurisdiction to resolve controversies of this nature. A number of cases dealing with the apportionment of waters between states have been resolved in this manner (the most recent culminated in the famous 1963 *Arizona* v. *California* decision).

A device often used to settle interstate water problems rather than invoking the original jurisdiction of the United States Supreme Court is the "interstate compact." An interstate compact involves an agreement between two or more states to resolve a controversy or a problem which involves the jurisdiction of more than one state. The United States Constitution requires that the consent of Congress be given to a compact before it is effective. Thus, the compact constitutes a contract of sorts between the federal government and at least two or more states.

Compacts are often used to create regional commissions and authorities designed to exercise broad legislative and enforcement powers. Federal water resource legislation occasionally will set out the terms of an interstate compact and require that the states ratify the compact before the legislation is effective. This works extremely well in instances when the legislation involves the building of dams and irrigation projects which are beneficial to the states involved.

A third, and often controversial, device which may be used in the settlement of interstate water problems involves the exercise of direct federal legislative power. We have already noted an example of this in the Federal Water Pollution Control Act, which provides for federal determination and abatement of water pollution on interstate waters. Another example is the creation of the Tennesseee Valley Authority, which exercises broad regulatory control over water resources.

The control and ownership of the nation's water resources has given rise to a very extensive, complex, and sometimes conflicting body of law. In large measure, the issues of control and ownership have been accentuated by a continuing conflict between the states and the federal government. The stage for this conflict was recently shifted from the courts to the halls of Congress with the introduction of a number of bills which would have clarified many areas of controversy (the Barrett Bill of 1956; the Kuchel Bill, S.1636, of 1966).* In general, these bills were aimed at enlarging state's rights in certain areas by limiting federal rights which have been established in past court litigation. It now appears very unlikely that the Congress will act to limit federal powers in the area of water resource development. The primary

---

* For an extensive discussion of these bills, see Morreale (1966:243).

reason is that over the past few decades it has come to be recognized that many water resource problems are national or, at least, regional in scope and require national or, at least, regional solutions.

Because of the complexity of the issues involved, the following discussion is intended to give only the briefest indication of the areas of conflict.

Typically, the conflicts between the states and the federal government have involved two basic and separate questions: first, the proprietary interests of the United States in water resources; second, the legislative jurisdiction of the United States over water resources.

In some cases, federal claims to western waters require no compensation to be paid those individuals affected, and the federal right of control is superior to the state right of control. The nature of the water-related interests of the United States may be seen in the following claims it has made and actions it has undertaken.*

The federal government has claimed the right to reserve waters of a sufficient supply to serve Indian reservations, national forests, military reservations, recreation and wildlife areas, and other "reserved" governmental lands. Such reserved waters are not subject to state control (for example, the federal government has claimed that in appropriating water for its own use on a military reservation, it need not comply with state appropriation law and a mandatory permit system).

The federal government has avoided paying the holders of state-created interests (as for the value of a dam site) compensation when it appropriated nonnavigable water power for use in connection with a federal dam.

It has destroyed and diminished economic values held by private owners in navigable waters by advancing federal projects, and avoided the payment of compensation on the ground that there exists a federal "navigational servitude."

The legislative jurisdiction of the United States to act in a manner that may conflict with state law and state-created water rights raises issues concerning the limits of federal constitutional authority to govern water use, the nature of its claimed proprietary interests in any given case, and the statutory limitations of the particular legislation involved.

Some of the rights which the federal government has asserted in the exercise of legislative authority and its role as lawmaker include: (1) the right to decide *if,* and, if so, upon what terms, hydroelectric power projects and dams may be built upon certain streams under licenses from the Federal

* For an extended discussion of the examples given here, see Sax (1965:345–423).

1955 Trends in the statutory law of ground water in the western states. Texas Law Review, 34:157.

1964 Washington water law. University of Washington Law Library (mimeographed).

Johnson, Ralph W.

1960 Riparian and public rights to lakes and streams. Washington Law Review, 35:580.

1961 Cases and materials on the law of natural resources. Mimeograph. University of Washington Law Library.

Meyers, Charles

1966 The Colorado River. Stanford Law Review, 19:1.

Morreales, Eva

1966 Federal-state conflicts over western waters—a decade of attempted clarifying legislation. Rutgers Law Review, 20:423.

Morris, Arval

1956 Washington water rights—a sketch. Washington Law Review, 31:243.

Sax, Joseph L.

1965 Water law: Cases and commentary. Preliminary paperbound ed. Pruett Press, Boulder, Colo.

Trelease, Frank, Harold Blodmenthal and Joseph Geraud

1965 Natural resources. West Publishing Company, St. Paul, Minn.

U.S. Geological Survey

1966 Mineral and water resources of Washington. Committee Print of the U.S. Senate Committee on Interior and Insular Affairs, 89th Congress, 2nd Session.

Van Ness, William

1966 Uncertainty in Washington water rights. University of Washington Law Library (mimeographed).